coolcamping
france
second edition

David Bowen, Anna Chapman, Dan Davies, Keith Didcock, David & Jane Hart,
Scott Manson, Sam Pow, Paul Sullivan, Dave Swindells, Richard Waters

The publishers assert their right to use
Cool Camping as a trademark of Punk Publishing Ltd.

Cool Camping: France (2nd edition)
First edition published in 2008
This second edition published in the United Kingdom in 2011 by
Punk Publishing Ltd
3 The Yard
Pegasus Place
London
SE11 5SD

www.punkpublishing.co.uk
www.coolcamping.co.uk

Map on page 9 supplied by Lovell Johns (www.lovelljohns.com)

A catalogue record of this book is available from the British Library.

ISBN: 978-1-906889-31-9 2nd edition
(ISBN: 978-0-9552036-5-7 1st edition)

10 9 8 7 6 5 4 3

introduction

Bienvenue to the second edition of *Cool Camping France.* We at *Cool Camping* towers are of the opinion that visiting the best, most beautiful, or fascinating, campsites in any country is nothing short of a dream job. But when it comes to exploring every Normandy nook or Riviera cranny belonging to our Gallic neighbours, sometimes even we have to pinch ourselves, so entranced are we by the *magnifique* surroundings.

The land of chateaux and *chocolat chaud,* foie gras, and *fruits de mer* is vast. Yet the sights that greet our travels daily are genuinely spellbinding: whether they're made from bricks and mortar, Mother Nature, or, more simply, sugar and cocoa beans. Turn a corner *et voilà!* suddenly we are face to face with buildings or archeological wonders dating back to the Revolution, the Renaissance, or even the prehistoric era. Connecting the towns and villages are incredibly beautiful landscapes that cry out for exploration on foot or bike. Nature is key to the country's popularity, along with a moderate climate; then there's the wine, the cheese, and other gastronomic delights, the variety of terrains and cultures, and the mellifluous language… France has truly got it all.

These days camping is a big industry in France, thanks largely to its weather, its expansive space, and the spiritual freedom the latter brings. Subsequently, the range of sites available is quite incredible. To ease your decision of where to go and which campsite to try first we've divided the reviews into regional sections. So should you fancy campsite-hopping across the Riviera, or hiking through the Pyrénées, camping out on a working farm, or indulging in a little yoga, then there's something here for you. Most sites are well set up for foreign tourists, and, in fact, we've met many of you along the way who have given us great, positive feedback about the first edition of *Cool Camping France.* Increasingly we're seeing Dutch and British owners behind the helm at new boutique-bolthole or mountain-hideaway sites. You're likely to meet many Belgians, Dutch, and Germans on your travels in any case, as well as the French, who have always been keen campers, of course. It was with much amusement that we bumped into the French CEO and the marketing director husband-and-wife team behind the Huttopia and Indigo chain of campsites (see page 54) in one forest, trying out a new model of their Nature Range tents. (Let's just say that only the French could emerge from something so small looking so chic and ready for a night on the tiles.)

The municipal sites, on the other hand, tend to be professionally run French operations that, while busier and noisier, offer fantastic economical holidays with activities to keep the whole family entertained. Should you seek a more traditional, intimate experience, with campsite owners who don't speak a word of English, well, we feature these, too (see, for example, Camping de l'Ouysse, page 136, and Le Moulin de Cost, page 204). Then there are the campsites close to the Spanish border in areas that celebrate a local dialect and local customs, offering an experience that feels very special indeed.

New to our second edition is the inclusion of a dozen-plus luxury sites. 'Glamping' isn't a term that appeals to everyone, but Mille Étoiles, see page 214, have been renting yurts since long before the glamping boom. Arguably it is a way of distinguishing a higher level of service and accommodation not found in traditional campsites. Mille Étoiles' wonderful range of yurts is perched on the forested edge of a canyon overlooking the Ardèche River, with a stunning wooden café-lounge, where guests may breakfast. Idyllic isn't the word. Nearby Haut Toupian (see page 218) is probably the most expensive campsite in the book, but a stay here is a 5-star treat. Super-stressed-out campers can languish in the pool, then enjoy a jet shower before sinking into snuggly duvets for a siesta, waking to dine in the peace and quiet of the Languedoc-Roussillon countryside. Total entrancement. We also feature tree houses, native American tipis, stargazing cubicles, and airstream trailers, so if you want to try something completely unusual, there's nothing stopping you.

Follow our Campsites at a Glance (CAAG) (see page 14) to browse sites that meet your personal criteria or choose a region that appeals. According to French tourism development agency ATOUT France, locals and tourists are avoiding the crowds and holidaying in Champagne, Burgundy, Limousin, Alsace, and Franche-Comté, but if you're travelling out of season all the sites will be enjoyable. The CAAG lists sites according to proximity to the sea, mountains, or rivers, as well as those close to the action. Our two longest categories show that France is a nation of dog-lovers (Camping Les Perron-Beauvineau, page 68, even offers dog kennels for hire) and that first-time campers are widely, warmly welcomed.

Coming back to those rivers for a second, is there really anything as pleasurable as canoeing or kayaking along the Rivers Ardèche, Cèze, or Allier, for instance, bronzing on the river banks, then trekking back to camp with an appetite to devour as much local cuisine as we can muster.

And so, buoyed with commitment to unearth those extra-special sites worthy of a place in the Top 100, our army of researchers has left no rural village, mountain hamlet, or seaside resort uncovered. Yes, you did read that right; we now have a whopping 100 sites for your reading pleasure, all of which adhere to the *Cool Camping* ethos: beautiful campsites in beautiful places, or unusual sites in unusual places. So whether you're camping in the shadow of a king's castle in the Loire valley, among the pines next to the crashing westerly Atlantic, or under the snow-capped peaks of the Alps, all of these campsites offer a truly unique experience. We've visited 4-star sites that we chose not to include because the welcome was not personal enough – *Cool Camping* recommendations are not about a list of services and amenities.

Also, many sites featured in the first edition have been given less space this time, to make room for new players. But less space does not mean they are any less special. All reviews are backed up by practicalities: information that might include the best regional food, the in-house massage, where to find the best market, as well as general directions. Camping in France creates lasting memories and, as we've said, it's easier getting around than you'd imagine. We hope this guide makes it even easier for you. Anyway, that's enough from us. It's your guide and your holiday, so turn the page: *entrez, entrez, nos amis...*

campsite locator

continued overleaf

ENGLISH CHANNEL

Dunkerque
Calais
Boulogne
belgium
Lille
Valenciennes
LUXEMBOURG
Dieppe
Amiens
Charleville-
Mézières
GERMANY
Cherbourg
St Quentin
Reims
Metz
Le Havre
Rouen
Strasbourg
Caen
PARIS
Chalons-sur-
Marne
Nancy
St-Malo
Versailles
Brest
St-Brieuc
Chartres
Quimper
Rennes
Orléans
Dijon
Besançon
Lorient
Le Mans
SWITZERLAND
Vannes
Angers
Bourges
Chalon-sur-Saône
St-Nazaire
Nantes
Tours
Cholet
Nevers
Annecy
Poitiers
Châteauroux
La Rochelle
Niort
Lyon
Rochefort
Limoges
Chambéry
ATLANTIC OCEAN
Angoulême
Clermont-Ferrand
Grenoble
ITALY
Brive-la-Gaillarde
Le Puy
Bordeaux
Valence
Cahors
Rodez
Millau
Avignon
Agen
Cannes
Mont-de-Marsan
Nîmes
Nice
Toulouse
Béziers
Marseille
Bayonne
Pau
Montpellier
Toulon
St-Tropez
Tarbes
Carcassonne
Narbonne
Foix
Perpignan
SPAIN
ANDORRA
MEDITERRANEAN SEA

campsite locator 9

campsite locator (continued)

1   2

3   4

cool camping top 5

Like a tense Grand Prix qualifying round, 100 stunning campsites jostled for a prize position on our Top 5 grid. These, er, magnificent *seven* raced to the front. Watch out for the chequered flag – and race to book your pitch...

`1` Les Eucalyptus, Riviera   p188

In pole position, this secluded Riviera-based beauty boasts a neighbouring vineyard, easy access to the Riviera's glammest beach, and all the decadence of St-Tropez is less than a billionaire's yacht-length away.

`2` Les Mathévies, Dordogne & Lot   p132

Spacious leafy pitches and onsite café that must be one of the cosiest in France; this place offers fabulous family camping plus proximity to the medieval town of Sarlat and all its delicious architecture and cuisine.

`3` Terre Ferme, Central France   p166

A roomy, rustic site bordered by natural woodland and a spring-fed pond, it's near the *autoroute* – perfect for a stop-off on a longer journey, or stay a while and lap up the *aire naturelle*.

`4` Haut Toupian, Ardèche   p218

The luxurious tents, sublime food, and idyllic location within the serenity of the Ardèche valley have set a new standard at the top of the glamping scale.

`5=` = La Serre, Languedoc   p236

Your own private universe; enclosed terraces shaded by ancient oaks. Onsite eco-events include tasting evenings with local farmers, who bring their organic wine and produce.

`5=` = Ferme Noemie, Alps   p178

An Alpine charmer with super facilities to match its spectacular surroundings.

`5=` = Le Brévedent, Brittany & Normandy   p26

A convivial site in the grounds of a chateau in a beautiful part of Normandy. Music and local calvados abound, and it's child-friendly and eco-conscious, too.

campsites at a glance

www.etangducamp.fr

WALK THIS WAY

Most of the sites are good for walking.

brittany &
normandy

rando-yourte

Rando-yourte, 1484 route de St Valéry, Hameau de Conteville, 76450 Paluel   00 33 2 35 57 04 71   www.rando-yourte.com

Nestled under apple trees in a titchy village near the Normandy coast sit six Mongolian yurts. The squat tents might be unexpected, but the French have embraced this form of camping and are prepared to wait months for the chance to spend a few nights living like Genghis Khan. But don't just drop in; you need to book well in advance.

Unlike the fiery 13th-century Mongolian emperor, this is a peaceful place and to aid you in the pursuit of R&R are an onsite sauna, steam bath, and masseur. The owners, the Dordets, might stipulate that the yurts aren't party pads, but they give every guest a bottle of local cider on arrival. And sharing with friends is the most economical approach to yurt life, with the largest two accommodating six people. However, be prepared to sacrifice privacy and learn to love snoring – the yurts are open-plan. Their brightly coloured interiors are lively – the ornate wooden furniture might be authentic, but Day-Glo orange is not hangover-friendly. Being healthy is the way forward here and there's a football goal, should you need a bit of shooting practice. The sea is a 20-minute walk away at Veulettes-sur-Mer, where the yacht club offers all sorts of nautical activities.

Rando-yourte is open 10 months a year, so it's great for a late-autumn French camping experience, when most of the regular sites have long since padlocked their gates. In Mongolia the yurt remains snug even when temperatures outside zoom down to minus 40; fortunately Haute-Normandie is a bit milder out of season.

COOL FACTOR Mongolian chic for cider-lovers.

WHO'S IN? Large groups, young groups – yes. Tents, campervans, caravans, dogs – no.

ON SITE Six yurts sleeping a maximum of 20. Two wash-rooms including 2 free showers. One baby-change and a washing machine. Bike rentals €5 per half-day. Continental breakfast €6. There are no cooking facilities. The nearest shops and restaurants are in Veulettes-sur-Mer ¾ mile (1.5 km) away. Massage, sauna, and steam room are €10 each for 30 minutes. No campfires.

OFF SITE There's a map of local walks and bike rides in each yurt. Unfortunately a barbed-wire-encased nuclear power station lies less than ½ mile (1 km) away on the road to Bertheauville. You're better off heading for the beach at Veulettes-sur-Mer, which can be reached offroad along the cliffs. Water sports are also available 2½ miles (4 km) inland at Lac de Caniel (00 33 2 35 97 40 55; www.lacdecaniel. com) in Vittefleur, which has warmer water, smaller waves, and a bowling alley. If it's raining the Estran Cité de la Mer in Dieppe (00 33 2 35 06 93 20; www.estrancitedelamer.fr) has the deepest aquarium in Europe.

FOOD AND DRINK Down local cider at Le Pressoir (00 33 2 35 97 51 49) in St-Valéry-en-Caux. Work up an appetite for a posh meal at L'Assiette Gourmande (00 33 2 35 97 18 84) 1¾ miles (3 km) away in Bertheauville with a guided tour of the chateau. The *menu du jour* is €26. Closed Mondays. The Saturday fish market in Dieppe is unmissable.

GETTING THERE From Dieppe take D925. Turn on to D79 after St-Valéry-en-Caux and head west. The site is 4½ miles (7.5 km) away in Conteville.

OPEN Closed December and January.

THE DAMAGE From €50 per night for 2 people.

camping d'étretat

Camping Municipal d'Étretat, 69 rue Guy de Maupassant, 76790 Étretat   00 33 2 35 27 07 67

Famed for its dramatic cliffs and pebbly beach, Étretat is a gorgeous medieval town on the north coast, which unlike many of its neighbouring resorts, escaped the D-Day bombings. Inevitably this little gem is a popular destination with discerning European campers and its small municipal site is often full by midday. Annoyingly you can't book, so arriving super-early in July and August is a must if you want to appreciate Étretat's comfortably flat pitches and unfussy charms. This is municipal camping par excellence – sparklingly clean bathrooms, friendly service, and an old-fashioned playground with no fancy stuff. Surrounded by trees, the site is the perfect spot for a snooze after a hard day's lounging at the beach. The bus from Le Havre stops right outside, making it suitable for car-less campers. Situated just 20 miles (32 km) from the port, it's a good option for your first or last night on French soil. But if you're too late for a slot, head 10 miles (16 km) up the coast to the casino-ridden Fécamp, where the bustling Domaine de Reneville site rambles down the hill, offering stunning views of the sea.

COOL FACTOR Chilled camping in a medieval town.

WHO'S IN? Tents, campervans, caravans, dogs, large groups, young groups – yes.

ON SITE Campfires allowed off the ground. Seventy-three pitches and 53 hook-ups – 20 with tents. Immaculate washrooms with 12 free showers. Two coin-operated washing machines €2.50, dryer €1.50. Playground.

OFF SITE Beach and cliffs ½ mile (1 km). Stunning walks along cliff-top golf course.

FOOD AND DRINK Les Galets Bleu (00 33 2 35 29 85 58) on rue Prosper Brindejont offers mussels with different sauces and chips from €10.90. Ice cream sold at Chocolats Hautot (www.chocolats-hautot.com) on rue des Docteurs Fidelin. Try the farm shop at Musée Agricole in Maniquerville (00 33 2 35 10 74 00; www.lafermenormande.com).

GETTING THERE From Le Havre take D940 to Étretat. In the town centre turn right on to rue Guy de Maupassant. The site is less than ½ mile (1 km) on the left.

PUBLIC TRANSPORT Bus no. 24 stops outside daily and runs between Le Havre and Fécamp.

OPEN Early April–mid October.

THE DAMAGE Tent and car plus 2 adults €11.30, child 4–10 years €2.50, electricity €5–€6.

le bois coudrais

Le Bois Coudrais, 35270 Cuguen   00 33 2 99 73 27 45   www.vacancebretagne.com

'Turn left at the crossroads and then look out for the *drapeau Britannique* on your left,' grinned a helpful couple. There's a French flag flying outside the site, too, but it's mostly British and Dutch campers who appreciate the friendly, family-run, traditional camping here. At night the peace and quiet is only disturbed by leaves rustling in the poplars, but the myriad birds deliver a dawn chorus, so if the other kind of twittering disturbs you, then best drive by.

The reward for getting up early is the sweet smell of fresh croissants delivered before 8am, and perhaps a chance to visit the goats, sheep, chickens, and ducks by the stream. Children so enjoy petting and feeding them that the animals need to be put on a diet come summer's end. In high season the owners bake cakes and make quiches, lasagnes, or salads, so campers can eat outside the bijou café-bar next to the pool. Inspiration and activities are on a map showing Mont St-Michel 20 minutes in one direction and the fairy-tale feudal castle at Fougères, with towers and turrets in all the right places, 35 minutes in the other.

COOL FACTOR Traditional camping in north Brittany.

WHO'S IN? Tents, campervans, caravans, dogs (on leads) – yes. Large groups – by arrangement.

ON SITE Twenty-five pitches, 19 with electric hook-ups. Bright block with free hot showers and good laundry. Washing-up facilities. Shady or sunny pitches. Kids' play and animal-petting areas. Heated swimming pool. Free wi-fi. Four *gîtes* plus equipped tent for hire. No campfires, BBQs okay.

OFF SITE Head to the visitor centre for a coffee, shop, play area, and start point for walks, strolls, and offroad cycling.

FOOD AND DRINK Auberge de la Cour Verte in Dol-de-Bretagne (00 33 2 99 48 41 41) is a welcoming mid-range auberge. Or treat yourself to the best seafood at Côté Mer, 4 rue Ernest Lamort, with *menus* from €27 (00 33 2 99 89 66 08; www.restaurant-cotemer.fr).

GETTING THERE From Combourg follow signs to Mont St-Michel on D796 and then Cuguen on D83. The site is signposted left about 1 mile (2 km) after Cuguen. From Pontorson take D90 to Trans-la-Forêt, then D83 towards Cuguen. The site is signed right before the village.

OPEN Late April–late September.

THE DAMAGE Camping, car, 2 adults €17. Extra adults €3.50. Child (up to age 14) €3. Electricity (10 amp) €3.

In the heart of Calvados country, near the idyllic village of Blangy, is the friendliest chateau-camping experience you can hope to find in France. Camping at Le Brévedent was first set up to pay for repairs to the Louis XVI hunting lodge after the Second World War. Fortunately for us it was the only way that the Marquis de Chabannes La Palice could afford to stay on the land, which had been in his family for 350 years. He also planted an orchard across the site. Now his great-grandson, Raphael Bony, heads up the operation and considers sociability to be a major aspect of his job – apples play a large part in this. Every night Raphael opens the bar in the main house so that guests can drink local cider and calvados, wander through the ground floor looking at oil paintings of his ancestors and shoot pool. Twice a week he hosts music sessions with his brother, Arthur, who plays the *cajón*, a Peruvian instrument. The Bonys are into French folk music, but they invite guests to play what they like. This year a Belgian family treated Le Brévedent to Mozart and Rachmaninov on the violin and piano. They were followed by a guy on the bagpipes.

Assumption Day on August 15th, is celebrated here, like many places in France, with fireworks. At Le Brévedent they host a spectacular display over the lake, BBQ, and an impromptu jam session.

le brévedent

Castel Camping Le Brévedent, route du Pin, 14130 Le Brévedent   00 33 2 31 64 72 88   www.campinglebrevedent.com

Any excuse for a party, Raphael now winds up the season with an official music festival. It might be far smaller than the Big Chill, but the line-up is just as eclectic.

Plastic bags have been outlawed on site and each guest is given a reusable green Le Brévedent sac to carry their morning croissants home from the shop. Living in sync with nature extends to the free kids' club in July and August, when they take advantage of the apple season. In the morning the children gather windfalls and hold apple-and-spoon races before pressing them into juice after lunch. The delicious results are distributed among passing campers at the end of the day. Teenagers are the only group who aren't specifically catered for at Le Brévedent, although they'd probably dispute this if they could get their hands on the cider.

In *Cool Camping* terms Le Brévedent is a big site, but its canny design results in a beautifully chilled atmosphere. The play areas are handily situated by adult distractions such as the restaurant, café terrace (with free wi-fi), and lake, where huge carp can be caught. The heated swimming pool and paddling pool have been tastefully cut into the slope in front of the main house. From here there's a spectacular view of the lake, which is where most people choose to camp. Behind the lake is a stream, the banks of which are populated by a

community of guinea pigs. Elsewhere ducks and chickens meander about the site among the apple trees and herbaceous borders.

On Sunday evenings, in the salon, Madame Gurrey (Raphael's granny) recounts tales of aristocratic eccentricities. She maintains that Raphael has inherited the relaxed charm of his great grandfather, who often failed to charge campers. Today you can hire a canoe for a scenic glide across the lake; the small fee should be per hour, but Raphael is laid-back about counting minutes. After all, there's no reason to rush here.

COOL FACTOR Amiable lakeside lounging in the grounds of a Calvados chateau.

WHO'S IN? Tents, campervans, caravans, large groups, young groups – yes. Dogs – no.

ON SITE Campfires allowed off the ground. One hundred and forty pitches with hook-ups. Three wash-rooms, the oldest one by the restaurant is due to be renovated in 2012, so best head for the newer ones. The showers are strong and free. Baby-change in each wash-room. Disabled facilities. Free activities include 3 playgrounds, heated swimming and paddling pool, games room in the lodge, fishing on the lake, *boules*, volleyball, badminton, football, mini-golf. The games room on the ground floor of the house is open all day and has a pool table. Tennis €5 per hour. Canoe hire €3 per hour. Bike hire €4 per hour. The onsite restaurant serves pizza in high season. Steak and chips is €10.50 and the 3-course *menu du camping* is €15. They also do takeaways. The café has a sun terrace with free wi-fi. The shop is extremely well stocked and sells local produce. Recycling facilities.

OFF SITE What could be better than a ramble or cycle through gentle, rolling fields full of sturdy cattle and traditional, timbered Normandy farmhouses? Each camper is given a map detailing 3 local walks. Hire a pony from the horse-riding centre ½ mile (1 km) away. Or, for wilder animal thrills, go on safari at Parc Zoologique Cerza (www.cerza. com), which has 700 animals including tigers, alligators, and a rare Indian rhinoceros. Pont-l'Évêque 6 miles (10 km) away, which retains period charm despite taking a pounding in the Second World War. Apart from being home to a deliciously stinky cheese, the restored Mont St-Michel cathedral is worth a look. Art fans love the picturesque port of Honfleur, 15½ miles (25 km) away.

FOOD AND DRINK Thursday is the day for foodies, starting with the morning market in Blangy-le-Château. It might be small, but it's incredibly charming and has a fine fish van selling oysters and mussels. Soak up the atmosphere and treat yourself to a coffee or cassis in the bar-tabac opposite. On Thursday afternoon the campsite organises a trip to Les Bruyères Carrées, a small distillery, which produces top-notch Calvados and cider. For a fancy meal head 1 mile (2 km) further along D140 to the delightful Le Mesnil-sur-Blangy, where Le Restaurant de la Galerie (00 33 2 31 64 77 13; www.restaurant-galerie.com) serves seasonal food (foie gras €14, duck €19) and doubles as an art gallery. Check out the cows at Ferme Spruytte (00 33 2 31 64 71 99), which makes and sells the local Pont-l'Évêque cheese. It's walking distance along D284.

GETTING THERE From Rouen take A13 to Pont-l'Évêque. Head ½ mile (1 km) south on the D579 towards Lisieux before joining D51 to Blangy-le-Château. From Blangy take D98 south 1 mile (2 km). The site is on your left before you reach the hamlet of Le Brévedent.

OPEN April–September.

THE DAMAGE Tent plus 2 adults €18–€28 (depending on season), electric hook-up €4, child under 7 years €2.20, 7–12 years €3.30.

la ferme de croas men

La Ferme de Croas Men, Croas Men 29610, Plouigneau   00 33 2 98 79 11 50   www.ferme-de-croasmen.com

Brittany and Cornwall share a Celtic-British history and a similar geography. Each is a westernmost promontory buffeted by Atlantic waves, with rugged capes and cliffs sheltering fishing villages and sandy beaches, while inland lie moors and the neolithic menhir monuments beloved by Asterix. Brittany, though, is almost 10 times the size of Cornwall and retains its own language and distinctive cultural traditions. In a part of northern Brittany blessed with place names like Plouezoc'h, Trudujo, and Beg ar C'hra you'll find La Ferme de Croas Men nestled in the rolling countryside. The flowery signs by the roadside were painted by Monsieur Cotty, who started the campsite 20 years ago and also created the many *objets trouvés* sculptures around the site. This is also a working dairy farm shared by four generations of the Cotty family and an ark-ful of animals. They raise and grow food for 45 cows, but there are also donkeys, goats, sheep, ducks, rabbits, chickens, and Max the Pig among the 30 or so breeds. Such a menagerie makes this site a great opportunity to introduce children to all sorts of animals.

This is much more than a glorified petting farm, though, for this place demonstrates how farm life has developed over the last century, with a museum of farm machinery next to Ty Coz, the original family cottage, which looks just as it might have in 1900, complete with a beaten-earth floor, massive table and benches, four-poster bed, vintage dresser, and grandfather clock, which stands opposite photos of the great grandparents.

Rather than being a dusty, hands-off rural museum, though, this room can be booked for a special breakfast – a stack of pancakes, fresh bread, and home-made jams just waiting to be devoured with tea, coffee, or hot chocolate.

The Cottys, among whom Raphael speaks excellent English, allow small visitors to watch the milking, feed the animals, and witness the farm in action throughout the day, asking only that adults are present to ensure safety and that animals are allowed to rest between 11am and 4pm. There are tractor rides and donkey-cart rides around the farm in July and August (keep a look out for over 150 different plants and trees), and plenty to see round about, with beautiful sunken-road walks starting from the farm itself.

The historic port of Morlaix is just 10 minutes' drive away, while the closest beaches and coves on Brittany's heather-covered northern coast, the wonderfully named Armorican Corniche, are about 15 minutes away by car.

Morlaix is famous for its colossal viaduct, the remarkable 16th-century house of Queen Anne of Brittany, and for beating off an attack by an English fleet in 1522. The English sailed up the estuary and found the town undefended and, in true medieval style, proceeded to pillage. But they made the mistake of lingering in the wine cellars until the locals returned to drive the inebriated intruders away, subsequently adding *'S'ils te mordent, mords-les!'* ('If they bite you, bite them!') to the town's coat of arms. Fortunately, there

are no worries about overstaying your welcome any more, with spacious pitches, cabins, or tents waiting for you just 20 miles (32 km) down the coast from the port of Roscoff. They're used to visitors here year-round as the farm is often visited by school groups, and one of the friendly features is 'Oscar', the name given to a building Monsieur Cotty constructed from boulders and stone blocks that Obelix would have been proud to lift. Inside this wonder is an equally massive table for campers and farm visitors to socialise and feast around, whatever the weather.

COOL FACTOR It's proper camping on the farm, but with every creature comfort.

WHO'S IN? Tents, campervans, caravans, and dogs (on leads), large groups, young groups by arrangement (there's plenty of room) – yes.

ON SITE Campfires allowed. Fifty large pitches, all with electric hook-ups. There are 2 wash-blocks, but people prefer the newer one in the middle of the site, which is bright and airy with efficient warm showers, laundry sinks, disabled access, a parent-and-baby room, washing machine, and chemical disposal point. Next door is a reception room with walking routes and tourist information, toys, books, and board games for the kids – especially good if it's a rainy morning. Family fun is right here on the farm, feeding the animals. There are 2 wooden roulottes (gypsy caravans), chalets, cabins, and wood-and-canvas tents to hire, too.

OFF SITE Morlaix hosts one of the local markets, which take place every day of the week. Only one of them is further than a 15-minute drive from the campsite, so fans of produits régioneux can get a daily fix if they fancy, and discover lovely Breton towns and villages in the process. There's a big indoor pool with slide and jacuzzi at Plouigneau, if the weather's awful, but otherwise there are so many beaches and coves to explore nearby – the sandy shore, surf, and sailing schools at Locquirec are recommended. Beyond lies the medieval town of Lannion and the pink-and-orange rock formations of the enticingly named Côte de Granit Rose (Pink Granite Coast) are just 25 miles (40 km) away.

FOOD AND DRINK Whether you choose to breakfast in the atmospheric old farm cottage or chez vous, it's a meal to savour on a farm where milk, eggs, butter, yogurt, preserves, honey, cider, and apple juice are either made right here or locally produced and can be bought at reception. Factor in local markets and this could be a real foodie treat. The Crêperie L'Hermine (00 33 2 98 88 10 91) on the quiet rue Ange de Guernisac, in the heart of Morlaix, makes a traditional Breton pit-stop after the Saturday morning market. Alternatively, go for a lunchtime treat of fresh seafood and fruits de mer on the terrace of the Brasserie de la Plage (00 33 2 98 79 30 70; see www.grand-hotel-des-bains.com) overlooking the beach and harbour at Locquirec, or stay for dinner in the swanky restaurant (00 33 2 98 67 41 02; see www.grand-hotel-des-bains.com).

GETTING THERE Plouigneau is close to Morlaix, just off N12 between Brest and Rennes. Take the Plouigneau exit off N12, but don't go into Plouigneau; head for Lanmeur on D64. Drive for 160 yards (150 m) and you should see the first of the pale-blue signs for the farm, 3½ miles (6 km) away. Follow them and you should be fine, but if you do get lost, head for Garlan and ask there.

OPEN April–October.

THE DAMAGE Camping with a vehicle plus tent or caravan and 2 adults €11.40. Extra people over 7 years €3.20, child €2–€2.80. Electricity (6 amp) €3.20.

camping des abers

Camping des Abers, 51 Toull Treaz, 29870 Landéda   00 33 2 98 04 93 35   www.camping-des-abers.com

Wetsuited kite-surfers revel in the often blustery conditions, but thankfully this spot is ideally adapted to cope with stiff sea breezes. Trees and thick laurel hedges protect the seaward side and define the pitches throughout the site, which rolls around a hillock, affording great views across the wide Baie des Anges.

A very different outlook greets campers in the morning, when the wind has died down, the sunshine has returned, and the sea has retreated, extending the sandy beach by up to a kilometre and exposing an archipelago of small grassy islands that can be explored between tides.

This is called the 'coast of legends' (Côte des Légendes, also known as Côte des Abers) and nearly all these dune islets have stories to tell – of Greeks and Phoenicians trading in tin and pewter with fellow Celts of Cornwall, of ancient megalithic tombs, or Irish missionaries living as hermits. The bay can be explored at high tide, too – diving, swimming, kayaking, sailing, surfing, and windsurfing are all options, and they're made more interesting by the site lying close to the estuaries of Aber-Benoît and Aber Wrac'h; river valleys 'drowned' by rising sea levels.

There are plenty of *animations* on site, too – children's art classes, courses in Breton cooking, dance classes, music events in high season, and Fest Noz (traditional Breton festival and dancing) events. If this all sounds too exhausting, just lie on the beach and contemplate the delicious takeaway meal to be delivered to the site in the evening.

COOL FACTOR Camping between the river and the sea, with ancient dune islands to explore.

WHO'S IN? Tents, campervans, caravans, dogs (on leads), large groups by arrangement – yes.

ON SITE A hundred and fifty-eight pitches, all with electric hook-ups. Three smart wash-blocks, with hot showers and laundry wash-rooms. Good kids' play areas and direct access to the beach. Music events Wednesdays and Sundays in season, with a Fest Noz Fridays. Children's art class 2–4pm, dance classes (jazz, step, hip-hop), t'ai chi. Games room. Free wi-fi and internet access. Motorhome service point. No campfires, but BBQs are okay.

OFF SITE Sailing, diving, and windsurfing courses are all offered locally. Neighbouring nature reserves are great for pony-trekking, fishing, cycling, walking, and bird-watching. Le Phare de Île Vierge (the Virgin Island lighthouse) is the tallest in Europe, so there are great views. There's a museum of seaweed-gathering in the Ecomusée de Plouguerneau (00 33 2 98 37 13 35; www.ecomusee-plouguerneau.com).

FOOD AND DRINK There's an *épicerie* (grocery shop) next to the campsite entrance. Takeaway food (crêpes, paella, Chinese food) is delivered to the site 5 days a week. Le Vioben in Port de l'Aber-Wrac'h, Landéda (00 33 2 98 04 96 77) is great for seafood.

GETTING THERE From Brest take D112, D788, and D13 to Lannilis, then D128 to Landéda. You'll see signs for Camping des Abers along route de l'Armorique and then Toull Treaz.

OPEN May–September.

THE DAMAGE Pitch, car, and 2 adults €13.60 (€15.10 from mid June to 31 August). Extra adults €3.35 (€3.70). Child up to 7 years €2. Electricity €2.50. Shower token €0.65 (€0.80).

la pointe

Camping La Pointe, route St-Coulitz, 29150 Châteaulin   00 33 2 98 86 51 53   www.lapointesuperbecamping.com

La Pointe lies just outside the picturesque town of Châteaulin, close by a tree-lined bend of the canalised River Aulne. The site is British-owned – Marcus and Julie took over from another English couple in 2008 – but it attracts a loyal following of French *campeurs*, along with British and Dutch regulars, who appreciate the warm, considerate welcome. The site sits in a conifer-lined valley at the foot of a deciduous forest, which was recently incorporated within the borders of the Parc Naturel Régional d'Armorique, with a tinkling stream running down one side.

The pitches are huge, separated by hedges and flowers, with terraces rising up the wooded hillside if you seek more shade and privacy – 300 trees were cleared in 2010 to ensure that the site wasn't too shady. Experienced campers themselves, the owners know what their customers want – there's a spacious play area for the kids and a chill-out room; outdoor furniture for lounging and a handy fridge-freezer. If you fancy having a BBQ, you'll find them for hire here, and there's a daily *boulangerie* delivery as well as fresh eggs and vegetables from the kitchen garden. Along with the woodland, the canal path is ideal for a walking, running, cycling, or fishing (the canal is a grade-two salmon stream), but adventure-sports junkies won't need to travel far either.

To get a bird's eye view of the Breton countryside, take a trip 5 miles (8 km) to the summit of Ménez-Hom, the highest peak in the Black Mountains. At just over 1,000 feet (330

metres) it's no Everest, and you can actually drive almost to the top, but it offers a panorama of Western Brittany and the Crozon Peninsula. The paragliders who use the peak get an even loftier view looking north towards Brest, south to Quimper, and west, where the coastline curves around the sweep of the Baie de Douarnenez and on to the stunning views of cliffs at Pointe du Raz.

There are more thrills on the extravagantly long, level stretches of sand near Douarnenez. The *char à voile* (sand-yachting) world championships were held at Pentrez beach and there are plenty of them lined up for hire if you fancy eye-watering, seat-of-the-pants speed. There are smaller coves beyond, such as Trez Bellec, where you won't be sandblasted by sea breezes. Perhaps this explains why the French don't bother with wind-breaks, those small fortresses of stripey canvas that British beach-lovers love, but sit stoically in the face of buffeting blasts. Surfers who want to catch the Atlantic swell can head for Pen Hir Point, but slower-motion adrenaline junkies will find pleasure here, too – Marcus and Julie are keen bird-watchers, who recommend the rugged cliffs around Pointe du Raz, and local marshland sites near La Feu, to fellow twitchers.

Another essential excursion is to the remarkable medieval town of Locronan, a perfectly preserved, cobbled, car-free haven (park just outside). It became famous in the 14th century for making sailcloth, although there are Celtic and early Christian traditions here, too, as it dates back

Châteaulin – a short walk
from the campsite

2,500 years. The sand-coloured granite houses and 15th-century church have made it a favourite location for film-makers, and it's so reminiscent of Hardy's Wessex that Roman Polanski's version of *Tess of the d'Urbervilles* was even filmed there. The town feels quite touristy in the afternoon, so it's probably best to go on a Wednesday evening, when there's an atmospheric 'starlit' market. In short, there's plenty to do around La Pointe. The visitors' book is full of comments like 'I only meant to stay one night and I'm still here a week later'. Which says it all, really.

COOL FACTOR The warm welcome comes with cool, shady pitches in the forest, even in high season.

WHO'S IN? Tents, campervans, caravans, and well-behaved dogs, large groups by arrangement – yes.

ON SITE Campfires are allowed (but not in the forest) – please ask first. Eighty pitches, all with electric hook-ups. The wash-block is large enough to accommodate a much bigger site, so there are plenty of sparkling-clean sinks and showers, plus laundry wash-rooms. Next door there is an information room and book exchange; there's free wi-fi, too. The communal room isn't fancy, but it has a table-tennis table and space enough to relax on a rainy day when you can't get out. The owners aim to introduce kayaks for use on the calm waters of the River Aulne, which forms part of the 200 miles (315 km) of the Brest–Nantes canal. There's a motorhome service point.

OFF SITE Châteaulin, a stroll along the river from the site, is a lovely, floral riverside town, good for a weekly market and supermarkets, restaurants, tennis, and heated indoor swimming pool. Beaches, water sports, and sand-yachting are 10 miles (16 km) away. Quimper, the medieval capital of Finistère, is a 20-minute drive away. Brest is about 40 minutes away, and that's where you'll find the Océanopolis aquarium (00 33 2 98 34 40 40; www.oceanopolis.com), which isn't cheap (adult €16.50, child €11.50), but it's great for a family day out. There's also an excellent open-air boat museum, Le Port-Musée, in Douarnenez (00 33 2 98 92 65 20; www.port-musee.org).

FOOD AND DRINK *Boulangerie* deliveries mean you can guarantee your pain au chocolat for breakfast, and fresh eggs and fresh vegetables are available, too. On Thursdays in high season it's crêpe night on site, but otherwise there are special ways to enjoy Breton crêpes close by. The Crêperie St Côme (00 33 2 98 26 55 86; www.creperie-stcome. com), on an old farm at St-Côme, near Pentrez beach, has 580 different crêpes to choose from. Marcus and Julie recommend Crêperie de l'Enclos in Pleyben (00 33 2 98 26 38 68), where they may add truffles, foie gras, peach, and other exotic gastronomic flavours, which helped earn it 2 'chef hats' in the 2010 Gault & Millau guide. In Châteaulin Le Miniscule (00 33 2 98 86 28 66) is an easy-going, friendly pizza and seafood bar/restaurant, where *moules frites* are around €10.

GETTING THERE It's about an hour's drive from Roscoff, but if you're coming from Rennes take N12 and then change to N164, signposted Quimper. Once you get to Châteaulin drive down to the river in the centre, cross the bridge, and follow signs to Quimper on D770. After ½ mile (1 km) turn left, signposted St-Coulitz, and the campsite is 110 yards (100 m) further, on your right.

PUBLIC TRANSPORT Châteaulin is 20 minutes by train from Quimper, which is on the express TGV line from Paris, so you won't have to have a car here.

OPEN Mid March–late October.

THE DAMAGE Camping, car, and 2 adults €16.50 (€13 on bikes). Extra adult €4. Child €2. Electricity €3.

Beach holidays have one small problem. After you've splashed about in the shallows and lounged on the beach for a few hours, getting sandy, salty, and suntanned, you really don't feel like performing an accidental striptease changing out of your swimwear and then stepping into a car that's also been gently roasting in an open-air oven. The solution is to get as close to the sea as possible. Camping du Letty has this covered, enabling you to stroll to the showers before ambling back to your *emplacement* refreshed and ready for action. Or inaction, of course. You don't have to be busy here, but as in many of the other larger coastal sites, there's plenty happening on site – Camping

du Letty comes complete with what one camper, who preferred slightly quieter scenarios, described as her *bête noire*, 'the whole hurdy-gurdy thing of discos, bars, and entertainment'. To add to this excitement, in 2011 there will be a brand-new swimming pool and aquapark, too, with slides and a retractable roof.

And yet, despite what this may suggest, campers can have a lovely, peaceful holiday here, if they so wish. A short distance along the *corniche* from the shops and restaurants of the summer resort of Bénodet, Camping du Letty is run by two generations of the Le Guyader family. Marc and his parents have their work cut out here as the

camping du letty

Camping du Letty, 32 rue du Canvez, 29950 Bénodet   00 33 2 98 57 04 69   www.campingduletty.com

site is spread over 25 acres (10 hectares) with about 600 pitches, but their enthusiasm and commitment are obvious. More to the point, the site has been established for decades, so the shade-giving trees are mature and the abundant hedges give each camping area a real sense of privacy and seclusion. In fact it's perfectly easy to forget that you're really in the midst of a veritable tentopolis.

Unlike some other sites there is no supplement to be paid for booking a sought-after beachside pitch, and once you're established you can stay for as long as you wish. The disco-cum-performance building is far enough away from the sleeping areas for people not to be disturbed – and it's not open at all on Fridays, because that is party night in Bénodet, and there's no point competing with that.

The campsite abuts Plage du Groasguan, a strip of golden sand along a slinky lagoon at the mouth of the River Odet. Across the placid water the Dunes Dominiales de Mousterlin stretch away, providing a sandy horizon that blocks out the sea's swell. The result is a choice between a backwater that's ideal for paddling or launching the kids on to the not-so-high seas (they can learn the ropes at one of the local sailing schools), while their parents lie back on the shore, or the alternative of the real beach and bigger waves, which is just a short hike away from the site. This one is overlooked by a

Philomene's macaroons are justly famous in Quimper

LES MACARONS
DE PHILOMENE

lighthouse that winks flirtatiously at every passing vessel after dark.

As you stroll along the shore, past the colourful art-deco changing rooms, and then further along Plage du Trez and around Pointe du Coq, you'll be getting closer to the old port of Bénodet, where river cruisers can ferry you upstream to Quimper. This is the place to come to for seafood that is so fresh that it may still be flapping about; perfect to fry up in a butter and white wine sauce. Because freshly caught food is surely the other main reason you like being right beside the seaside.

COOL FACTOR The sandy beach is next to the site and the living is easy.

WHO'S IN? Tents, campervans, caravans, and dogs (on leads), large groups and young groups by arrangement – yes (but everybody must keep quiet after 10pm).

ON SITE Six hundred pitches, most with electric hook-ups. It's a 4-star site with masses of services and facilities, including 6 **wash-blocks** around the site – one even has a shower for dogs. They charge €0.60 for showers, though. There's also a well-equipped *salle du musculation* (gym), a kids' club, a library, free wi-fi, an *épicerie* (mini-market; sells cold meats, too), squash and tennis courts, volleyball and archery areas, sauna and massage rooms, and even a salon for girls to do their hair and make-up before going out (it's usually girls, but no doubt everybody's welcome). New swimming pool coming in 2011. Takeaway food, from pizzas to main meals, is available every lunchtime and evening. Canoe and kayak hire and water sports on the beach. Motorhome service point. No campfires, but BBQs okay.

OFF SITE Why go off site? Only kidding. There are plenty of great cycle or canoe rides around the nature reserve and waterways adjacent to the site. Bénodet has more beaches, the *grande promenade* along the *corniche*, ferry trips across the River Odet to Ste Marine or upriver to the impressive medieval centre and double-steepled cathedral of Quimper, ancient capital of La Cornouaille (Cornwall). In the other (easterly) direction, the fishing port and resort of Concarneau, complete with its remarkable rampart-enclosed fortress island, Ville Close, lies along the coast, with the artist-favoured Pont-Aven further beyond, around 21 miles (35 km) away.

FOOD AND DRINK The Monday-morning market in Bénodet (or Wednesday in Ste Marine), or the Champion supermarket, may tempt you off site. There are plenty of bars and restaurants along Bénodet's seafront, but if you're looking for a more refined atmosphere head for the restaurant at the Grand Hotel l'Abbatiale (00 33 2 98 66 21 66; www.hotelabbatiale.com) at the old port, which specialises in the day's catch (*menus* from €22) in a room that is smart without being stuffy. Alternatively, arrive early and you may decide to buy your own fresh fish at the shop around the side of the hotel to fry by the seashore.

GETTING THERE From Quimper north, take D34 and follow signs to Bénodet. At the Rond Point de Penfoul, bear left on to D44 (avenue de Fouesnant) and follow for 1 mile (1.5 km) until Rond Point de Ty Pin. Turn right on to route du Letty, then fourth right on to rue de Canvez and second left down impasse de Creisanguer. Site entrance at end of road.

PUBLIC TRANSPORT Take a train from Paris to Quimper, catch a ferry to Bénodet, then take a taxi to the site.

OPEN Mid June–early September.

THE DAMAGE This can get complicated, so... 2 people (7 years plus), with a car or motorhome on a pitch €20 in low season and up to €25.50 from mid July to mid August. Add €2.30 for a dog, €2–€3.35 for a child aged 2–6 years, and €1.50–€4 for electricity, depending on ampage.

bois des écureuils

Camping Bois des Écureuils, 29300 Guilligomarc'h   00 33 2 98 71 70 98   www.bois-des-ecureuils.com

French campsites often have magnificent trees, but this five-acre site isn't decorated by *arbres* so much as dwarfed by them – all of Squirrel Wood stands tall and beautiful. Silver birch, green oak, beech, and chestnut branches tower over tents and campervans nestling contentedly in the sun-dappled shade. It's a discreet site that quietly revels in its own tranquillity, tucked into the farmlands of southern Brittany, with simple amenities providing all that self-sufficient campers really need. The nearby village of Guilligomarc'h (don't try saying that after a bottle of *cidre*), with its honey-coloured stone and white shutters, has a baker, butcher, *épicerie*, bar/restaurants, and friendly locals. It also lies between the valleys of the Scorff and Ellé rivers, which present the best fishing and scenery for biking and hiking trips. Just north of Locunolé, the scary-sounding Roche du Diable on the River Ellé is a favourite spot for canoeists who love their water white and definitely on the rocks. The only mystery is why this site is only open June to August, after which the red squirrels have the run of the place for the next nine months.

COOL FACTOR Beautiful trees are always cool, especially in the shade.

WHO'S IN? Tents, campervans, caravans, and dogs (on leads), large groups by arrangement – yes.

ON SITE Forty pitches, many with electric hook-ups. Clean block with plenty of hot showers and toilets, laundry sinks and a washing machine, plus a small shop for basics. Bicycles, tents, and fridges available to hire. No campfires, BBQs okay.

OFF SITE Bike-riding, walking, and gentle drives are the best way to get around, or kayaking on the rivers. It's 12 miles (20 km) to sandy beaches and lazy estuaries.

FOOD AND DRINK Guilligomarc'h and Arzano both have *boulangeries* and *pâtisseries*. In old Quimperlé go for Crêperie Ty Gwechall (00 33 2 98 96 30 63) or the Restaurant Le Bistro de la Tour (00 33 2 98 39 29 58) serves *cuisine de terroir* with *menus* from €19.

GETTING THERE From Quimperlé take D22 through Arzano. Turn left on D222 to Guilligomarc'h. Go through the village, following signposts for the site on to a minor road. The campsite is on the right.

OPEN Early June–end August.

THE DAMAGE Camping, car, 2 adults €11. Child to 7 years €1.50. Extra adult €3. Electricity €2.50.

croas an ter

Camping de Croas an Ter, Quelvez, 29360 Clohars-Carnoët   00 33 2 98 39 94 19   www.campingcroasanter.com

In Britain you'd be thrilled to find a site like this. A calm country location next to a farm, with magnificent trees and plentiful hedges for shade and privacy; a variety of pitches (sunny, shady, overlooking fields); a wash-block that looks brand new, complete with showers like you wish you had at home; a huge volleyball/badminton court, and children's play area with table-tennis tables.

There are walks (or bike routes) that begin from the site, through the forest, or past the fields and marshy reed beds. The walk along the River Laïta from Posmoric Port to Le Pouldu is really lovely – no wonder Gauguin and friends moved here in 1889. You can visit the house-museum where they stayed and painted the beautiful dining room. It's only a step to the closest seaside; the flower-filled market town of Quimperlé is nearby, and Pont-Aven, where Gauguin founded the post-Impressionist school, is a half hour's drive.

In France there's so much more competition that campsites have to be this good. If you really want a piscine to dip into you can go to a nearby site, but we can't promise such a friendly welcome.

COOL FACTOR The comforts of a country campsite 5 minutes' drive from beautiful beaches.

WHO'S IN? Tents, campervans, caravans, and dogs (on leads), families – yes. Large groups of teenagers – no.

ON SITE Eighty-three pitches, all with hook-ups. Sparkling wash-block with baby-changing, wheelchair access, excellent showers. Bike hire available. No campfires. BBQs okay.

OFF SITE The kids might like the Animal Park (Parc Animalier du Quinquis) in Clohars-Carnoët (00 33 2 98 39 94 13; www.parcanimalierduquinquis.com). The Gauguin-focused Maison-Musée du Pouldu is well worth a visit (00 33 2 98 39 98 51; www.museedupouldu.clohars-carnoet.fr).

FOOD AND DRINK There's an *épicerie* and pizzeria close by and good markets in Quimperlé, Guidel, and Clohars-Carnoët, but for eating out head to Doëlan. Bar Le Rive Gauche (00 33 2 98 71 56 50) stands out for its seafood.

GETTING THERE From Quimperlé (or off N165 motorway) take D49 direction Le Pouldu. About ½ mile (1 km) after the crossroads with D224 at Lann Justis, the site is signposted 110 yards (100 m) to your left.

OPEN End May–mid September.

THE DAMAGE Camping, car, 2 adults €12.20. Extra person over 7 years €3.60. Electricity €3.20.

château du deffay

Château du Deffay, 18 Ste-Reine-de-Bretagne, 44160 Pontchâteau   00 33 2 40 88 00 57   www.camping-le-deffay.com

After driving for hours through English summer storms and the soft, steady rain of northern France, waking up in the sunshine beside the lake is a little like falling down the rabbit hole and arriving in wonderland. The chateau itself is mostly used for conferences, but the lake is on show, with pedal-boats, (gentle) exercise equipment, and strolls around the waterside for when you feel like doing more than admiring the view.

The ranks of mobile homes on the far side of the lake may not please the eye, but the site and its facilities are lovely, and the heated swimming pool, with its retractable roof, means that even a grey day here need not be a washout.

There are plenty more ways to get wet nearby. The Parc Naturel Régional de Brière is a huge expanse of marshland, resulting from the sea's incursion 7,500 years ago, leaving swathes of reeds and bullrushes crisscrossed by narrow waterways. Some land has been reclaimed, but it remains the second-largest marsh in France, so it's a perfect place to find thatched-cottage, picturebook villages such as Kerhinet, local crafts such as basket-making, or for watching birds, especially on guided punts. Look out for Cetti's warblers, black-winged stilts, and whiskered terns, some of which will be time-sharing by flying the few miles inland.

The beautiful sheltered bay of La Baule boasts the longest sandy beach in Europe – at 7½ miles (12 km) we're not arguing – so you're sure to find your own patch, but you'd best go up to La Mine d'Or at Pénestin if you are looking for surf action.

COOL FACTOR Lakeside charm near seaside and marshes.

WHO'S IN? Tents, campervans, caravans, and dogs on leads, large groups by arrangement – yes.

ON SITE A hundred and twenty spacious pitches, all with electric hook-ups. Excellent wash-block, plenty of toilets and hot showers plus good washing-up, laundry facilities, and washing machines. There's a big caged trampoline and play area for the kids. Tennis, fishing, heated pool, ping-pong, and pedal-boats are free (go-karts can be hired). There's a bar, restaurant, and shop May to mid-September, and a kids' club during high season. Bike hire and canoe/kayak hire can be arranged. Motorhome service point. Wi-fi €3 per day. No campfires, but BBQs okay.

OFF SITE Ideal cycling country when the wind's behind you, but great fun to hire canoes/kayaks to explore the marshes or go horse- or pony-trekking nearby. Wide selection of beaches and water sports are 20–30 minutes' drive.

FOOD AND DRINK For a great gastronomic experience, Eric Guerin's flamboyant La Mare aux Oiseaux, *menus* from €40 (00 33 2 40 88 53 01; www.mareauxoiseaux.fr) in the middle of the marsh at St-Joachim, deserves its rave reviews.

GETTING THERE Halfway along N165 between Nantes and Vannes, come off at J13 and follow D33 towards Ste-Reine-de-Bretagne. Three miles (5 km) from the town you'll see Château du Deffay signposted to the right.

PUBLIC TRANSPORT Railway station in Pontchâteau.

OPEN May–September.

THE DAMAGE €3.30–€5.50 per adult and €2.30–€3.80 per child (2–12 years) per night, plus €8.50–€12.50 for a pitch, depending on season. Two adults and pitch early August €23.50. Electricity €3–€4.30. Two-person chalets €189–€623 per week.

kota cabana

Kota Cabana, 2 ave de la Libération, 72350 Brûlon   00 33 2 43 92 17 85   www.chateau-enclos.com

Glamping doesn't get more glamorous than this: a double-decked luxury tree house perched in the branches of sequoia and cedar trees overlooking the elegant second-empire Château de l'Enclos. Don't expect any pretence about cooking or preparing food; raising a champagne glass to your lips and carrying a toothbrush up the 30-odd steps is the closest you're likely to get to chores.

Retired businessman Jean-Claude Guillou and his wife Annie-Claude already had a charming three-bedroomed guest house in the grounds of his 19th-century chateau at Brûlon, but the equilateral triangle formed by three magnificent conifers presented an opportunity to create a lofty platform that mixes Baltic style with the *joie de vivre* of Brazilian beach life, hence 'cabana', and couples have stayed happily here ever since.

The octagonal bedroom is built of untreated pine, so the aroma of natural resins permeates the pile of cushions in a room decorated with jokey references to Lapland reindeer. On the deck there's a captain's bell, which signals that the basket of breakfast goodies is ready to be winched up, and a table and chairs to enjoy them *en plein air*, with views across the garden (look out for llamas, sheep, goats, and miniature donkeys) and beyond to the Vallée de la Vègre. In 2010 a second, lower deck was added; a chill-out area that's ideal for kicking back with a book and an aperitif. A further innovation is a brand-new, authentic roulotte, with its own private terrace and offering a very different, yet equally de luxe, experience.

COOL FACTOR It's camping in a tree house or a genuine Bohemian gypsy caravan. Enough said.

WHO'S IN? Couples – yes. Kids, pets, complications – no.

ON SITE Hosts both speak excellent English and enthusiastically show guests the grounds and animals – 7 acres (3 hectares) of landscaped botanical gardens and a collection of tame creatures. There's a basin and toilet in the tree house, but the shower is in an annexe next to the house. The roulotte has a shower. Three superior *chambres d'hôtes* (bed-and-breakfast) options are also available.

OFF SITE Most people treat this as a one-night or weekend affair, but that's no reason not to enjoy a tour of the valley of the River Sarthe before driving 20 miles (32 km) to Le Mans to visit the circuit of the 24-hour race and the Musée de l'Automobile de la Sarthe (00 33 2 43 72 72 24).

FOOD AND DRINK It's wisest to eat out. The Guillous recommend Auberge de la Grande Charnie (00 33 2 43 88 43 12; www.aubergedelagrandecharnie.com), about 8 miles (12 km) away in St-Denis-d'Orques, and suggest a *menu* emphasising *cuisine de terroir* of the Valley. Book ahead.

GETTING THERE Take A81 from Le Mans. Come off at J1 on to D4 for Brûlon. Follow the road through the town, up the hill. The entrance is on your right.

PUBLIC TRANSPORT The TGV stops in Le Mans and if you're staying here a 20-mile (32-km) cab fare won't add much to the bill.

OPEN The cabana and roulotte are heated and available all year round. Best to book well ahead.

THE DAMAGE €160 per night for Kota Cabana; €140 per night for the Roulotte de Lamane. Breakfast included.

forest view

Forest View, L'Espérance, 61110 Dorceau   00 33 2 33 25 45 27   www.forestviewleisurebreaks.co.uk

Yorkshire exiles Pete and Karen Wilson took over Forest View in 2005 and have transformed the wilderness they found into a comfortable, easy-going site that lies by a quiet crossroads between the edge of the Forêt de Saussay and a landscape of gently rolling farmland. While the forest is huge and forms a significant part of the Parc Naturel Régional du Perche, the site itself could easily be called Lake View because it's the reflections in the fishing lake that most people love to gaze at.

The lake is stocked with rudd, roach, pike, and tench, but there's a firm no-killing policy, so even if you land a giant carp it must go back in the water. There's crazy golf and a small pool in the orchard to dip into, but most people come here to ride horses or bikes, to paint, watch birds, or walk in the woods of tamarisk and hawthorn. Perhaps they are thinking of Proust as they do so – the town of Illiers-Combray, where he used to spend the summer and which provided the setting for *Swann's Way*, is 20 miles (32 km) to the south-east. This region is often bypassed in the rush to get south to the Loire and the Dordogne. It's a land of forests, ancient abbeys, and fortified manors with massive circular towers and beautiful gardens. The area is famous for its lace, its powerful Percheron horses, and for unspoilt thousand-year-old villages such as Chapelle-Montligeon, where an early-20th-century, gothic revival cathedral, Notre-Dame de Montligeon, rises somewhat bizarrely above the fields. And it's known for its wonderful cider and hospitality, both of which can be sampled when you get back to camp.

COOL FACTOR Cool views, warm hospitality, hot meals, and cold ice creams. Plus a whole lot of history.

WHO'S IN? Tents, campervans, caravans, and dogs (on leads), large groups by arrangement – yes.

ON SITE Twenty pitches, 12 with electric hook-ups. There's also a *gîte*, B&B, and tent hire. The 2 showers and toilets are powerful and spacious. There's a shop for essentials, fishing, and mini-golf, and a small pool. Wi-fi is €2 per day. No campfires, but BBQs okay.

OFF SITE Hikes and rides from the site. Bretoncelles and Rémalard have markets every day. L'Aigle has a big Tuesday market and Nogent-le-Rotrou has one on Saturdays. Horse-riding at the Château de Villeray. Sensational stained glass, soaring spires of Chartres Cathedral 27 miles (44 km) away.

FOOD AND DRINK Campers can book a 4-course meal in the function room on Wednesday evenings. It's great to visit the cider-making farm at L'Hermitière (00 33 2 37 49 67 30; www.cidrerie-traditionnelle-du-perche.fr) and a 15-minute drive away is the beautiful dining room at Hôtel Le Montligeon (00 33 2 33 83 81 19; www.hotelmontligeon.com), which features wonderful local *cuisine de terroir du Perche*, and has *menus* (from €15) in English.

GETTING THERE N12 from Paris. Just past Dreux bear left on to D828 and then D928, always direction Le Mans. Approximately 6 miles (10 km) after passing through La Loupe, turn right on to D620 to Bretoncelles. Turn left in Bretoncelles and then right on D38 signposted 'Rémalard'. The site is on your right just before crossroads at L'Espérance.

OPEN Late March–October.

THE DAMAGE Prices by the pitch, so tent pitch is €9 (€13 July, August), caravan €12 (€16), including electricity. Pets €1.40 per day.

around paris

huttopia versailles

Huttopia Versailles, 31 rue Berthelot, 78000 Versailles   00 33 1 39 51 23 61 www.huttopia.com
Huttopia Senonches, Étang de Badouleau, 28250 Senonches   00 33 2 37 37 81 40

If you enjoy a good pun and are seeking a campsite that feels rustic, has an element of luxury, and is close to Paris, then Huttopia Versailles might be just the ticket. Despite being one outlet of many and owned by an internationally expanding company, the overall experience is far from cult-like or corporate. In fact – I'm lovin' it.

Developed into a fringe of woodland, Huttopia Versailles has a peaceful vibe. Only 20 minutes from the Eiffel Tower and with the Palace of Versailles even closer – an easy 1¾ mile (3 km) walk – Huttopia is still enjoyable for more than location alone. The site has a number of subtle touches, adding to the ambience of comfort. One of the shower blocks, bedecked in hotel-quality fittings, has a wood-burner wafting a fragrant aroma of pine into the air. Much more appealing than, say, damp feet. And a family shower room with basins and plenty of space to hold three makes life easier for parents. Understandably, families adore Huttopia. There is a nice compact play area next to the terrace, which is beside the restaurant and pool. The terrace is a useful place for families to create a base when they are relaxing on site, as the kids can be seen wherever they wander. The tent spaces are open and high at the rear of the camp, behind the 'huts' of the site's name. Mature trees shade much of the area, which means the ground can feel a little uneven due to tree roots. It's easy enough to find a level spot, though, and besides – nature is lumpy.

City outskirts sound a little too urban? Want a more ecological experience but still with the option of a Paris visit? In that case around 93 miles (150 km) from Paris, Huttopia has just opened its newest addition at Senonches (south-west of Paris, near Chartres). Here nature and setting are at the fore, within a spacious encampment in France's second-largest state-managed woodland. Near a swimming lake, and with a great deal of nature-related activity on hand, Paris may be within reach, yet motivation to visit it is in short supply.

Horse-riding, mountain-biking, and hiking are all facilitated here, and fishing in the Étang de Badouleau, adjacent to the camp, is easy. The site is car-free and campervans are limited to pitches near the entrance, lending a more back-to-basics feel than Versailles. As with all Huttopia destinations, though, the reality is far from basic.

The forethought injected into the site means you'll not be rubbing sticks together for warmth nor searching out the 'soft' leaves. Brand-new, superbly equipped toilet- and wash-blocks are scattered around, and tent pitches are based in their own generous clearing, supplemented with a picnic table. There is a ready-made bivouac and BBQ meeting point, with arranged tables to sit at and socialise. Activity-wise, nature trails and even treasure hunts can take you through the forest. In high season sport tournaments are arranged for those with a flair for it, and a weekday morning-club with art and nature-based play keeps children occupied. An evening programme for adults, including story-telling, outdoor cinema, live music,

Huttopia Versailles

and board games make this a rather special break from the norm.

Huttopia has reserved itself a very secure pitch in the camping world and deserves to be congratulated for the new site at Senonches. This site illustrates that while the brand has grown beyond a family concern, it still has the soul and the desire to explore new forms of hospitality. The same, while utterly different, Huttopia Versailles and Senonches can be effortlessly combined into a single holiday, giving both Paris and the nearby Parc Régional du Perche an opportunity to shine.

COOL FACTOR The location near Paris, as well as the high quality of facilities and fittings, make Huttopia Versailles a viable option for a city break, with the bonus of being in nature. Senonches is an idyllic, peaceful escape, beautifully thought out and easily within reach of Paris, boasting a wide range of imaginative activities for all ages.

WHO'S IN? Tents, campervans, caravans, cars, families, couples – yes. Cars left at the gate in Senonches.

ON SITE Versailles has 130 marked pitches, 20 chalets, and tent space is variable. Fifteen excellent showers in 3 blocks, cleaned 3 times a day. Excellent baby-change and disabled facilities. Swimming and paddling pool with pleasant poolside area, café-restaurant serving home-made organic pizza (meals from €10), bar until 11pm. Climbing frame near café, with soft wood chippings, swings, table tennis, badminton, *boules*, table football. Senonches has 128 large and private pitches for tents, each with its own picnic table. Shower- and wash-rooms are dotted around – some under canvas and some in wooden huts. Fixtures, water pressure, and cleanliness are good. Good baby-changing facilities. Swimming lake, with a bar/restaurant stretching over it on stilts that serves grilled meats and pizza. Upstairs has a good stock of board games. There is a vast array of children's activities daily, concerning nature and art, and adult activities of an evening. Site shop sells essentials and some local produce.

OFF SITE Leaving the Huttopia Versailles campsite and walking straight down the road for 160 yards (150 m) brings you to the closest supermarket. Continue another 440 yards (400 m) and you arrive at the railway station to central Paris (www.parisinfo.com). The Palace of Versailles (www.versailles-tourisme.com) is a 1¾-mile (3-km) walk, or you can hire cycles on site. Reception has plenty of information. The town of Senonches is charming and appears to have dropped from the sky into the centre of the forest. There is an 11th-century castle and plenty of interesting architecture. Parc Régional du Perche is 450 acres (182 hectares) of natural and cultural heritage, with fortified manor houses, farmsteads, and villages. Cycling or walking is best for exploring the region. Chartres is 25 miles (40 km) away with a medieval old town and cathedral. Both Chartres and Senonches have great restaurants to discover.

FOOD AND DRINK There is a good American-style café in Versailles called Sisters Café (00 33 1 30 21 21 22), which is open for lunch until 3pm and in the evening until 11pm. Otherwise, head into Paris and take your pick.

GETTING THERE Versailles: from Paris Orly Airport – 15 miles/24 km (25 mins by car). Huttopia have helpful route-planners for both sites (see www.huttopia.com).

PUBLIC TRANSPORT The train to central Paris is 440 yards (400 m) from the Versailles campsite.

OPEN Versailles: March–November.

Senonches: April–November.

THE DAMAGE Versailles: 2 people, tent, car €25–€36.

Senonches: 2 people, tent, car €18–€25.

alsace lorraine & champagne

la citadelle

Camping La Citadelle, rue Vauban, 55600 Montmédy   00 33 3 29 80 10 40   www.lorraineaucoeur.com

To say north-eastern France has endured a troubled history would be an understatement. Shifting borders tossed the region from one country's ownership to another and back again. Montmédy is not the most famous battleground near the Meuse, yet 2,000 years of history in the citadel's evolution make it a fascinating base.

Camping La Citadelle earns its place in this book by its location far more than by its charms. It is a small site with low hedges dividing up private areas, or the opportunity to pitch a tent outside this grid formation. Tucked under the Citadel's walls, sharing the same exposed hill, the campsite is shielded from winds by mature trees and the citadel itself, just a stone's throw away. A short walk takes you to the extraordinary defensive outer ring. Fantastic views can be enjoyed by circumnavigating the ancient walled buildings, or the 'small circuit' with its views more towards the still partially ruined town. Within the magnificent walls are places to eat, an information office, and a mixture of derelict and beautifully restored buildings with an impressive church at the centre.

COOL FACTOR The campsite's location, its views, and the opportunity to explore a monumental creation of, and memorial to, war.

WHO'S IN? Tents, campervans, caravans, pets – yes.

ON SITE Thirty-two pitches and a free area for tents. Clean wash-block, disabled toilet and shower, 2 basic hot showers, 2 toilets. Small playground with slide/swing. Café and other facilities shared within the Citadel itself, home to artists' studios and galleries, built into the formidable inner walls.

OFF SITE The Meuse Valley has beautiful villages, farms, and open landscapes. The overwhelming pull for tourism is Verdun. North-east of the city saw the longest, most costly battle in recorded history, during the First World War. Now woodland, battlefields, and destroyed villages betray the scars. Tourist maps provide detailed information.

FOOD AND DRINK Le Panoramique in Montmédy (00 33 3 29 80 11 68) is a traditional, reasonably priced restaurant (€14–€59).

GETTING THERE From Verdun follow D964 along the Meuse. Turn right on to D17 at Mouzay. Look for D947 junction. Follow until D963 – you are at Montmédy.

OPEN Early May–late September.

THE DAMAGE Tent and car plus 2 people €8.60.

ferme du bois joli

Ferme du Bois Joli, 12 rue Haute Gaston Parant, 55210 St-Maurice-sous-les-Côtes   00 33 3 29 89 33 32

France's Bienvenue à la Ferme (Welcome to the Farm) initiative was set up in Lorraine to build a bridge between tourism and the mostly agricultural heritage of local villages. Staying on a farm has plenty going for it; it is likely to be less touristy, fresh goodies may be delivered direct to your awning, and you may be able to have a more authentic experience. Around 400 farms have opened up and, what with Lorraine having a rather successful quiche named after it, staying at a couple sounds like a good idea.

Pitches in an old farm orchard are shaded by plum, apple, or pear trees. Facilities are basic, but the trade-off is worth it when you consider the quiet location, views, and proximity to Metz and Nancy. From the higher side of the site, tucked into the base of a wooded hill, you can sit in peace, munching a fresh plum, with the church spire in the foreground and, way beyond, softly undulating farmland. Walking can find you atop a hill, in deep woods, or next to a small lake. Jumping into a car or on to a bicycle widens the options to include water sports or stunning national parkland.

COOL FACTOR Peace and quiet, views, an authentic and untouristy site in a good location with a farm experience adjacent to a regional park.

WHO'S IN? Tents, campervans, caravans, pets, large or small groups – yes.

ON SITE Twenty-five spacious pitches with 18 electric hook-ups between the trees, basic hot showers and toilets in adjacent blocks, outdoor sink, and tap access. Children's area. Fresh fruit falling from the trees and expansive views. Walking in the woods directly behind the site.

OFF SITE Lac de Madine for water sports, golf, horse-riding, and supervised beaches only 6 miles (10 km) to the south.

FOOD AND DRINK One speciality is *potée Lorraine* (boiled meat with cabbage), accompanied by wine from Moselle or the Côtes de Toul. The mirabelle plum and brandy deserve attention, as does locally made quiche. The village restaurant is a 10–15-minute stroll away.

GETTING THERE From Reims take A4 (toll) towards Verdun and Metz, taking exit 32 south and the first exit after the toll booth. Take D904 and D908 to St-Maurice-sous-les-Côtes. The campsite is signed from the village centre.

OPEN Mid April–mid October.

THE DAMAGE Tent and car plus 2 people €7.50.

les grèbes

Les Grèbes du Lac de Marcenay, 5 rue du Pont Neuf, 21330 Marcenay   00 33 3 80 81 61 72   www.campingmarcenaylac.com

Marcenay, in the Châtillonnais area of Burgundy, is one of 23 villages famed for Chardonnay and Pinot Noir wines. At one time the lake here was used by local monks as their source of piscatorial sustenance: however today it attracts a somewhat more diverse collection of people, who come to sunbathe on its sandy banks, row, or paddle across the large expanse of water, or watch the wildlife. And, fortunately, there's also a lovely campsite nestled right next to it.

Les Grèbes du Lac de Marcenay is everything that a campsite should and could be. It's got all the ingredients for an old-school camping experience: a remote location far away from any road noise, a substantial lake, an incredibly friendly and helpful welcome in the guise of Dirk Jansen, the owner, and a laissez-faire attitude to where you pitch your home for the duration of your stay. That it's off the beaten track won't appeal to people who like to be within walking distance of a choice of bars and restaurants, but we kind of feel that this isolation is all part of its appeal.

When Dirk took on the site it was a tired municipal affair in desperate need of someone who could let its natural character shine through. He says that one of the first things he did was remove the barrier at the entrance and throw away the rules and regulations telling campers what they could and couldn't do. 'People don't want to see that when they are on holiday', he explains in his dulcet Dutch tones. Since then, he's been quietly turning it into a relaxed lakeside idyll. And after all the years that he's worked running and owning campsites, you can tell that he still has a passion for it and has a hundred and one plans for things he wants to develop – when time and funds allow.

The site itself seems to attract a mixture of people; young couples touring around France who just want to stay for a few days, and older couples who come back year after year and stay for weeks at a time. It also seems to attract cyclists, who use it as a base to explore the area. Being away from any traffic, the site feels like a safe place for kids to run around and have fun without causing undue parental anxiety.

It's a lush, green, wooded plot with reasonably spacious pitches (or, at least, spacious by French standards). Each one is set in a clearing that is partially surrounded by shrubs or trees, so there is a real sense of privacy. On one side are open fields and vineyards and on the other is the lake, which is about 3 miles (5 km) all the way round and on the edge of a forest. And despite Dirk's various plans, the site's greatest asset will always be the ancient natural feature that gives it its name. There is something very special about living near the water and the tall trees that line its banks. Unfortunately you can't actually camp on the lakeside itself, but you are literally a hop, skip, and a jump away across one of a couple of footbridges that links you to the water's edge. So you could very easily take a bottle of wine and a blanket and sit on the sand, watching the sun set, and not have to worry about getting lost as you scuttle back to your bed.

Although individual campfires aren't allowed next to the pitches, there is a communal area just outside the main site overlooking the lake, where Dirk regularly sets up a fire and BBQ for everyone to enjoy. He also plans to have a small outside bar, so campers can enjoy *une bière* and some *saucisson*

and tell stories around the campfire, too. All in all, Les Grèbes du Lac Marcenay is a very special campsite. Its relaxed, welcoming atmosphere and beautiful setting somehow capture the true spirit of camping in France and make the experience of staying here a real joy.

COOL FACTOR Relaxed, remote, lakeside chilling.

WHO'S IN? Tents, campervans, caravans, dogs, large groups (owner checks details before confirming) – yes.

ON SITE Ninety pitches, all with electric hook-ups, if needed. There are 13 clean toilets and 17 good showers, free for residents, and there are 2 disabled toilets and showers and a baby-changing room. A small play area is provided for children, with kids' bikes and a free-standing outdoor pool. In the main reception there is a games area with a pool table and free wi-fi. The laundry area is also in the main reception building. There is a facility for freezing ice packs. No individual campfires are allowed, but there is a communal fire just to the side of the main site.

OFF SITE If you fancy a bit of lake-orienteering you can borrow the Canadian canoe for free. Or, if you'd rather stick to dry land there are three different walks around the lake, ranging from 3 miles (5 km) to 6 miles (10 km). Dirk will rent bikes to you at a reasonable €3.50 for 2 hours and lend you some local maps. Or you can try pony-trekking next door for €18 an hour (ask at campsite reception). There's also a hidden bird-watching tower for the more ornothologically inclined. And if the attractions of the lake aren't enough, there's a recently opened assault course in the trees at Forêt de l'Aventure d'Auxerre-Laborde (00 33 6 69 06 34 17; www.foret-aventure-auxerre.com), which is a 45-minute drive and costs €14 for kids and €22 for adults. If you like the idea of nosing round other people's cast-offs, you'll be able to find a car-boot sale (*vide grenier*) most weekends in one of the

nearby villages (ask reception for a list). We found that this was more tailored towards locals than tourists, but there's bound to be something to pique your interest.

FOOD AND DRINK You can pre-order fresh bread and pastries at reception every day and they carry a small selection of food and drink, including the local tipple: we're in Crémant de Bourgogne country after all. For those interested in fully immersing themselves in local culture, there is free wine-tasting in Marcenay courtesy of Monsieur Guilleman (00 33 3 80 81 40 03). Just around the corner, in Balot, there is a snail farm, which you can visit and even taste the produce for €7 per person. For traditional French food served in what feels like someone's front room, complete with dressers and a mounted boar's head, with its friendly welcome and reasonably priced fare Auberge de la Baume, also in nearby Balot (00 33 3 80 81 40 15; www.aubergedelabaume.com), is well worth a visit. For a special treat, why not try the Michelin-starred, 12th-century chateau-hotel, Abbaye de la Bussière in Bussière-sur-Ouche (00 33 3 80 49 02 29; www.abbayedelabussiere.fr)?

GETTING THERE The site is on D965 between Laignes and Châtillon-sur-Seine. Follow signposts to Lac de Marcenay and 'Camping'.

OPEN May–September.

THE DAMAGE 2 adults, tent €15.50, extra adult €5, child (2–11 years) €4.

camping de troyes

Camping de Troyes, 7 rue Roger Salengro, 10150 Pont-Ste-Marie   00 33 3 25 81 02 64   www.troyescamping.net

Camping de Troyes is perfectly situated if you're looking for a stop-off point en route to the south of France or a base from which to explore the Champagne region. The centre of Troyes, with its medieval wooden-framed buildings that almost topple into each other, is only a short drive away. It is well worth spending a day meandering through the tiny streets and imagining what life would have been like as a musketeer in the Middle Ages.

When you first arrive at Camping de Troyes you could be forgiven for thinking that you were walking into a motorhome nightmare. But keep the faith and head to the back of the site, where you'll find a tent haven surrounded by shrubs and trees. Suddenly you'll realise why it's worth a few nights' breather. Although you can easily feel you have your own private space, the plot itself isn't exactly sprawling, so being at the end of the site doesn't mean a long walk if you get caught short in the middle of the night. The site is modern, but not overly manicured, and the pitches aren't regimented. The overall feel is 'organised' and you'll leave refreshed, ready to go on your way.

COOL FACTOR Great stop-off point when heading south.
WHO'S IN? Tents, campervans, caravans, dogs – yes. Large groups allowed, but owner checks details before confirming.
ON SITE One hundred and four pitches, 26 for tents, 22 hook-ups, 3 in the tent area. Heated outdoor swimming pool, games room, restaurant. Twelve free showers, 11 toilets and wash-block. Disabled facilities and baby-changing room. Bike hire, small shop, and daily bread-delivery service. Small play area, kids' bikes for hire. Ice-pack freezing. No campfires.
OFF SITE Troyes is one of the Champagne region's historic capitals with many medieval streets. It has its own beach at Lac de la Forêt d'Orient.
FOOD AND DRINK The onsite restaurant is fairly basic. For something more interesting Libanais (00 33 3 25 70 60 68) serves home-made Lebanese food.
GETTING THERE From Troyes, head 2½ miles (4 km) north to Pont Ste-Marie (signposted) then follow signs for Municipal Camping.
PUBLIC TRANSPORT Troyes is easily reached by train or bus. A bus service runs from the centre to close to the site.
OPEN April–mid October.
THE DAMAGE 2 people, vehicle, tent €18.90, extra adult (13 years plus) €5.45, child (2–12 years) €3.40.

camping de belle hutte

Camping de Belle Hutte, 1 bis Vouille de Belle Hutte, 88250 La Bresse   00 33 3 29 25 49 75   www.camping-belle-hutte.com

Is it possible for parents to buy a child's love with a holiday and still take pleasure in it themselves? Camping de Belle Hutte might provide an answer, with superb facilities set before a Vosges Mountain backdrop. With grandchildren of the original owners now working reception, awareness of both children's and parents' needs must be instinctive. It's a quiet, safe, fun environment, squatting between wooded mountains with walks and cycle routes. A large heated pool, complete with slides, has claimed the finest views down the lush green valley. The camping area at the far end has open pitches and blends into the woods. More private hedge-enclosed spaces are closer to facilities. Terraced over three levels, some pitches have better views, yet all feel comfortably tucked in.

Belle Hutte evolves as the owners tweak the visitor experience. With wi-fi in all corners and new toilet blocks, what will the owners think of next? Offsite activities, courtesy of nature, and thoughtful consideration of how to spend time on site make this a great base for those with healthy intentions, who also enjoy a day by the pool.

COOL FACTOR Family-orientated with enough to keep everyone happy – all the possibilities of the Vosges.

WHO'S IN? Tents, campervans, caravans, pets, large groups or small groups – yes.

ON SITE In the heart of the Parc Naturel Régional des Ballons des Vosges, the site has 130 pitches, 24 good showers, 2 baby-changes and 2 disabled facilities. Large, new pool; tiered smaller pool; 2 slides. Washing machine, tumble-drier, drying room, ski room. Games room, table tennis, trampoline, TV, snack bar, and bar. Mini-market, bread supply, gas supply. Ticketing and fishing license purchase.

OFF SITE Quarter of a mile (500 m) from a lake with surrounding woodland. Routes for cycling, hiking, skiing. Fishing possible.

FOOD AND DRINK Auberge de la Chume du Firstmiss, (00 33 3 29 63 26 13), Auberge Breitzhousen (00 33 3 29 63 22 92) and Auberge Huss (00 33 3 89 82 27 20) are all good.

GETTING THERE From Paris A4: Paris, Metz, Nancy, Epinal, Remiremont, La Bresse. In La Bresse take D430 eastwards 5 ½ miles (9 km). Site signposted.

PUBLIC TRANSPORT Paris to La Bresse by train.

OPEN Mid December–mid November.

THE DAMAGE Tent and car plus 2 people €19.

les perron-beauvineau

Camping Les Perron-Beauvineau, route de Spoy, 10200 Meurville   00 33 3 25 27 40 56   www.champagne-perron-beauvineau.com

As any red-nosed soul will expound between hiccups, France has a somewhat well-deserved reputation for its wine. It produces some of the most esteemed inebriants in the world, rendering a certain dedicated exploration into the subject essential. A pilgrimage of gratitude could begin with the most famous region, producing the most famous wine – Champagne. Of all the tipples in existence, none other comes close for sparking the imagination or exuding sheer glamour.

The Perron family have spent 110 years and five generations of history in the pursuit of champagne, working their business through biblical upheavals of war and pestilence. Marilyn Perron recently had the idea of evolving oenological tourism for the Aube area and opened the gloriously intimate and ecologically clean Sauleraie – a campsite with a dual purpose.

In the first instance it is a convenient retreat for those wishing to explore the Aube area's forests, lakes, plains, and rolling hills by bicycle or on foot. A short walk brings you to Meurville – a beautiful village nestled between vineyard-topped slopes, where more than a dozen families make champagne. In the main square by the church a tourist map provides a label-by-label guide around the village producers, each virtually within staggering distance of each other. A little way out of town it's possible to walk in the vineyards themselves, or take the Champagne Tourist Route that winds between them. Workers harvest the grapes from late August onwards, making this

a good time to visit. The second purpose of La Sauleraie is as an approved bird sanctuary with a small wild lake and nesting boxes for every winged creature, from predators to prey. Wild ducks and geese frequent the lake, and the introduction of pollinating prairie plants and shrubs is under way in order to attract a wider pool of species.

Settled around the lake, the campsite has a rural feel without being disconnected. Vineyards and fields creep up the slopes and there are mature weeping willows, pines, and hedges softening the space. Nature-lovers have been well catered for and a limit of six tents on one side of the lake ensures that it feels spacious even when full.

If the weather is appalling, or a little more luxury is desired after sipping bubbly, the Perrons have built three themed log cabins. These *fustes* sleep up to four people and are sympathetic to the environment, with sheepskin insulation and vegetal roofs. Small and perfectly formed, each has its own features and comfortable decoration. The Tsukiyo cabin has a basin and a small fountain outside; Salama has mature pine trees and hammocks; while Kalyani enjoys a terrace. Although these cabins share the camping loo block and lack a kitchen sink, breakfast can be provided and a stay of five nights or more will find you rewarded with a bottle of champagne.

Everyone who visits the site is invited into the rather grand family cellar and tasting-room in Meurville. Here you will find out more about the Champagne Tourist Route, be introduced

Perron cellar in Meurville

Champagne Route vineyards, with views towards Meurville

to their own brands of fine wine, discover how the drink is made and why so much struggle surrounds its production. The variables that affect a vineyard during a year are genuinely staggering. Understanding this undoubtedly aids appreciation and enjoyment of the different vintages.

Perhaps the most memorable aspect of staying with the Perrons is the opportunity to be guided through the region by such a dedicated, respected champagne producer. The Perron passion for the business shines through. Chin-chin.

COOL FACTOR Staying in an intimate sanctuary under the rolling Champagne hills, with a host who has been making bubbly for 5 generations and wants you to try it. This is a place to relax, unwind, and recharge your batteries alongside nature – and fine wine.

WHO'S IN? Tents, campervans, caravans, dogs, nature-lovers, families – yes. Large groups, noisy intentions – no.

ON SITE Six pitches with electricity for tents or campervans, 3 small log cabins sleeping 4. Newly built, very clean, tiled shower block with 2 washbasins, 2 good showers, 2 washing cubicles, 1 disabled cubicle with shower/toilet, and facilities for washing up. Cycle shelter. Cycle hire possible through the campsite. Two dog kennels. The site playground has a trampoline, table tennis, sandpit, 'sprung' animals, swings, wooden blocks/climbing frame. A second playground, conveniently in the village at the Perron cellar, has a large climbing frame and swings. A lake, with a bridge to an island hide for bird- and animal-spotting. Several bird boxes and nesting boxes. *Boules* facilities. Permanent BBQ. Picnic tables. Site office is in the village at the Perron cellar. No campfires.

OFF SITE The regional capital of Troyes is recommended and is only 30 miles (50 km) from Meurville. Numerous museums and medieval buildings pack the narrow streets. During the second week of June it hosts various Champagne Fairs. The Champagne Tourist Route is a 373-mile (600-km) signposted circular trip through vineyard country, and local tourist offices can point you in the direction of growers with cellars open to the public. Running between Bar-sur-Seine

and Bar-sur-Aube the trail leads through Meurville and can be picked up there. About 19 miles (30 km) north-west of Meurville is Lac d'Orient, an activity-heavy lake with a beach and water sports. It is one of 3 man-made lakes in parkland once owned by the Knights Templar. The Aube has countryside of gentle rolling hills and big skies. It is a place to take a walk or hire a mountain bike and explore. By car there are villages that beg you to stop. Switch off the satnav, leave with a full tank of petrol, and see where it takes you.

FOOD AND DRINK Meurville is a village of 180 inhabitants. The nearest quality restaurants are La Toque Baralbine in Bar-sur-Aube, 5½ miles (9 km) away, Le Moulin du Landion in Dolancourt, 4½ miles (7.5 km) away, and Marilyn Perron's personal recommendation La Petite Auberge in Arsonval, 6 miles (10 km) away, which serves typical local food such as rabbit in champagne.

GETTING THERE From Paris follow A5a and then A5 beyond Troyes until the turn off for D4 north. Meurville is signposted as a left turn off D4. The site office is in Meurville village opposite the Les Perron-Beauvineau cellar sign, on route de Spoy. Phone from the village, where someone will guide you to the site.

OPEN April–October. A good idea to book early.

THE DAMAGE 2 people, 1 tent/campervan, 1 vehicle €11. Electricity €3.50, pet €1.50. The *fustes* (cabins) 2 people €50, 3 people €60, 4 people €70.

haut des bluches

Camping du Haut des Bluches, 5 route des Planches, 88250 La Bresse   00 33 3 29 25 64 80   www.domainehautdesbluches.labresse.fr

Ahh... there's nothing like a babbling brook to keep the plumbing clear. Located high above sea level, in the Parc Naturel Régional des Ballons des Vosges, Camping du Haut des Bluches has just that. Nestled in one of the mountain range's most outstanding valleys, just outside the town of La Bresse, this sprawling site feels smaller than the 140 pitches it boasts. The river that divides it and the terracing that breaks up the open areas may be responsible. In the summer plenty of shade is provided by copious trees, which, coupled with the site's impressive views, make it a superb place to practise inner calm, breathe in the quiet, and breathe out any stress. That said, if you're heading into the Vosges Mountains, relaxation is probably the last thing on your mind.

This site is the most convenient base from which to start a serious hiking, mountain-biking, road-biking, or skiing holiday. If you're not utterly exhausted just thinking about it, then everything is at your fingertips to ensure you'll wake in the morning with muscles screaming in pain. The local *commune* manages the site extremely well, with good-humoured staff to help with the planning of sport-torture. The site is the main departure point for many mountain-biking, fishing, hiking (including snow-shoe walking), and orienteering circuits – handy maps provided. However, if operating the clutch is more your style of work-out, then the winding mountain roads, tranquil lakes, and breathtaking views are easily within your grasp. The choice is yours.

COOL FACTOR Kick-off base for mountain-biking, hiking, and more. A good night's sleep and stunning surroundings.

WHO'S IN? Tents, campervans, caravans, pets – yes. Noisy groups after 10pm – no.

ON SITE One hundred and forty pitches; 13-room chalet, each room sleeping 2 to 6; 24 good-quality showers, 2 baby-changing rooms, 2 disabled rooms. Wi-fi. Washing and drying. Bar, small shop, freezer, café. Restaurant with *plat du jour* €10–€12. Games room, table football, and pool. Table tennis, children's slide, 'sprung' animals. Children's club.

OFF SITE Free children's access to La Bresse pool. Routes for cycling, hiking, snow-shoe walking, skiing, and fishing. A drive along the mountain-top route des Crêtes (D430) provides excellent views. Continue to D67a and Lac de Longemer and D417 to Lac de Céradmers beaches and water sports. Lac des Corbeaux affords fishing and extraordinary views. Three skiing areas: 37 pistes at La Bresse-Hohneck, 6 pistes at Lispach, 8 pistes at La Bresse-Brabant.

FOOD AND DRINK You'll find more than a dozen auberges along D430 serving food. Most notable are the Auberge de la Chume de Firstmiss (00 33 3 29 63 26 13), the Auberge de Breitzhousen (00 33 3 29 63 22 92), and the Auberge Huss (00 33 3 89 82 27 20).

GETTING THERE In La Bresse take D430 eastwards for 2½ miles (4 km). The site is signposted.

PUBLIC TRANSPORT TGV from Paris Est to Nancy, regional RER to Remiremont, local SNCF bus to La Bresse.

OPEN Mid December–1 November.

THE DAMAGE Tent and car plus 2 people €13, electricity €8.

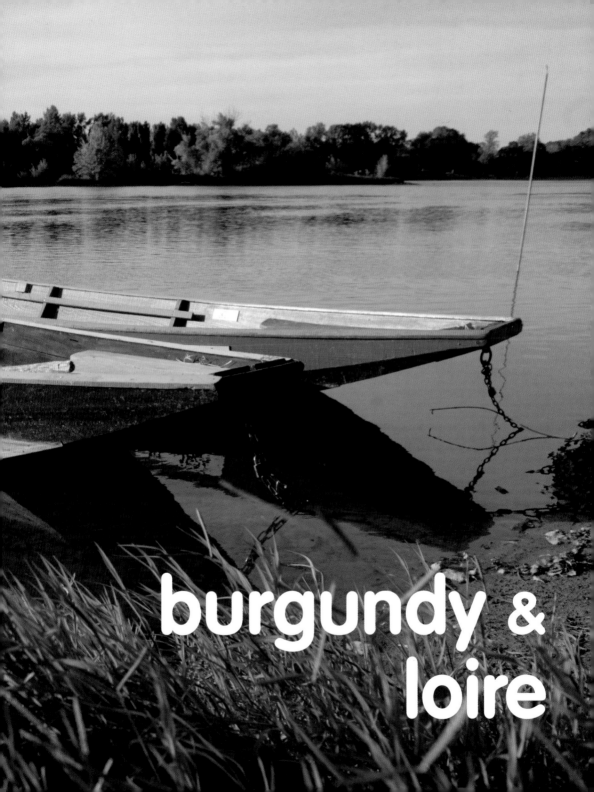

burgundy &
loire

camping au bois joli

Camping au Bois Joli, route de Villeprenoy, 89480 Andryes   00 33 3 86 81 70 48   www.campingauboisjoli.com

Au Bois Joli means 'pretty wood' and is a fine indication of where you're heading with this site. Perhaps all woodland areas have their charm, yet there is a little extra magic about this site and the trees that arch over it. Approaching Andryes down open and meandering roads, dissecting vast farm-scapes that blend at the horizon with rich blue skies for much of the summer, it is impossible to resist a smile. The site and its region are firmly deserving of investigation.

Perhaps it's the wealth of Burgundy sunflowers arching aloft before the summer harvest that makes even the most inanimate entity appear jolly. Or it could be that the inspiring, vast skies endorse an air of drifting creative thought. Whatever the explanation, it's blindingly obvious why Robert and Henriëtte de Vries elected to settle here, amid the cheerfully swaying branches.

Au Bois Joli was created with a sharply observed philosophy in mind: respect for nature, for peace of mind, and for a carefully nurtured atmosphere of good will. The site layout, its location, and ambience merge effortlessly towards this end, yet only a daily investment of hard work and passion maintains the balance. The camp is quietly adjusted around the campers all day, with the owner's high expectations catapulting the site way ahead of 'average'. It has been awarded a prestigious Clef Verte for its ecologically sound methods and astounding reverence for nature. In turn, nature seems to be thanking Au Bois Joli, with Robert and Henriëtte proud to record each new winged visitor or blooming flower to appear. If you're lucky and catch either host during a quiet moment, it's absorbing to learn about the site's unique micro-environment and how they tend it. For example, more than a dozen varieties of orchid have blossomed on their watch and careful grass-cutting ensures each new shoot is given its chance. A total of 110 wild plants have been noted and 61 different types of bird have paid a visit thus far.

The consideration for environment is also extended to their human guests. Parents on holiday with young children can often endure more work than relaxation, but Camping au Bois Joli tries to address this with a site grown for safety. A tree that lends itself to climbing has a stone-edged entrance guiding towards lower branches and soft wood chippings below. The ample play areas have the same soft precautions, with enough corners, obstacles, and hideaways to feed fertile minds. Children even have a wash-block of their own.

Adults can luxuriate in the shade of mature trees or blister in the sun beside the pool, all the while soaking up epic views. For a small deposit, books can be borrowed from the site library or a free magazine can be borrowed from the racks outside reception. At the highest point of the site a gate leads to a wild wood, for which access has been negotiated, and within moments it's possible to be quite alone. Alternatively the prepared welcome pack, tailored to the length of your stay, has suggestions for offsite activities that demand varying degrees of exertion.

It is difficult to be critical of a campsite when the owners are meditating upon greater improvements that seem superfluous, given the high standards already achieved. Plans are afoot to arrange the camp track for one-way traffic to improve safety, even though it hardly seems required. This reviewer has rarely trusted gushing praise in reviews, so in order to bring a critical conclusion to this one: the grass needs combing, the trees are not symmetrical, and the site isn't open all year. I suppose the latter could be construed as the only real shame.

COOL FACTOR Relaxation and tranquillity, in contact with abundant nature. An outstandingly well-maintained site with exceptional views and open pitches.

WHO'S IN? Tents, campervans, caravans, nature-lovers, families, mature adults – yes. Loud intentions, busy desires, late-night owls – no.

ON SITE Weekly campfires lit by the owners at the discretion of the weather – if it's too dry, windy, and dangerous it'll not happen. Under no circumstances must a fire be lit without permission due to the delicate natural balance and risk of forest fire. Ninety-five pitches on site, with a wide, open area among trees for pitching tents anywhere. Thirteen superb shower booths, ample toilet blocks, disabled access for toilets, showers, and washing up, dedicated wash-block for children/seniors with low-access facilities. Two washing machines (€4.50 including powder), free spinner. Excellent climbing frame, mock castle, slides, sand pit, 'sprung' animals for children. Clean and well-maintained swimming and paddling pool facing epic landscape, with decent poolside area. Café with terrace, shop selling organic produce, daily bakery delivery, library, and magazine rack. In the high season you can pre-order hamburgers and fries. Free wi-fi in an all-weather marquee, with independent power sockets. Partially 'green' electricity supply, freezer available. Plenty of local information regarding wildlife, walks, cycle routes, and places of interest. Table-tennis tables, volleyball, skittles, basketball hoop, *boules*, and badminton available.

OFF SITE One must-see is the astonishing contemporary construction of a medieval fort at Guédelon, which is being built using only 13th-century tools and materials. Work began in 1997 and completion will be in about 2035. Auxerre, Avallon, and Clamecy all have farmers' markets twice a week. The campsite is an official cycle kick-off point for the newly renovated paths beside the canal between Auxerre in the north and Clamecy to the south. This 38-mile (62-km) stretch is one of a total 500 miles (800 km) of canal being worked on. Vézelay, a world heritage site, is a short drive from the campsite and well worth exploring.

FOOD AND DRINK Auberge des Sources (00 33 3 86 41 55 14; www.auberge-des-sources.com), beyond Clamecy, has a good reputation as does the warm and inviting 2 Pieces Cuisine (00 33 3 86 27 25 07) in Clamecy itself. The latter has a great candle-lit terrace on the junction of 3 pedestrian streets, and the family feel of the place is wonderful. La Grange Batelière, (00 33 3 86 81 82 38; www.lagrangebateliere.fr) also comes recommended by owners Richard and Henriëtte and is at Coulanges-sur-Yonne.

GETTING THERE From Auxerre, take N151 (Bourges). In Coulanges-sur-Yonne take D39 to Andryes. After 1¾ miles (3 km), in the centre of Andryes, you will see Camping signs.

OPEN April–November.

THE DAMAGE Car, 2 people €19.80 (high season). Child to 11 years €4.

la forêt du morvan

La Forêt du Morvan, 58370 Larochemillay, Nièvre   00 33 3 86 30 47 93   www.campinglaforet.nl

There's always something a little magical about forests. They're dark, dripping, mysterious places full of unseen dangers, lurking beasts, and the constant fear of getting lost. Even on the sunniest of days a dimly lit forest interior can feel like a very quiet, twilit world, where even the birds seem to keep away.

Luckily the site at La Forêt du Morvan isn't quite in the heart of the forest and has cleared enough space for its 25 pitches to let the sunshine in and give the birds free reign to fly about and tweet. Well, not Tweet™ exactly, but you get the point. The Morvan is almost half a million acres (226,000 hectares) of prime French countryside, officially made a Parc Régional in 1970, and now something of a playground for the not-so-rich and not-so-famous. Hills, lakes, and forests are the main attractions, best explored using a combination of shoes, pedals, and oars (or an outboard, if you're lazy). Just make sure you take a map.

There are two main camping areas on the south-facing slopes of the site; one above and one below the main buildings. Below has a bit more in the way of trees and shade, while the pitches up above are more open and have slightly more expansive views down across the valley.

One handy feature is the availability, for hire, of private bathrooms, which is a great idea for families. You can keep your clobber in there and you don't have to cart it around every time the kids need a scrub-down. It's not cheap, but worth it if you're here for a week.

COOL FACTOR Fresh-air camping in nearly half a million acres (226,000 hectares) of prime French forest.

WHO'S IN? Tents, campervans, small caravans (large ones may not get down the drive), dogs – yes.

ON SITE Facilities in the old barns, with hot showers, private bathrooms, kitchen facilities. Arts and crafts, weekly campfire, kids' disco, tractor tour, sports competitions.

OFF SITE Autun's the nearest town of any significance, with a Roman amphitheatre and 12th-century Gothic cathedral and it's also the base from which to explore the lakes of the Forêt de Planoise. Try the Base Nautique du Moulin du Vallon (00 33 3 85 86 95 80) for itineraries for sailing, pedaloes, canoes, and kayaks. Lots to do and visit (ask the owners). Nice walks from the campsite (maps provided). Campers informed daily about regional events.

FOOD AND DRINK Best to bring your own supplies (kitchen facilities on site). Twice a week you can join the owners for a regional 3-course meal. At weekends there's a pizza night. Order takeaway snacks, but if you want to eat out head to L'École Buissonière(00 33 3 86 30 47 21) in Millay, or Auberge de Poil (00 33 3 86 30 22 20).

GETTING THERE The site's halfway between Nevers and Beaune, north of Luzy, south of Villapourçon. Take D27 north or south, between Larochemillay and Le Puits. The site's off the main road 2 miles (3 km) north of Larochemillay.

PUBLIC TRANSPORT There are trains to Autun, but unfortunately no bus serving D27.

OPEN April–October.

THE DAMAGE Family pitch (5 people) and tent €15–€27.50 per night, depending on season. Rented tent (sleeps 5) €30–€60. Private facilities cost €7.50 per night in high season. Discount for singles and couples.

domaine du bourg

Domaine du Bourg, 4 chemin des Terriens, 03230 Gannay-sur-Loire   00 33 4 70 43 49 01   www.domainedubourg.com

Domaine names are a tricky business. Not those 'double-yew double-yew double-yew dot' Internet domain names, but the names of little French estates. Call them something fancy like Domaine de Beauregard and the neighbours think you're pretentious. So this place keeps it pretty simple. Domaine du Bourg, it says on the gate: Small Market Town Estate. And what's inside's fairly straightforward, too. Dutch owners, Peter and Trudi de Lange, have converted some old farming buildings into a cracking, pretty sizeable, home, along with four *gîtes*, three *chambres d'hôtes*, and some *gîtes d'étape* dorm rooms. Beyond the huddle of buildings is over seven acres (two-and-half hectares) of camping ground with only 18 pitches.

The small market town in question is Gannay-sur-Loire, a pretty sleepy little place, if the truth be told, but the quiet roads and gentle countryside are ideal for exploration by bike. These are available for hire from the site and come equipped with maps. There are plenty of water sports to try out, including kayaks, which you can hire from the site.

The site's also on the new EuroVélo6 cycle route, stretching across eight countries from the Atlantic coast to the Black Sea. The French section starts at St Nazaire and follows the Loire through Orléans and Nevers, before swinging north through Switzerland, Germany, Austria, and Slovakia and south through Hungary and Serbia, finishing in Romania. So there's no real excuse for coming here and just lounging around.

COOL FACTOR Smallsville camping with plenty of room to stretch out.

WHO'S IN? Tents, campervans, caravans, dogs (as long you scoop any poop) – yes.

ON SITE At the time of writing the facilities were limited to a couple of WCs in one of the buildings and 2 hot showers and a washbasin in a roulotte (gypsy caravan) in the camping field, along with outside dishwashing facilities. However, there is a new bespoke facilities block. Elsewhere there's a small pool and a covered seating area (where meals are served), which is handy as a day area.

OFF SITE This is a fairly quiet area, so the best thing is to capitalise on that quietness and hire a bike or kayak. Bikes can be rented from the site at €9 per day and kayaks are available at €14 per half-day and €23 per full-day, including transport to and from the river.

FOOD AND DRINK There's a small Proxi convenience store, a *pâtisserie*, a butcher, and a very 'local' little café-bar in the village.

GETTING THERE From Nevers take D13 and D116 to Decize. Head out of town on D978a and turn left on to D116 for Gannay-sur-Loire. Once in the village and over the river you'll see a triangular green with a road veering off to the left. Follow that road for 110 yards (100 m) and the site's on the right.

PUBLIC TRANSPORT The closest you can get to the site is 8–10 miles (12–16 km) away at one of the nearby railway stations (Fours, Cercy-la-Tour, and Decize are closest).

OPEN Easter–end October.

THE DAMAGE Pitch €6 low season; €9 high season. Adults €2–€2.75, kids up to 12 years €1–€1.75. No charge for dogs.

camping de nevers

Camping de Nevers, rue de la Jonction, 58000 Nevers   00 33 6 84 98 69 79   www.campingnevers.com

All great countries have a great river or two and France's pièce de résistance has to be the Loire. Its fancy urban cousin, the Seine, may slink its way through the boulevards of Paris, but it's the Loire, winding its way past shady banks and leafy vineyards, that's the country's golden artery. And while the broader reaches around Blois and Tours are swarming with tourists in high season, you can be smart and head a little up-river to Nevers. This is a great little former Roman town with a medieval heart and a fantastic cathedral that you can sit and admire from your tent.

The campsite is divided into two, with shady spots up top, where most of the caravans and campervans park up, and a lower level running down to the river bank, which tends to be where the tents pitch. Sadly there's not much access to the river, but you can still enjoy watching it idle by and in the morning see the mist slowly rising from the waters. And the best bit is that the town's just a ten-minute stroll across the river, allowing you to sit back and take in the views before summoning the will to go and explore.

COOL FACTOR Loire-side camping with views to Nevers.
WHO'S IN? Tents, campervans, caravans, dogs – yes.
ON SITE The reception, café, and facilities are all well maintained. There's a heated shower room with hot showers and unisex WCs, and an outside area for dishwashing. There's also a washing machine (€4) and dryer (€3). Up in reception there's a computer for Internet access at €1 for 15 minutes.
OFF SITE The town across the river is worth exploring, from the old streets around the ducal palace to the marvellous cathedral of St-Cyr-et-Ste-Juliette.
FOOD AND DRINK Apart from the small café on site, it's best to head over the bridge into the town. At Au Bureau on place St-Sebastien you can sit out on the pavement terrace, enjoy a coffee or beer, and watch the world go by.
GETTING THERE Through Nevers follow signs for Moulins and Bourges. The site is on the opposite bank, on your left.
PUBLIC TRANSPORT Nevers is easily accessible by train and bus from Paris, Lyon, and Dijon and the campsite is only a 10-minute ride from the bus and railway stations.
OPEN Mid April–mid October.
THE DAMAGE 2 adults, tent €13.50 (low season); €14.50 (high season). Extra adult €2.50–€3.50 and kids to 7 years €1.30–€2.80.

Le Château de Sully-sur-Loire

hortus, le jardin de sully

Hortus, Le Jardin de Sully, 1 route de St-Benoît, 45600 Sully/St-Père-sur-Loire   00 33 2 38 36 35 94   www.hortus-sully.com

A couple of millennia ago the Gallo-Roman Empire established a base here to control one of the rare crossing-points of the River Loire, and began something of a trend. More than a thousand years of layered history sits beneath the contemporary 14th-century medieval chateau of Sully-sur-Loire, and on the opposite side of the river bank sits the mercifully less hostile form of Le Jardin de Sully. Less hostile, though perhaps industrial and worn-looking in places, Le Jardin's open tent pitches still enable commanding views across the river that led Joan of Arc, Voltaire, and Louis XIV to seek sanctuary in the castle.

This is a large, well-equipped site, with everything you need for a relaxing stay, yet it is somewhat uninspired. It's reasonably priced for the region and, if you are even remotely interested in medieval history, wildlife, or outdoor sports, the Loire Valley will lure you away from dawn till dusk. The Loire's well-preserved castles, wild river banks, and historic villages begin here with Sully-sur-Loire, establishing Le Jardin's excellent positioning as a leap-off point to explore the region.

COOL FACTOR Open pitches with views across the Loire. A short walk down the bank can have you paddling in the water, or relaxing and watching the wildlife from your tent.

WHO'S IN? Tents, caravans, campervans, large groups, families, pets, nature enthusiasts – yes.

ON SITE Eighty pitches, 50 tent hook-ups, 10 hot showers, some looking tired. Free mini-golf, tennis, table tennis, swimming pool, playgrounds, *boules*. One disabled toilet/shower, baby-changing facilities. Wi-fi connection, snacks, pizza, small shop, licensed bar. No campfires. BBQs okay.

OFF SITE Ride a horse and carriage around town or tour Château de Sully-sur-Loire (adult €6, child €3) – 30-minute walk or 2 buses leave 110 yards (100 m) from the site.

FOOD AND DRINK Little in Sully. In Orléans try La Parenthèse (00 33 2 38 62 07 50), and Les Terrasses de Loire (00 33 2 38 53 45 98; www.lesterrassesduborddeloire.com).

GETTING THERE From Paris: A6 direction Lyon, A77 to exit 19 'Bourges, Vierzon, Giens'. Continue on D940 to Gien, D952 direction Orléans to Ouzouer-sur-Loire. Left on to D119 to St-Père-sur-Loire. Turn right towards St-Benoît. The campsite is 440 yards (400 m) on the left.

OPEN All year.

THE DAMAGE 2 people, tent €15; electricity €3.50.

les roulottes

Les Roulottes, 41350 Les Marais, Huisseau-sur-Cosson   00 33 6 67 74 94 93   www.lesroulottes.net

Gypsy caravans are a popular option in campsites all over France, but usually these 'roulottes' are no more Romany than President Sarkozy, being simply wooden-walled chalets with curved roofs. One of life's pleasures is actually finding out where they are, because signs on nearby roads are few and far between – these might encourage the idly curious. The 'roulottes' advertised on French campsites are invariably nothing like as authentic or atmospheric as the five circus caravans Monsieur Séné has here. His roulottes are stationed either in their own little field or in a woodland arbour by the stream, and they present a retrotastic traditional camping experience, full of simple pleasures. The caravans are of different vintages between the 1920s and the 1970s and have been restored and decorated accordingly, painted in rich reds, greens, mauves, and carmines, filled with life-affirming patterns and vintage furniture. They may be small, but it doesn't feel that way. Minimalism doesn't get a look in and they're full of character.

Nuzzling up to the banks of a river so slow it looks like a long pond, the site is surrounded by trees; as private as you could wish for. It's a great hideaway and children love the freedom to play in and around the roulottes and the stream. A hammock swings between trees, there's a stack of wood for the fire, canoes to paddle in, and a riding centre ½ mile (1 km) away. Plus there are bikes here, allowing you to take advantage of a local network of routes to explore the grand chateaux. However long you stay, the time will just fly by.

COOL FACTOR Is there a retro-cooler way to camp in comfort?

WHO'S IN? Couples, families, dogs – yes.

ON SITE Campfires are positively encouraged as it's the principal cooking method. There's just a small toilet and shower in one of the roulottes. There are bikes and canoes to use while you're at the site.

OFF SITE There's a network of cycle routes (www.chateauxavelo.com) to explore the chateaux and countryside. Chambord, with 440 magnificent rooms, is close, with a huge park and woods. A short drive away, in Blois, you can experience hundreds of years of architectural styles and stories of murder and derring-do (and that's just the chateau), plus the Maison de la Magie (00 33 2 54 90 33 33; www.maisondelamagie.fr) museum of magic.

FOOD AND DRINK There are many shops within 1 mile (2 km) to get supplies to cook on the open fire, or there's a hob and a microwave if it's really raining. Alternatively, head into Blois, where Au Bouchon Lyonnais (00 33 2 54 74 12 87; www.aubouchonlyonnais.com) combines the local cuisine with dishes from Lyon in *menus* from €20.

GETTING THERE From Blois follow D33 towards Huisseau-sur-Cosson. As you approach the town, you'll see Château des Grotteaux. Turn left and carry on past the entrance. Just after crossing the river, take the dirt track to the left and drive 550 yards (500 m) until you pass through a small tunnel. The gated entrance to Les Roulottes is immediately on your left.

OPEN All year.

THE DAMAGE €450 per week in July and August, reducing to €310 the rest of the year. For a 5-night stay rates are €380/€250; weekend (Sat–Mon) rates are €250/€200.

ferme de prunay

Ferme de Prunay, 41150 Seillac   00 33 2 54 70 02 01   www.prunay.fr

Gazing at the turrets and gleaming towers of Azay-le-Rideau, Villandry, or Valençay, which are so picture-book pretty they look more like Disneyland Paris than *la vraie France*, it's easy to forget that not all of the chateaux decorating the Loire Valley exemplify state-of-the-art Renaissance luxury. Chinon, by contrast, is a fortress, all practical purpose and no frippery, while Amboise was heavily defended long before François I made it a centre of culture and learning and invited Leonardo da Vinci to add his genius to the court. The chateau at Blois (like Amboise, it's no more than 20 minutes' drive from Ferme de Prunay), was also built with defence in mind, a reminder that this region was fought over for many centuries, not least by the English.

Ferme de Prunay looks perfectly peaceful now, but the farm originally formed the core of a Gallo-Roman fortified village. The ancient moat that curls around two sides was built to keep marauders out, but now it provides a gentle afternoon's fishing practice. Similarly, when the owner, Michel Fouchault, dug out the swimming pool, he unearthed many graves and bones, but hopefully that won't bother *campeurs* as they dive into the heated *piscine*. Traditions run deep here, but it's perfectly safe and calm now: the farm has been in the Fouchault family for six generations, and Fouchault *fils* plans to continue the tradition, so you can make advance bookings in confidence.

Beyond the floral borders of the site they cultivate 494 acres (200 hectares) of cereal crops,

and that feeling of spaciousness extends to the enormous pitches, some of which are big enough to accommodate a car, a caravan, and a few badminton courts. There's never any danger of feeling hemmed in between caravans and motor homes here, and there's a real variety to the pitches, too. The French tend to prefer privacy; they like their own space, with hedges and trees around them. The Dutch, who live in a relatively small, crowded country, like the freedom of open space and expansive views, so they usually opt to be next to the fields. As for the British, well, they may go for one or the other.

Many of the pitches have their own plum or apple trees, which campers are welcome to plunder, or you can join the Dutch overlooking a huge bank of wild flowers (planted to attract butterflies and bees) and the open fields. Those who choose the views should know that their freedom comes with a price tag, as they're further away from the wash-block. But it's worth it; a blooming horizon is wonderful to wake up to.

The Ferme de Prunay also operates as a *ferme pédagogique*, or teaching farm, with school visits off season. Those opportunities continue throughout the summer, so children and their parents may learn how corn is ground and how to bake bread, for instance, or go on guided local walks, which may pass by a local goat farm or vineyard, with opportunities to buy the wine, cheese, and honey. This could be a model campsite, as they get so much right. The bikes around the site are all free

Leonardo at Amboise

to use, as is a fridge, cooker, the pool, and sports and leisure amenities. There are also volleyball and basketball areas and acres more space to play in front. It's an easy-going place, especially for families. Kids really love the tractor-train rides and walking up the forest path to see the animals – take your pick from pigs, rabbits, chickens, donkeys, goats, turkeys, and a horse. Meanwhile, just 6 miles (10 km) away, is the turreted wonder that is Château de Chaumont and some of the finest grand Loire chateaux and gardens are but a short drive in every direction.

COOL FACTOR Camping on the farm a short ride away from great rivers and grand castles.

WHO'S IN? Tents, campervans, caravans, and dogs (on leads), large groups and young people – yes.

ON SITE The wash-block has the option of family shower rooms, but though still effective, the block is basic and showing its age. It's the only drawback of a superbly organised site, which has welcome letters and information in English, French, Dutch, and German. The bar is open from 8am (for bread and croissant deliveries) until 9pm and also sells ice creams, basic bar food, and pizzas. There are tractor-train rides around the site (high season), animal petting and kids' play areas, table tennis, volleyball court and basketball areas at the front of the site, which is where (supervised) campfires take place. No campfires, but BBQs okay.

OFF SITE There are discount vouchers available on site to get into many tourist locations in the Loir-et-Cher département, including the wonderful chateau at Blois 10 miles (16 km) away, where Joan of Arc was blessed in 1429 before she left with her army to drive the English from Orléans (00 33 2 54 90 33 32; www.chateaudeblois. fr). The Maison de la Magie (00 33 2 54 90 33 33; www. maisondelamagie.fr), a spectacular House of Magic museum, is situated across the Place de la Château from the castle and equally merits a visit. The beautiful town of Amboise is well worth the 20-minute drive along the Loire both for its chateau and Le Clos Lucé (00 33 2 47 57 00 73; www.vinci-closluce.com), the house where Leonardo da Vinci lived his final 3 years, which is now a museum displaying models of his amazing drawings. It's possible to hire canoes to use on the Loire itself, or the rivers Loir and Cher, which feed into it.

FOOD AND DRINK The farm is a member of the regional tourist organisation 'Bienvenue à la ferme' and can recommend many local suppliers, listed in a French brochure, including La Cabinette for goats' cheese in Onzain, 5 miles (8 km) away (which also has the best range of shops locally), or their favourite organic Touraine wine produced at Domaine Château-Gaillard in Mesland, about 2 miles (3 km) from the site. Among the many local markets they recommend those in Amboise on Friday and Sunday mornings on the banks of the Loire. There are many restaurants to choose from in Blois and just about anywhere near the castle is good. Nonetheless, L'Orangerie du Château de Blois really stands out as a special gastronomic treat. In a beautiful building with stunning interiors and a lovely terrace opposite the castle, its *menus* are from €34 (00 33 2 54 78 05 36; www.orangerie-du-chateau.fr).

GETTING THERE From A10 take the Blois exit, then follow directions for Angers and Château-Renault until Molineuf, then follow signs for Chambon-sur-Cisse and then Seillac on D131, where you'll pick up the roadside signs to Ferme de Prunay.

OPEN April–early October.

THE DAMAGE 2 adults plus pitch €14.30 (€22.50 in high season). Extra adult €5.10 (€9.20), under-5s €3.10 (€3.60). Electricity €3.60.

domaine du bien vivre

Domaine du Bien Vivre, 13-15 route du Petit Village, 41140 St-Romain-sur-Cher   00 33 2 54 71 73 74
http://domainedubienvivre.pagesperso-orange.fr

It's enjoying the simple pleasures with family or friends that makes for a good life, like eating *en plein air* while the sun sets, then staying outside as the stars come out, sipping wine from grapes that ripened just a stone's throw from where you are sitting. The rows of Cabernet vines stand to attention in front of you; there are open fields to your left and paths into the forest directly off the site to your right. A set of swings sums up the kids' entertainment, but there's plenty of space to play around this *aire naturelle* site, with just 25 pitches ensuring it's never too hectic. There are some hedges to give a little privacy and that's it, really. Quality Touraine wine is produced and sold right here and you can buy goats' cheese and other *produits fermiers,* too. Like much of the Loire Valley, it's ideal walking and cycling country, or a relaxed base from which to explore La Route des Vins and the grand chateaux – the flamboyant Renaissance castle estates of Cheverny, Valençay, and Chenonceau, and the more martial 11th-century castle keep at Loches, are all no more than 20 minutes' drive away.

COOL FACTOR Camping so close to the vineyards that you can almost pick the grapes from your tent.
WHO'S IN Tents, campervans, caravans, dogs (on leads) – yes. And plenty of Dutch tourers, too.
ON SITE Twenty-five pitches, 10 with electric hook-ups. The wash-block is fairly rustic. Two basic-looking *gîtes*, and a rentable static. No campfires, but BBQs okay.
OFF SITE A base from which to explore the Loir-et-Cher *département*. For a break from wine *domaines*, the koalas at ZooParc de Beauval (00 33 2 54 75 50 00; www.zoobeauval. com) are just a 10-minute drive away.
FOOD AND DRINK Enjoy woodfire-grilled *entrecôte* and *cuisine de terroir* (*menus* from €16) in a former wine cellar at Le Busquet (00 33 2 54 71 44 44; www.le-busquet.com) or eat goat and lamb from the *menu fermier* under the covered terrace at Ferme Auberge de La Lionnière (00 33 2 54 75 24 99; http://frederic.bouland.pagesperso-orange.fr).
GETTING THERE Take exit 12 off A85 and follow signs for St-Romain-sur-Cher. At the second crossroads, turn right down route du Petit Village and it's on your left.
OPEN April–September.
THE DAMAGE Pitch €3, adults €2.90, and kids to 7 years €2, so this is a bargain. Electricity €3.

The River Cher runs beneath the old mill

le moulin fort

Camping Le Moulin Fort, 37150 Francueil   00 33 2 47 23 86 22   www.lemoulinfort.com

The Loire is a lovely, lazy river in the summertime; all meandering channels, shifting sandbanks, and wide-angle panoramas. But being smaller, its tributary, the River Cher, is even better to camp alongside, and this charmingly appointed site occupies a long strip of bank that Ratty and Mole would appreciate, planted with weeping willows, with families tucking into their picnics on either side of the water.

It is a great view and explains why Le Moulin Fort has such a relaxed air and keeps campers coming back for return visits. But it's worth rousing yourself for the short canoe paddle (or bike ride) to see Chenonceau reflected in the Cher. Stunning chateaux are around every corner, yet Chenonceau stands out for its combination of beautiful, bravura architecture and grand Renaissance gardens. Amboise has its spectacular royal chateau, too, not to mention Leonardo da Vinci's house and museum, Le Clos Lucé, yet it's easy to understand why some campers choose to stay and chill by the pool, play mini-golf with the kids, or simply enjoy watching the water slide by.

COOL FACTOR Camping on the river doesn't get better.

WHO'S IN? Tents, campervans, caravans, dogs (on leads) – yes.

ON SITE A hundred and thirty pitches, 120 with electric hook-ups. The 2 wash-blocks have clean, warm showers and laundry areas. Pool and kids' pool by the mill house. Canoes and bikes for hire. Crazy golf and play area. Library and table tennis. No campfires, but BBQs okay.

OFF SITE Chenonceaux has ivy-clad shops and hostelries. Amboise best on Friday or Sunday for the riverside market.

FOOD AND DRINK Pre-ordered bread and croissants delivered daily in the season. Food available in the mill house. For a more gastronomic meal cross into Chenonceaux to enjoy fine dining at La Roseraie (00 33 2 47 23 90 09).

GETTING THERE Follow D976 east from Tours on the south bank of the Cher. Turn left on to D80 towards Chenonceaux, but just before the bridge take the road to the right and the campsite is along the banks of the river.

OPEN April–September.

THE DAMAGE Tent, caravan/campervan plus 2 adults €13.50–€22 depending on season. Extra adult €3–€5 and child (4–12 years) €2–€4. Electricity €4.

le chant d'oiseau

Le Chant d'Oiseau, 49390 Mouliherne   00 33 2 41 67 09 78   www.loire-gites.com/campsite.asp

The open grassland and forests surrounding Le Chant d'Oiseau make an ideal habitat for the tawny owls and barn owls that live in the loft above one of the three *gîtes*. All sorts of other birds, from herons and hen harriers to buzzards and goldfinches, love it around here, too, which is surely how the house got its moniker. The name appears on a map from 1750, but the house could be centuries older – the date 1626 was incised into the stone walls of the hayloft by workers tallying up bales. Stu and Syb Bradley are passionate about the house and region, learning its history and photographing its finer features; a knowledgeable source of recommendations on places to visit.

The Bradleys moved their family here from Doncaster in 2005 and brought an easy-going conviviality from South Yorkshire that blends in perfectly with the Loire region's reputation for *la douceur de vivre* (Flaubert called it 'the most sensual river in France'); enjoying life at the same leisurely pace at which France's longest river flows through the valley. They're relaxed about campers arriving late, and offer to come and find those searching for the site after dark, even making them a nice cup of tea on arrival – just what the welcome visitors cherish after a long drive from a channel port. An earlier arrival means you can join your hosts for a glass of wine from Chinon and Saumur in the 'barn' (of which only the lower walls remain), which serves as an alfresco wi-fi area, communal eating space, retreat for shade-lovers, and home to two BBQs and a bread oven that Stu made himself.

It was worth the effort: the wood-fired oven makes a superb pizza oven once a week, when campers can join Stu and Syb, and meet each other, under the awning. On Mondays and Fridays during the summer they serve a four-course French meal here, too, and they heat up the oven on Sundays to bake the troglodyte (and Angevin) favourite, *fouée*; small parcels of bread dough into which savoury or sweet fillings can be added: goats' cheese, pork pâté, *rillettes, confiture*… delicious!

These events are all optional, but it's an option that can make camping so much more appealing. The Bradleys had decades of experience camping and caravanning in Cornwall and France, and have tried to incorporate here all the best features of sites they've experienced, as well as weekly wine-tasting evenings led by a local *vigneron* and campers getting together to eat and socialise. This social aspect of camping is continued on their Facebook site (www.facebook.com/Le.Chant), while the lengthy questionnaire in their welcome pack shows that the Bradleys are open to suggestions on improving the site.

Animals are very much part of the Bradley menage. Apart from the owls and visiting birds, there are two dogs, two cats, and eight chickens that also share the site, the latter clucking around the tents and providing fresh eggs. Deer are a common sight and wild boar live in the woods, so it's not surprising that the sport of Kings, which originally attracted French royals to the Loire, now draws *chasseurs*, but modern hunters arrive in cars,

on mopeds, and quad bikes, all communicating by mobile phone. The Bradleys aren't fans of the hunting season because it can be dangerous just walking the dog in the woods if trigger-happy hunters aren't careful, but fortunately shooting doesn't begin until September, so the forests are perfectly safe throughout the summer.

Stu and Syb were once avid surfers and originally intended to set up a site in Cornwall, but that proved too expensive. Now, they're delighted they live in an area where the climate makes camping comfortable six months a year.

COOL FACTOR Birdsong and conviviality in the countryside in the heart of the Loire.

WHO'S IN? Tents, campervans, caravans, and dogs (not in high season), large groups (by arrangement) – yes.

ON SITE Campfires allowed off the ground. Twelve pitches, 8 with 6-amp hook-ups. The 2 showers and 2 toilets (plus 3 basins) are freshly tiled, clean, and homely, with wheelchair access. There may be a wait in high season. There are 2 brick BBQs in the 'barn', which campers are welcome to use, plus a gas cooker, fridge, kettle, microwave, and food-preparation area in the Kampers' Kitchen. Stone-cooked pizzas are cooked once a week and 4-course meals, prepared by Stu and Syb, are available 2 nights a week during the season, so campers can be convivial and cooking need not be an everyday chore. Wi-fi, table tennis, a pool table, a small swimming pool, bikes, and book exchange are all available, and there's a kids' play area. Three *gîtes* on site means multi-generation family/friends holidays are easy.

OFF SITE Medieval Mouliherne and its twisted-spired church is 3 miles (5 km) away, and there are peaceful walks and bike-rides through the woods and fields. The elegant city of Saumur, with its fortress-chateau, multi-arched bridges, and houses built in local tufa limestone, is a 25-minute drive. Stu (and the Michelin Guide) rate the Musée des Blindes tank museum (00 33 2 41 53 06 99; www.museedesblindes. fr). The town also has a great market on Saturdays on place de St Pierre and is an appellation renowned for its sparkling white wines. There are lovely chateaux also at Gizeaux,

Montgeoffroy, and Montsoreau (all around 30 minutes away) and the monastery and abbey at Fontrevraud are impressive; Richard the Lionheart, Henry II, and Eleanor of Aquitaine are all buried there.

FOOD AND DRINK In the Kampers' Kitchen you can buy locally produced *confitures*. Cooked food is available, and milk, fresh eggs, ice creams, and local wine is also for sale. Bread and croissant deliveries (amazing *croissants aux amandes*), booked the night before. Le Grand Bleu (00 33 2 41 67 41 83) is a lovely family-friendly seafood restaurant on rue du Marché in old Saumur. Alternatively, in Auverse, there's L'Oeil de Boeuf (00 33 2 41 82 38 19; www. loeildeboeuf-auverse.com). Stu confesses he may be biased recommending it, as his son-in-law is chef and his daughter greets diners.

GETTING THERE It's easiest to get to the nearby village of Mouliherne and follow signs to Le Chant d'Oiseau 3 miles (5 km) from there. Otherwise, it's off D58 between Vernantes and Mouliherne, but it's very easy to miss. Count 3 miles (5 km) from Vernantes or Mouliherne and then look for a crossroads. If it says Plaisance on one side and you can see 2 birds on the other, follow the direction of the birds for about ½ mile (1 km).

OPEN All year.

THE DAMAGE Caravan, motorhome, and trailer-tent plus 2 adults €15 Oct–May (€19.50 high season). Tent €10 (€16), extra people over 5 years €5 in high season. Electricity €5 (high season only).

atlantic coast

la vendette

Noirmoutier La Vendette, 23 allée des Sableaux, 85330 Noirmoutier-en-l'île   00 33 2 51 39 06 24   see www.camping-indigo.com/fr

The old paved causeway that crosses the tidal mudflats from the mainland may look like the best way to approach the island of Noirmoutier. But the Passage du Gois is only open at low tide, so campers crossing from Beauvoir-sur-Mer need to beware, even if the trusty satnav cheerfully insists on guiding drivers along the causeway as waves lap around the wheels. Fortunately there's also an impressive toll bridge that arrives at the southern tip of the long, low-lying island, which feels a lot further south than it has any right to.

Given that it is only a little south of Brittany, 30 miles (50 km) below the mouth of the Loire, Noirmoutier can feel almost Mediterranean, especially when there's no fresh Atlantic westerly blowing and there's barely a ripple of water disturbing the reflections of the pleasure boats across the sheltered bay.

The Impressionist painter Renoir was drawn here in 1892, attracted by the mild climate. No doubt the whitewashed Midi-style villas, with their terracotta tiles and blue shutters, appealed too. However, his best-known work from the visit, 'Noirmoutier', looks remarkably like the pine and green oak trees, and sandy scrubland would have been here in the Bois de la Chaize long before the Huttopia chain's Indigo brand of sites brought campers to the coastline.

Camping at La Vendette isn't like sleeping on the beach, it *is* sleeping on the beach, except with nice showers, good facilities, and great company, all being well. Only a fence, which everyone seems to appropriate for drying towels, separates the sandy shoreline from the sand you pitch your tent or park your caravan on, with the option of pine-tree shade or full sunshine, depending on how desperate you are for *du soleil*. And a lovely beach it is, too, sweeping around the wide bay and along the coastline of the northern half of the island, in case you fancy a really long walk before breakfast.

The appeal of the site centres on this beach and its relative proximity to the island's town, Noirmoutier-en-l'Île. There's a short cut to it through a nature reserve that's ideal for bike-riders and hikers, but cars are obliged to meander around a longer route before they reach a pleasant town with sleepy sun-bleached streets, a dry-moated 12th-century castle, a Romanesque church, and plenty of cafés and restaurants. Here you can fortify yourself for a trip to the great beaches and villages on the north side of the island – Plage des Lutins, close to L'Herbaudière, is a real surfers' favourite.

A roulotte (gypsy caravan) close to the site's reception serves chips, pizzas, and sandwiches, but BBQ-ing or home-cooking is most popular, especially around the stylish wood-and-canvas Canadian-style tents (of which there are 80).

At low tide hundreds of people may scour the beach with rakes and buckets in search of oysters, cockles, and clams. Campers do it, too, but a cheap and equally cheerful alternative is to buy the local fishermen's latest catch in town, or stop at one of the excellent roadside cafés selling *huîtres* (oysters)

or *moules* (mussels), while crossing the island. Often these can be found right next to the salt marshes, which formed the backbone of the local economy (a quarter of the island used to be salt marsh), and provide great viewing points for egrets, avocets, shelducks, and other migratory birds.

After your seafood supper, suitably enriched with local *fleurs de sel* salt and Breton *cidre*, you can simply sit and watch the sea as the subtle blues, pinks, and purple-greys merge around the horizon, because there's really no need to rush around here, unless you need to catch the causeway at low tide.

COOL FACTOR You're as close to the beach as you can get, but it feels sheltered.

WHO'S IN? Tents, campervans, caravans, dogs (on leads), families, couples, large groups, young groups – yes.

ON SITE For a site with 500 pitches, the kids' play area is relatively small. The nearest shop is outside the municipal campsite, not far from the main gate, with more supermarkets to be found further into Noirmoutier-en-L'Île. There are 5 wash-blocks, with plenty of hot showers, toilets, and stylish washing facilities, though some women, when asked, said they would definitely prefer it if the showers were not 'mixed' areas. *Jetons* (tokens) for washing machines are available from reception, where bike-hire and wi-fi access is also available. BBQs are fine, but campfires are not allowed on site, nor on the beach, though people do light their own beach fires.

OFF SITE There are bike trails across the island, some of which are cycles-only, criss-crossing the Marais salt marshes. When there's not enough excitement to be had on the beach, the water chutes, slides, torrents, and geysers at the Océanile Aquatic Park (00 33 2 51 35 91 35; www.oceanile. com) should deliver it. Alternatively, there's surfing and kite-surfing, sailing, fishing, horse-riding, or kayak and canoe hire to help you discover the labyrinthine Routes du Sel (the salt routes). And there's a nature reserve that's great for spotting sea- and marsh-loving birds next to the site.

FOOD AND DRINK There's a *boulanger* who comes to the site each morning at around 8.30am with fresh bread and croissants. Make sure you buy, catch, or collect some seafood, whether it's covered in scales, shells, or exoskeletons, to eat on site, preferably after an aperitif of Pineau made in the Vendée or the Charente. Among the many restaurants in Noirmoutier-en-l'Île, the ivy-clad Le Grand Four, right next to the castle (00 33 2 51 39 61 97; www.legrandfour.com) comes highly recommended for gastronomic thrills (*menus* from €23). Or try the family-friendly seafood and crêpes selection at Le Transat (00 33 2 51 35 72 27), which has a very friendly atmosphere and offers panoramic views over the port of L'Herbaudière, about 3½ miles (6 km) from La Vendette.

GETTING THERE The sites (there are several along the Les Sableaux beach) are well signposted from the main road through the town. La Vendette is the last of them on the left, with a large indigo-blue sign over the entrance.

OPEN 2 April–10 October.

THE DAMAGE A pitch (tent/caravan/motorhome, 2 people, vehicle) €13.30 (€19.90 in high season) or €15.50 (€24.10) for a beachside position, which is cheeky. Each extra person is €3.30 (€4.80), kids from 2–7 years are €1.60 (€2.70), but babies are free. Electricity is €4.50. If you're planning to stay for longer, consider renting one of the Canadian-style tents, especially before or after the French holidays (the last week of August), when there are special promotional deals.

l'étournerie

L'Étournerie, 85320 Château Guibert   00 33 2 51 28 77 68   www.letournerie.nl

Camping *à la ferme* in a basic *camping rural* site is one approach to simplified summer living, but L'Étournerie is even smaller than that. It's a non-classified campsite, which means it must have no more than six pitches. Sisters Jacky and Renée and their families also have a chalet and a stylish *gîte*, so the site is a truly bijou alternative. It's not basic, though, as it has a small heated swimming pool, meals can be ordered, and it sits in its own land in the hills of the southern Vendée.

The site is run by three Dutch families, who have realised their dream of living in the beautiful light and sweet air near the Atlantic coast and have created a place specifically for people who enjoy the same sort of things. The only noise is likely to come if the geese, the goat, and the chickens are disturbed, but as they don't even have foxes to worry about, that doesn't happen often.

The Vendée and its sandy beaches traditionally attract mainly French tourists – Jacky and Renée speak French, English, and German as well as Dutch – but the links with Holland go back a long way. Dutch engineers helped build the dykes and drain the marshes of the Marais Poitevin in the 17th century. Now nicknamed 'Green Venice', it's a maze of waterways and islets that's best explored in boats, but there are walks and cycle routes, too. The site also has access to a nearby reservoir, where you can fish, swim, or mess about in rubber boats. Although not designed for sports and leisure, this is a great site to hike around or cool off in on hot summer afternoons.

COOL FACTOR Tiny site in peaceful countryside.

WHO'S IN? Tents, caravans, dogs (on leads) – yes. People needing to be entertained, campervans – no.

ON SITE Six pitches, some with shade, all with electric hook-ups. Clean, bright toilets and showers, fridge, washing machine, and dryer available. Small (heated) pool and *boules* area. Geese, chickens, and a goat to admire.

OFF SITE Lake 328 yards (300 m) away is nearly on site. Guides to walks and cycle routes within 30 miles (50 km), plus golf courses and vineyards. Surf beaches on Atlantic coast, but Renée recommends the sheltered sands of La Faute-sur-Mer (www.lafautesurmer.com). 'Green Venice', aka the Marais Poitevin, lies to the south, but for historical spectacle and fun family experience at Château Puy du Fou (www.puydufou.com).

FOOD AND DRINK Meals available on site, as is local Pineau des Charentes, on occasion. The nearest shops are 2½ miles (4 km) away in Mareuil-sur-Lay-Dissais, as is 'L'Aubraie, a grill/pizza restaurant with terrace/gardens on the river (00 33 2 51 97 78 74; www.laubraie.com).

GETTING THERE From A83 take J6 (direction Bournezeau). In the village take a left towards Mareuil-sur-Lay-Dissais (D48). After 110 yards (100 m) turn right towards Thorigny (D36). In Thorigny, go left towards Château Guibert (D60). Pass through, lake on the right, and continue on rue du Lac through Bellenoue. On the right is a picnic/play area. Take next right. At the T-junction turn right again, after 110 yards (100 m), turn left at the sign, drive across the field and park behind the conifers.

OPEN Roughly May–September (*gîte* open all year).

THE DAMAGE 2 adults plus tent/caravan, including electricity €19–€22. Additional adults €6.

camping de l'océan

Camping de l'Océan, 62 allée de la Négade, 33780 Soulac-sur-Mer   00 33 5 56 09 76 10   http://camping.ocean.pagesperso-orange.fr

Soulac-sur-Mer, claims the tourist office, is 'close to everything except boredom'. They're not fibbing. This seaside resort on the Bay of Biscay is dense with activities to suit all ages, all within easy walking/cycling distance of each other. Starting at La Pointe de Grave, 88 miles (141 km) of cycling tracks run south down the Médoc coast to Les Landes, taking in wild beaches, stunning lakes, chateau vineyards, and scented pine forests. Long, sandy stretches front Soulac's compact town, where bijou boutiques and eateries suit all tastes. The resort has been protected from urbanisation, the streets look cute in their neo-classical splendour, and the locals appear to be a friendly bunch.

We're on the northern tip of the Médoc, where the Gironde Estuary meets the Atlantic Ocean on the Côte d'Argent (Silver Coast). The drive from Bordeaux takes close to two hours, or you can journey south across the estuary from Royan. Soulac is a calm, quaint resort. Locals claim it was the country's first beach resort and celebrate their heritage every June at a lively carnival. At the end of the last decade the town weathered two big storms that ate away at the coastline. Safely situated 328 yards (300 m) back from Plage de l'Amélie is Camping de l'Océan, undeniably the nicest campsite on the Soulac block. Their set-up is exemplary. A snack bar, reception, and wash-rooms are designed to blend in with the surroundings. Everything you need is on site, but if it's not, just grab a bike and get pedalling until you find it. Soulac won't leave you wanting.

COOL FACTOR Stress-free haven for beach-lovers, surfers, families, solo travellers, and everyone in between.

WHO'S IN? Tents, campervans, caravans, dogs – yes. Large groups, young groups – no.

ON SITE Three hundred pitches. Ten communal hook-ups, 3 washing areas (Le Soleil, La Mer, La Fôret), 30 strong, hot showers and 40 WCs, including disabled. Shop and snack bar open daily in July and August. Washing machines, tumble-dryers (€5/€2). Wi-fi €15 per hour (cheaper in town). Ten communal BBQs. Tennis free June and September, otherwise €6 per hour. TV and games room, table tennis. No campfires.

OFF SITE Cycling trails offer an exciting way to explore. Horse-riding, skate-boarding, and sky-diving easily accessible (www.soulac.com). The Romanesque Notre-Dame-de-la-Fin-des-Terres basilica is a UNESCO World Heritage Site. The oldest lighthouse in Europe is at Le Verdon-sur-Mer. If the Atlantic surf is too wild there are sandy lake beaches at Hourtin lakes, a 45-minute drive away.

FOOD AND DRINK Restaurants in Soulac take cash or cheque only. Le Panier de Becassine (00 33 6 63 30 94 36) serves Italian and fish dishes in a homely atmosphere.

GETTING THERE Head north-west out of Bordeaux on D1 towards Castelnau-de-Médoc, then D1215 towards Soulac-sur-Mer. Turn left on allée Montaigne towards L'Amélie-sur-Mer and look for a left turn on D101. Campsite signposted down track.

PUBLIC TRANSPORT Regular trains in summer from Bordeaux to Soulac. Prebook a taxi (00 33 5 56 09 79 57).

OPEN All year.

THE DAMAGE Pitch with 2 adults €23.50. Child 2–10 years €3, under 2 years free. Hook-ups €4. Dogs €2.50.

la prairie

La Prairie Aire Naturelle, St Hélène-de-l'Étang, 33121 Carcans   00 33 5 56 03 37 60   philip.roll@btinternet.com

Aire naturelle campsites appeal to anyone who rates personal space above fancy amenities and organised fun. Typically found in attractive back gardens of French family homes, only 25 pitches are permitted and they're spacious. To find a peaceful, unspoilt *aire naturelle* site so near to beaches and lakes is as good as it gets for nature-loving campers *en France*. Welcome to the home of English-born Mr Roll. His garden is a pretty, assymetric field with a few trees at each end and a couple of barns in between. When the weather is so hot that only sea breezes will keep you from melting, the coast is just 3 miles (5 km) away. And when the Atlantic currents are too strong to swim in, you're on the middle edge of the biggest natural lake in France, Lac d'Hourtin-Carcans. Hourtin beach, north, is a family favourite and further south is Lac de Lacanau, famous for international surfing competitions every August. White, sandy beaches and still waters offer supervised swimming and water sports. The nearest is Maubuisson; turn right out of the campsite and follow the signs and you'll be windsurfing in minutes.

COOL FACTOR All-weather water sports and cycling action in a beautiful part of France.

WHO'S IN? Tents, campervans, caravans, dogs, young groups (vetted) – yes. Large groups – no.

ONSITE Twenty-five pitches with 20 hook-ups. Shower block with 3 showers, 3 WCs and 1 disabled WC. Table tennis, 6 communal BBQs.

OFF SITE Maubuisson Nautic operates out of a booth on the lake (00 33 5 56 03 47 49) renting canoes €8 per hour, pedalos €13 per hour, catamaran lessons from €35 and windsurfers €12 per hour, lessons from €25.

FOOD AND DRINK A cluster of café-restaurants overlook the lake at Maubuisson. Pizza Marina (00 33 5 56 03 39 39) is the spot for huge platefuls of seafood salad.

GETTING THERE D6 to St-Médard-en-Jalles, then D1215 to Ste-Hélène. D104 and D207 to Carcans and right on D3. The campsite is on the left, turn down the long drive, around a few bends and look for the sign on the left.

OPEN Mid April–mid October.

THE DAMAGE 1 person €6.50, 2 people €9, dog €2.50 (no charge for 'handbag dogs'). Hook-ups €2.50. 2 static caravans sleep 6 €275–€300 per week.

cap de l'homy

Camping Municipal du Cap de l'Homy, 600 avenue de l'Océan, 40170 Lit-et-Mixe   00 33 5 58 42 83 47   www.camping-cap.com

Run by the local council, helping to keep costs low, this large municipal site advocates a back-to-nature approach that appeals. It has been going for 35 years and is already welcoming three generations of campers. July and August are always full, with families as well as dozens of beginner-to-intermediate surfers here to tackle the Atlantic's best waves. Two surf schools are next to the site, and with few other distractions, lessons are a must.

Half of the busy summer months' allocation is saved for personal callers, who often turn up overnight and fall asleep behind the wheel waiting for the gates to open (no traffic is permitted on site at night), hoping to grab one of the few seafront spots – lovely sandy pitches at the foot of the dunes, just yards from the beach.

The site extends well back from the sands into the large, yet serene, unspoilt, and virtually isolated floors of La Fôret de Lit-et-Mixe. With miles of cycling and hiking trails campers spend hours scrambling through the well-tended rows of pines. That's if they're not paddling in the ocean or simply enjoying the peace, of course.

COOL FACTOR Peaceful escapism under pines on a secluded, never-ending stretch of fine sand.

WHO'S IN? Tents, campervans, caravans, dogs, groups – yes.

ON SITE Of the 474 pitches, 156 are for tents without electric hook-ups and 39 with. Pitches for disabled marked 'H' on online site plan. Six shower blocks and WCs. Small play area, volleyball court, *boules/pétanque* court, and games room with table tennis. No BBQs or campfires.

OFF SITE Site on coastal cycle path through forest. For surf lessons book in at Cap Surf School (00 33 6 86 21 54 32) or Esprit Océan (00 33 6 63 21 95 19).

FOOD AND DRINK An hour's drive east is Mont-de-Marsan, where grapes are grown for Armagnac liqueur.

GETTING THERE From Bordeaux follow A63 towards Bayonne. Come off on D38 for Mézos and St-Julien-en-Born. Follow D652 through Lit-et-Mixe and 1 mile (2 km) on turn right on D88 and follow the road through the forest.

PUBLIC TRANSPORT Railway station in Dax. Bus to site.

OPEN May–September.

THE DAMAGE 2 people, tent/caravan, electricity €16.90 (without €12.70). Dog (on lead) €2.10. Canvas bungalow sleeps 5 people (no dogs) €570 per week.

panorama du pyla

Camping Panorama du Pyla, Grande Dune du Pyla, route de Biscarosse, 33115 Pyla-sur-Mer   00 33 5 56 22 10 44
www.camping-panorama.com

Arcachon – what a great surprise! This glitzy west coast resort is home to a natural, powerful, and somewhat elegant tourist attraction. It might only be a sand dune, but what a sand dune it is. The King Kong of all sand dunes in fact, busting all other imitations out of the water.

Traffic is bumper to bumper during summer months on the single autoroute to La Teste-de-Buch that leads to the suburbs of Arcachon's 'Winter Town' maze of magnificent Victorian villas. These ornate wooden-balustrade holiday homes belong to wealthy Bordelais and Parisians appear surprisingly tropical against the wooded hillside. The town was once the party destination *du jour*, and its forest walls whisper with tales of century-old aristocratic soirées. Next to the campsite the view is just as impressive. The largest sand dune in Europe was an 18th-century 'accident' that the wind slowly blew in over time. It measures 1¾ miles (3 km) in length, and is 550 yards (500 m) wide and 115 yards (107 m) high. From the campsite below, matchstick silhouettes can be seen trekking towards the summit, the reward for their 30-minute climb being a sublime pinky-blue sunset that engulfs the Bay of Arcachon, from the campsite across the waters to Cap Ferret.

Tourists aren't the only visitors flocking to this one-mile-wide bay. The Banc d'Arguin nature reserve, a UNESCO World Heritage Site, is a nesting home for thousands of birds that are attracted to the shallow coastal waters and protected mudflats of Île aux Oiseaux. But all guests are outnumbered by the zillions of oysters that thrive here. Dotted along the Cap Ferret Peninsula are 100-year-old oyster-farming villages, where colourful *cabanes* sit on stilts, storing the daily catches gathered in sprawling fishing nets.

Cap Ferret is an upmarket but laid-back shoppers' paradise serviced by regular, 20-minute ferries that zip back and forth from La Pyla, near the campsite. But if shopping's off the menu, make sure oysters are on. Pick a restaurant with views across the bay and feast on shellfish that is plated over ice within minutes of being caught. Afterwards, walk off lunch by climbing the 258 steps of the Pointe du Cap lighthouse. The view at the top is of a landscape that hasn't been destroyed by waterfront hotel or property developments; therein the beauty of Arcachon. You can eat back at camp if you'd prefer. Fresh fish, sea scallops, meat, foie gras, *plats du jour*, salads, and desserts are for the taking (Camping Panorama du Pyla is part of the Yelloh! Group that runs 45 sites in France, and their standards are high).

Obviously, a stay here isn't cheap, but it's worth every centime. The fancy à la carte restaurant, ice-cream parlour and crêperie, two swimming pools, and kids' entertainment create a boisterous atmosphere in high season, to say the least. The ergonomics work, however, with amenities grouped near the entrance to the site so that the noisier activities precede the quiet calm among the coniferous trees. Terraced slopes allow personal space at numerous pitches, but for greater seclusion

aim for a spot by the side of the dune. These pitches are still near the beach – the sea glistens through the trees – but you're further away from any of the pedestrian paths. Temperatures average 22°C (72°F) in summer, though sea breezes make the midday heat bearable. If climbing the dune feels like walking on hot coals, use the steps etched into the slope at the start of every summer. After the sun has set and you've washed the sand off, steam oysters over a bed of pine needles (it's what the locals do) and dream about the wonderful surprises that lie in store tomorrow.

COOL FACTOR A unique destination. Silvery-blue sea in front of you, Europe's biggest sand dune on your right, and oysters for breakfast (possibly).

WHO'S IN? Tents, campervans, dogs – yes. Caravans, large groups, young groups – no.

ON SITE Four hundred and fifty pitches, includes 50 for tents at the seafront (less shaded and sheltered from the elements, but with great sunset and sunrise views). All have electricity hook-ups. Seventy clean, modern wash-rooms with showers and 60 WCs. Two rooms for disabled (although, it must be pointed out, wheelchairs will have difficulty in the sand). Two outdoor pools, La Panorama restaurant, small shop, bar, beauty centre, bouncy castle, sauna and jacuzzi (both free to guests), tennis court, bike hire, mini-golf, mini-market, cash machine, laundry (€3), drier (€4), free wi-fi access. Baby cots for hire. No campfires.

OFF SITE Ferries run between Arcachon and Cap Ferret and make trips within the bay (www.uba-bateau-arcachon.com). The famous Médoc cycle trail starts at Cap Ferret and runs up the Médoc Bleu coastline along 88 miles (141km) of flat trails to the northern tip of the Gironde Estuary at Pointe de Grave. The trail passes the Lacanau lakes, Montalivet-les-Bains and Soulac-sur-Mer (see Camping de l'Océan, p106) passing magnificent ocean beaches and pine forests. Paragliding tandem flights with or without an instructor (if qualified) courtesy of the onsite École Winover (00 33 6 14 15 32 73). For a personally guided wine and food tour of the famous Médoc region in Bordeaux, full-day, tailor-made outings include collection from your campsite, a vineyard ramble, winery tasting, and 3-course lunch followed by visits and tastings at 2 more wineries, from €185 per person (medoc@winetour-france.com). Or visit at the end of June via Bordeaux, where every 2 years a wine festival with a mile-long 'wine road' of outdoor bars, wine stands, and food booths is staged (www.bordeaux-tourisme.com).

FOOD AND DRINK Commercial oyster-farming started in 1859 so, naturally, seafood is popular here. Pinasse Café in Cap Ferret has waterside views and an excellent ambience (00 33 5 56 03 77 87; www.pinassecafe.com). Tour an oyster farm in La Teste-de-Buch in Port de Larros. Many oyster huts (*cabanes*) offer tasting (*dégustation*) sessions. At camp, the crêperie and ice-cream café is situated in the middle of the site, making it hard to resist late-afternoon refreshment.

GETTING THERE From Bordeaux follow A63/A660 towards Arcachon. Come off at La Teste-de-Buch (signposted Dune de Pyla) and follow signs.

PUBLIC TRANSPORT Fast TGV trains run from Paris and stopping trains from Bordeaux to Arcachon, from where buses run past the site 6 times a day. Or book Bordeaux airport collection with the site, from €80 for 4–8 people.

OPEN 15 April–5 October.

THE DAMAGE Two adults €17–€43, child under 3 years free, otherwise €4–€6 per night. Bike hire €12 per day. Tennis free in low season, otherwise €9 per hour. Cots free except in high season €3. Bungalow €39–€170 per night.

dordogne & lot

Out of Africa meets Ibiza chic in this leviathan of taste and scale. It's hard to imagine a more stylish campsite, but don't be fooled by the uber-cool bar complete with shiny chrome taps, de rigueur grey tables, Ben and Jerry's fridge, and leafy piazza – Les Ormes is as rough and ready as you want it to be. Apart from the high-luxe tents, there are 100 great tent pitches for traditional camping in shady meadow areas. Of course, you could indulge in a bit of fantasy glamping if an extravagant wind blows, and this is what you can expect: 25 safari tents, each individually finished, hidden in mature groves, and perfectly set apart so as to nurture your Robert Redford/Meryl Streep delusions.

Each 'Gibson' tent has its very own verandah, twinkling candelabra, and lavish interior that seems to jump right out of the pages of a *Tatler* shoot; chaise longue, scatter cushions, fresh flowers, retro furnishings, and cool self-catering facilities, all finished off with a dash of élan. There's even a raised outdoor platform with a tent atop, should your kids want to escape you, but it's close enough should the bogeyman come a-calling. For the best valley views be sure to ask for the Mojave tents.

By the restaurant, on a gentle elevation, there are hammocks strung between the trees so that you can maximise the splendid views of the sunsets, which incandesce in the low-

les ormes

Camping Les Ormes, 47210 St Étienne de Villeréal   00 33 5 53 36 60 26   www.campinglesormes.com

slung hills. The crowd is mid-thirties to forties, the atmosphere decidedly laid-back; perhaps something to do with the chillsome tunes wafting by, along with the smell of deliciously grilled food from the gastro bar. As to facilities, there's a great deal to keep you busy and ensure you never need to leave the site. After a faux African sunrise and delicious cappuccino and breakfast in the whiter-than-heaven café, head off to the tennis court, or to the pond for a spell of fishing, or maybe it's volleyball, or a wander over to the petting zoo… oh now they're just showing off! And I didn't even get to the black granite swimming pool with the hip silver bus that doubles as a snack bar.

Kids are in their element here, perhaps because the site's huge but secure, so their parents are able to really relax, safe in the knowledge that if one of them tries to escape, the chances are a hundred per cent they'll be spotted by one of the many staff who drive around in beat-up, ancient Renaults. Apart from the kids' pool there are swings and climbing frames, and if they really want to get feral there's the mature elm woods – from which the place takes its name – to run wild in. There's even a kids' restaurant, where they can eat with their new buddies, undisturbed by annoying crinklies.

As to the final hundreds and thousands on this magnificent *gâteau*, there's a very tasteful boutique

where you can buy jewellery and pashminas in the possible event you get a little romantic or have forgotten your other half's birthday – it happens. Yes, if Carlsberg did campsites it would probably look something like this. For a bunch of Dutch travellers who came together through their wanderings in Indonesia and the Far East, there's nothing remotely laissez-faire or unfinessed about Les Ormes. Like all products of genius they make it look easy, but cast a deeper look and you'll see this finely wrought site is achieved by a consistent level of excellent service and creative imagination.

COOL FACTOR Les Ormes redefines 'comfort' with its laid-back ambience, efficient facilities, and general panache.

WHO'S IN? Tents, campervans, dogs (on leads), glampers – yes.

ON SITE Two large toilet and shower blocks, laundry, a great tennis court, granite swimming pool, and stylish pool bar as well as a kiddies' pool. There's a sandy beach by a lake rippling with fish, a petting zoo with friendly goats, a Mediterranean-style restaurant with the best steaks this side of Argentina, a well-stocked bar that would keep Olly Reed busy for a week, and a boutique selling jewellery. On the wellbeing side, there are yoga classes, kids' art courses, and onsite massage should you put your back out while doing absolutely nothing. There's also a kids' café and, perhaps more importantly, a Ben and Jerry's fridge bursting with your favourite Phish food and Chocolate Fudge Brownie flavours.

OFF SITE The nearest town of any real interest is beautiful Bergerac, which takes its name from the celebrated wordsmith with the oversized proboscis. You can see a statue of him in the old town; that is if you're not too busy stocking up on wine in one of a clutch of excellent wine-sellers. Red is the colour to go for here. The region is famous for its vino and there are great deals to be had. The old town undulates through a series of sun-dappled courtyards to the river and it makes for a lovely morning visit, wandering through the narrow alleys and getting lost. Closer to home there are a number of fortified medieval villages (*bastides*) including Villeréal, Monflanquin, and Monpazier, all with arcaded squares and vibrantly French with weekend markets selling everything from foie gras to local produce. Keep an eye out, too, for *vide greniers* (translates as 'empty the attic'), France's version of a car boot sale. You never know, you might just pick up something interesting. Come August, the towns recall their medieval past with the costumed festivals of the Vallée du Dropt. If you fancy a wine *dégustation* in a beautiful historic setting, head to Château de Monbazillac to try their sweet white wine. There's also an 18-hole golf course right next to the campsite.

FOOD AND DRINK Etincelles (00 33 5 53 74 08 79) in nearby Ste-Sabine-Born village has a Michelin star and is celebrated for its authentic French fare. To be honest, though, the campsite restaurant has a terrific menu, with staple dishes such as steak and couscous, and you may not need to go anywhere else.

GETTING THERE A10 towards Bordeaux. Just before Orléans take A71 direction Paris/Blois. After around 50 miles (80 km) – just before Vierzon – turn onto A20 to Toulouse/ Limoges. Near Brive-la-Gaillarde, pick up A89 to Bordeaux and exit at J15, direction Bergerac, then follow N21 and D121 through Bordas and Castillonnès to Villeréale from where the site is clearly signposted.

OPEN 1 May–15 September.

THE DAMAGE Tent, 2 people €10. Child under 8 years €8, under 7 years €4. For various prices for safari tents please refer to Les Ormes website.

simply canvas

Simply Canvas, Bonac, 47120 St-Jean-de-Duras   00 33 6 81 76 85 94   www.simplycanvas.eu

Sandra and Santi, the owners of Simply Canvas, couldn't be accused of being orthodox – they met in a Vietnamese monastery – she was a nun, he was a monk. After leaving for the world outside, destiny brought them to the Dordogne, whereupon they were married. The end? Not quite. They then set up a campsite that sought to encapsulate peace and equilibrium. As such, a zen-like calm filters through every inch of Simply Canvas. Chickens wander past fat Buddha statues in the allotment, kittens bounce across the lawn as hammocks swing gently in the breeze – tune in, turn on, doze off. Wander through the lavender grove to the graphite-black, kidney-shaped swimming pool – it's like that because it soaks up and retains the heat of the sun.

The accommodation is equally relaxing, with six safari tents furnished in traveller's paraphernalia – ornate globes, wicker furniture, peacock feathers… Each tent faces its own direction to maximise privacy. The site operates an honesty tab, so it's up to you to declare how many glasses of chilled rosé you've been tucking into while watching the extraordinary pink sunsets they fire up nightly. There's a high-beamed, candy-lit barn that is a playroom for kids on stormy days, venue for yoga classes, and also the kitchen and dining room. Because there are only six tents the atmosphere is intimate; you'll soon get to know your fellow guests, be it sitting alfresco or meeting on the way to the personalised shower each of you enjoys (your name is chalked on the door).

COOL FACTOR Zen calm meets colonial comfort.

WHO'S IN? Tents, campervans, dogs (on leads), glampers – yes.

ON SITE Everything you need is on site, from free electric Dutch bikes, sun-heated swimming pool, table-tennis table, lounge-lizard hammocks, volleyball, kids' swings, communal fire and BBQ; personalised shower and toilet. There's even frisbee tennis in the field next door. There are 6 safari tents and linen is changed daily.

OFF SITE Head for Bergerac for a *dégustation* of its famous red wine. En route, there's scores of roadside vintners. To see the lush valleys from a different angle treat yourself to an afternoon's hot-air ballooning (00 33 5 53 89 02 23; www.domainededurand.com).

FOOD AND DRINK Breakfast on site is an informal affair; you can eat outside the barn at the endlessly long table, which gives on to great views of the fields, or take it inside. Christine returns from the village every dawn laden with fresh baguettes, pains au chocolat, and croissants. In neighbouring Eymert, Le Pub Gambetta (00 33 5 53 23 33 41) on the central town square is welcoming and authentic.

GETTING THERE From Bordeaux, follow signs for Périgueux/Libourne, joining the A89 shortly before Libourne. Exit at J12 Ste-Foy-la-Grande, D708 to Margueron, then take the left turn in the village towards Miramont-de-Guyenne. After about 3 miles (5 km), turn left when you see the sign for Briquet/Bonac. Follow this road for 240 yards (220 m) until the white portal on your right, and you have arrived.

OPEN May–September.

THE DAMAGE Family safari tent €560 in low season, €680 in high season.

chez rambaud

Camping Chez Rambaud, 87440 Les Salles-Lavauguyon   00 33 5 55 00 08 90   www.chez-rambaud.com

The Limousin countryside rolls with wave upon wave of buttery hills, peppered with distinctive honey-hued cattle and pointy-hat chateaux. Chez Rambaud is truly out in the sticks, about a mile from sleepy Les Salles-Lavauguyon on the Richard Coeur de Lion route. It's so well hidden it might take a few goes to find it, but its vantage point on a gentle hill is the perfect place to pitch up. The site is small yet wide-horizoned. It's also immaculately clean, but not to the point where you'll feel bad if you drop a few baguette crumbs. Owners Nicky and Neil welcome you in their flower-filled garden, after which they leave you to your own devices. Since the site is bijou there are no painful odysseys to get to the sparkling toilet and wash-block.

The site is still in its nascency, so there's not a great deal for kids. For the adults this isn't a problem as there's a great library packed with thrillers. But fortunately for *les enfants*, a few miles away beautiful Lac de Lavaud has a sandy beach and swimming area – even if the water is a bit creepy. There are bags of local things to do, too, from wine-tasting, rambling, and cycling to exploring markets and summer festivals. If you fish you're in luck, for the Charente and Vienne rivers are nearby and the site owners can help you acquire a permit. There's plenty of farmhouse produce for sale. Nicky has taught herself animal husbandry and also grows lettuces, potatoes, tomatoes, and courgettes; coolher home-made sausages can be bought for monumental fry-ups.

COOL FACTOR A hidden gem crowded by lush fields, swimable lakes, rolling forests, and traditional villages.

WHO'S IN? Tents, campervans, and dogs (on leads) – yes.

ON SITE Electricity points at every pitch, of which there are 6. The wash-block is spotless and the showers warm and powerful enough to wake you from your slumber. Laundry facilities and special access for those with reduced mobility. Petting farm. Campfires not permitted, BBQs off ground okay.

OFF SITE The historic cities of Angoulême and Limoges are both within range. So, too, is the eerily preserved site of Oradour-sur-Glane, its peace belying a macabre day in 1942 on which 642 people were killed by the Waffen SS. The village was looted and set on fire and it has been kept in exactly the state it was left, with burnt-out cars and derelict buildings. On a lighter note golf, bird-watching, kayaking, and horse-riding can all be organised. If you have time, hop on the Velo Rail in nearby Confolens and pedal for miles on a disused railway line. Ask Nicky for information about local markets. For antique buffs there are plenty of *vide greniers* (car boots), where you might happen upon a real gem.

FOOD AND DRINK You're in gastro country; the area is renowned for its chocolate, walnuts, and artisan food. For lunch or dinner try Hôtel de France, Rochechouart (00 33 5 55 03 03 87), more French than Gainsbourg and much prettier, with wonderful views and a rustic seasonal *menu*. The *steak haché* (€12) is delicious.

GETTING THERE From Angoulême follow D12 and N141 to La Rochefoucauld, then hop on to D13, following the sign for Sauvagnac. Les Salles-Lavauguyon is the next village.

OPEN All year.

THE DAMAGE Pitch plus 2 adults and car €14.50 per night. Child (up to 10 years) €2 per night; dog €1.50. Hook-up €4.

Chez Rambaud
Confiture D'Oranges
(Marmalade)

la ribière sud

Camping de la Ribière Sud, 87230 Pageas, nr Châlus, Haute-Vienne   00 33 5 55 78 58 62   www.la-ribiere-sud.com

Known as France's Lake District, the Limousin is celebrated for its wonderful rolling hills, fox-red cattle, and hordes of Brits trying to escape their compatriots from the Dordogne. It's also an area integrally tied to the history of the Crusades and Richard the Lionheart, who met his end in the village of Châlus.

Camping de la Ribière Sud is just a few minutes away, set in 22 acres (9 hectares) of sleepy woodland and meadow on the former site of a tree nursery. It's a relatively new site run by two northerners (from the north of England, that is), Anne and Harry. Harry's an electrician by trade, so everything works like clockwork. Anne is gaining repute as an oil painter and her work appears in the local gallery as well as back home. The site's centrepiece is a wonderfully painted, genuine Mongolian yurt. Inside it's a hobbit hole of gypsy chic, wooden struts delicately illustrated by the hands of nomadic craftsmen; outside, a wonderful canvas dome bound in camel hair. But you don't have to stay in here if you've brought your own canvas – there are plenty of pitches in the shade of the towering poplars, all with electricity.

Wild boars sometimes pop in for a sniff around, as do the local deer, beneath the ever-present shadows of buzzards. By night you'll be sung to sleep by the soporific hoot of owls and coos of wood pigeons. The nice thing about La Ribière is the scale of the grounds – you can wander in wild glades and prairie grass without meeting a soul.

COOL FACTOR Mongolian splendour and comfort meets woodland serenity in this simple, immaculate campsite.

WHO'S IN? Tents and campervans, by the time you read this another yurt will have landed, dogs (on leads) – yes.

ON SITE There are 6 generously sized pitches with separate power points. The wash-room block is brand new and has piping-hot, eco-friendly power showers. There are disabled facilities. Kids' amusements, such as swings and climbing frames, are yet to be developed, though the wild grounds are rich pickings for their imaginations. Campfires are allowed.

OFF SITE The capital of Limousin is Limoges, famed for its pottery and gastronomy (Limousin beef is delicious, as is the indigenous cream and cherry tart), and is a short drive away. The ruinous Château de Châlus-Chabrolith (open to the public) is where Richard the Lionheart met his maker when he was struck in the eye by a crossbow bolt. North-east of Limoges (between Guéret and Bourganeuf) is Forêt de Chabrières, not only a wonderful place to go walking and picnicking, but also home to Les Loups de Chabrières (www.loups-chabrieres.com), where you can see wolves close up.

FOOD AND DRINK Hôtel du Centre in Châlus (00 33 5 55 78 58 62) does great daily specials such as escargots, Quiche Lorraine and salads and steaks. *Plat du jour* €9. There's also an Intermarché supermarket in town for all your self-catering needs.

GETTING THERE From Limoges go south towards Périgueux on N21, through Séreilhac. Camping de la Ribière Sud is 5 miles (8 km) south on the left, just past Domaine de la Ribière (fishing lake) before a right-hand bend.

OPEN All year.

THE DAMAGE Yurt (max 2 people) €395 per week. Tents €20 per night, including electricity.

moulin de feuyas

Camping Moulin de Feuyas, 24800 St-Romain-et-St-Clément   00 33 5 53 55 03 99   www.moulindefeuyas.fr

Discovered in 1953 on a farmer's land, Grotte de Villars is the largest underground network in the Dordogne, with over 9 miles (13 km) of subterranean galleries, caverns, and forests of 60-million-year-old stalagmites and stalactites once hollowed out by a river. It's an otherworldly, cold, and touchingly beautiful, land; a place to hush the mouths of babes and leave you speechless. The *son et lumière* show is spectacular. Take a moment to imagine prehistoric shamans entering these caves with firebrands powered by animal oil, the caverns their sacred, honoured temples.

Half an hour from the caves, in a peaceful setting next to a waterfall and former flour mill, Maité and Guy Lafon run a working farm of Limousin cattle. There's something a little *Under Milk Wood* about the place; dogs doze in the 'wetnosed' yards, and cats yawn as donkeys bray. The pitches, typical of *camping à la ferme*, are few (only eight). What makes these pitches special is their location under the shade of mighty acacias and beside a babbling brook. Although there are no cooking facilities, you are free to make your own BBQ. This site is really a place to come equipped with your own camping accoutrements, though you can buy seasonal veg.

There are swings for the kids by the stream and a little menagerie of geese, rabbits, and chickens to distract them. What's really rewarding is how quiet the place is (minus the animal noises), and the feeling that you might be asked at any moment to milk a cow or to deliver a foal.

COOL FACTOR   Rustic, simple, and back to basics. Waking up to the sound of geese, a babbling brook, and braying donkeys never sounded so good.

WHO'S IN?   Tents, campervans – yes.

ON SITE   Eight pitches, a basic shower and toilet block, though no allocation for babies and disabled campers. One menagerie, 2 donkeys, swings, and fresh farm produce. You might even get a coffee if you smile. Campfires are allowed.

OFF SITE   Exploring the Villars grotto; just a stone's throw from the site (00 33 5 53 54 82 36; www.grotte-villars.com), it's a must. The rolling valleys around the site are ripe for cycling, so hire a bike in neighbouring Thiviers (00 33 5 53 62 18 14) for €10 per day. The Voie Vert (Green Way) is 8 miles (12 km) of former railway line. These days it's used as a walking trail, snaking peacefully through verdant valleys. Hippocamp 9 miles (13 km) away, is the place to go for horse-riding (00 33 5 53 52 61 99).

FOOD AND DRINK   But for vegetables there's no food for sale on site. Nearby Thiviers has a *supermarché,* where you can stock up before you arrive. Restaurant Le St-Jean (00 33 5 53 52 23 20) in the nearby village of St-Jean-de-Cole is recommended for its hearty, affordable fare. There's a weekend fruit and veg market in Thiviers, as well as a number of *pâtisseries* dotted around the central square.

GETTING THERE   From Limoges take N21 down to Thiviers, from where you need to head downhill to the supermarket. The site is signposted from here. The road should take you past a quarry on your right, then follow the road a few miles.

OPEN   April–September.

THE DAMAGE   Tent (2 persons) €8 per night, child €2, electricity €2.

belle vue

Camping Belle Vue, La Contie, nr Hautefort, 24390 Boisseuilh   00 33 5 53 51 62 71   campingbellevue24@orange.fr

What at first might seem like a modest-sized campsite – a mere six pitches – soon wins you over with its intimate ambience and view over the fields to the chateau. Crowning the village of Hautefort, this grand old building was once lived in by a countess who survived a number of husbands. By night it lights up like a chandelier, and should you visit on a Wednesday evening you'll find people in period dress strutting around its ornamental lawns to the accompaniment of classical music. Sitting in the northern tip of the Dordogne, just below Limousin, Hautefort is a charmingly low-key village, with a clutch of antique shops, galleries, and rustic bars.

The campsite is well catered for with its cosy Stable Restaurant, which is decked out in blue-checked tablecloths, exposed brick walls, and a selection of local *vins rouges*. There's also a little shop selling basics, and in the evening you can place an order for mouth-watering fresh pastries and bread to be delivered piping hot next morning. Owners Cal and Simon, originally from the UK, wanted to escape the rat race and find a slower pace of life. As well as welcoming hosts they're also great cooks and replicate local dishes accompanied by vegetables grown on site. While striving to maintain rusticity, they've created a comfortable, efficient oasis of calm. Admittedly there's not much to do here, but the surrounding area is a literal smorgasbord of potential activities. Settle back and savour the honeysuckle perfume in the air and feel your pulse lowering by the minute.

COOL FACTOR Terrific valley views, a peaceful vibe, and friendly hosts keep visitors coming back.

WHO'S IN? Tents, campervans, dogs (on leads) – yes.

ON SITE Six pitches and a 6-berth, fully equipped, self-catering tent (€300 per week). The wash-block is clean, water warm, though without nappy-changing facilities or provision for disabled campers. The self-catering facilities and fridge are more than adequate. There's also a washing machine. Sadly, there's little to keep kids amused, though the swimming pool is welcome. Campfires not permitted on site, though there is a disused barn for larger parties and BBQs.

OFF SITE Oodles of things to do, from riding the Velo Rail (pedal karts) on disused railway tracks, to horse-riding, and hot-air ballooning (00 33 6 83 43 36 01; www.perigord-montgolfiere.com), which will set you back around €200, but is unforgettable. You might want to head for the river and hire a kayak. In July and August the tourist office organises tours to foie gras and walnut farms. Finally the prehistoric paintings of Lascaux are nearby (a short trip down D704).

FOOD AND DRINK The cuisine at the onsite Stable Restaurant is typically French; ex-chef Cal whips up dishes like Provençal beef casserole. Mains are €8. The onsite shop sells drinks and ice creams. Auberge du Parc in Hautefort (00 33 5 53 50 88 98) has affordable French fare (mains €13), while La Table d'Erillac is more upmarket with specialities such as boar. A 2-course meal starts at €20.

GETTING THERE East of Périgueux, pick up D5 through Cubjac and Tourtoirac to St-Agnan; head south on D71, keeping an eye out for signs to Hautefort.

OPEN 1 March–11 November.

THE DAMAGE Tent (2 people) with electricity €19, kids (under 12 years) €3.50, dogs €2.

le capeyrou

Camping Le Capeyrou, 24220 Beynac-et-Cazenac   00 33 5 53 29 54 95   www.campinglecapeyrou.com

In the heart of the Périgord Noir region, along one of the most jaw-droppingly perfect stretches of the Dordogne Valley, is the village of Beynac-et-Cazenac. Nestled under the vigilant gaze of the Château de Beynac this magical little village clings to the hillside as if it's been flung there by a giant. With its turreted witch's hat buildings and storybook red-tiled roofs, it's clearly medieval, though people have lived here since the Bronze Age. Pull up a chair at a riverside café, order a cool beer, and ponder Viking longships prowling up-river as they penetrated the valley in the 9th century. Head upstream to La Roque-Gageac to hire a kayak, then float downstream past cliffs and castles peeking through the vernal river bank.

Situated in this 'five castles valley' in the heart of the Périgord Noir, Camping Le Capeyrou sits beneath the fortress of the Château de Beynac. Waking to the sound of the nearby Dordogne River it's hard to imagine a more enchanting view than this. The site itself is well catered for, with a generously sized swimming pool, volleyball court, and homely bar, with 120 pitches enjoying plenty of mature shade. Pitch up by the river banks or in the meadow, away from civilisation. Come evening the bar, with its exposed stone walls and outside patio, is a pleasant spot for sundowners. Inside the recreation room, its walls festooned with old bicycles, there's a huge hearth and grill, where people bring their own meat to BBQ (there's a butcher a few minutes from the site). And if you're feeling decidedly British there's even a darts board.

COOL FACTOR Huge lush grounds beside a gently flowing river and one of the best castle views in the south of France.

WHO'S IN? Tents, campervans, glampers – yes.

ON SITE Two shower blocks, disabled facilities, baby rooms. No food on site. Inviting swimming pool, toddler pool, kids' climbing area. The best pitches are by the river. Volleyball court plus table-tennis tables and laundry facilities. Three safari tents recently added. Campfires allowed.

OFF SITE The surrounding area is famed for the presence of Cro-Magnon Man some 20,000 years ago. Within a 19-mile (30-km) radius there are plenty of troglodyte caves to explore, including world-renowned Lascaux. There are also more than 100 castles to visit. Fishing is a must, with local rivers choking on trout, salmon, and pike. If horse-riding (€16 per hour) and canoeing from Canoë Dordogne (00 33 5 53 29 58 50; www.canoesdordogne.fr) don't grab you, why not take a gentle river ride in a traditional *gabarre* from neighbouring La Roque-Gageac (€8.50 adult/€6 child)? Hot-air ballooning can also be arranged.

FOOD AND DRINK There's a little *supermarché* by Le Capeyrou's entrance, beside which is a *pâtisserie*; it might not look like much, but their walnut cake is exported all over the world. In Beynac head for the impossibly romantic restaurant, La Petite Tournelle (00 33 5 53 29 95 18) up a higgledy-piggledy street. Try the grilled duck, and the chocolate cake is pretty sumptuous, too. Prices from €16.

GETTING THERE Head towards Sarlat-la-Canéda. Beynac-et-Cazenac is 5 miles (8 km) south-west of the town, off D57. Coming from Bergerac, follow the River Dordogne.

OPEN April–September.

THE DAMAGE Tent (2 persons) per night €18. Child per night €3.20. Electricity €4.

les mathévies

Camping Domaine des Mathévies, 24200 Ste-Nathalène, nr Sarlat-la-Canéda   00 33 5 53 59 20 86   www.mathevies.com

The medieval town of Sarlat-la-Canéda is a maze of cobbled squares and imposing turreted buildings – in no time you'll be lost like Theseus in a benign labyrinth. Follow the nostalgic music of the accordion… didn't you pass that chap in the beret just a moment ago?

Losing your bearings is half the fun. The alleyways bulge at the seams with foie gras shops, for this is the wellspring of the hallowed pâté and renditions of geese abound at every turn in sculptures and posters. Take in the 12th-century cathedral over a cool *pression* at one of many alfresco bars before weaving your way through rolling countryside to Domaine des Mathévies.

Natalie and Patrick McAlpine, the campsite's owners, first met in India. Their subsequent travels brought them to this neglected campsite and they set about tastefully transforming it into the eco-minded sanctuary it is today. Imagine a place where adults are as well catered for and contented as their kids and where you can sit back with a frothy latté, play *pétanque* over a leisurely glass of St-Émilion as a paraglider is swallowed up by the salmon-pink sunset below.

Set on a gentle incline with masterful views over the wooded valley, there are 27 pitches to choose from, many of which enjoy shade from walnut, cherry, fig, apple, and plum trees, and all of which have electricity hook-ups. If you're arriving late and don't fancy pitching up for the night there are also some cosy Davy Crockett-style cabins dotted subtly around the site (we like the deep-brown ones for absolute escape). They can house you and your brood and sleep up to six.

Beside the Cosy Nook Café there's also a self-contained traditional *gîte* with all the mod cons (like Sky TV and a CD player), while still retaining exposed stone walls and beamed ceilings. Perfectly sized for a family, with two double bedrooms, it's recently been refurbished. The real ace, though, is the spectacular sunset view you enjoy from the back and the privacy the place affords; giving you all the amenities plus the chance to retire to your own little palace.

The site itself is a real playground for kids, with a toddlers' play area near the Cosy Nook Café (so you get to relax with them in plain view). Natalie and Patrick have two kids and it's this empathy for the little ones that seems to have led to so many thoughtful details to keep them happy; a particular fave is campfire night every week, where they can toast marshmallows (accompanied by an adult) and swap stories over the flames.

There's also a tree house for older kids and a terrific climbing area. If that's not enough to keep them occupied there's a children's pool as well as a larger swimming pool for adults beside the tennis courts and table-tennis table.

The Cosy Nook Café lives up to its moniker with swallow-you-up couches and delicious bar snacks and, with its exposed honey stone walls, it has to be one of the most inviting campsite cafés in France. Fresh bread and croissants are delivered every morning; the best spot to take breakfast is

Sarlat is bursting with foodie shops and twisting alleys

under the shade of the linden trees. And just in case you sneaked your computer in with you to do a little work, the Nook has wi-fi as well as satellite TV for movies or sport in the evening.

You may well find yourself staying much longer than planned with the gastronomical Mecca of Sarlat so close, coupled with perhaps the most charming, friendly site in the Dordogne.

COOL FACTOR One of the friendliest sites in the south. The hosts are delightful, the views stunning, and there's bags for you and the kids to do.

WHO'S IN? Tents, campervans, though they are in the definite minority here, but just as welcome as regular campers with cars, dogs (on leads) – yes.

ON SITE There's a designated fire pit for BBQs and nocturnal gatherings. This is a really friendly, but by no means raucous, place with plenty of Dutch customers, so don't be surprised if you find yourself drinking red wine by the flames long after your bedtime. The café-bar houses a good selection of holiday reads, has wi-fi, and sells a selection of basic supplies such as milk. There's a brand-new shower/wash-block with baby-changing facilities and toilets for disabled campers. There are 27 pitches and 6 wooden cabins. Apart from the tennis court and swimming pool there's also a volleyball court. If the unthinkable happens and it rains, the yoga barn morphs into a kids' area with board games, drawing materials, and plenty more things to keep everyone busy.

OFF SITE There are stacks of things to do locally if the active mood takes you: be it lunching in Sarlat-la-Canéda or popping into a roadside wine-seller's for a quick *dégustation*. Quality wine here is dirt cheap and Patrick can advise you on where to stock up on the best-value vino. The owners can also organise horse-riding at a local farm or you can take Maisy, the campsite dog, for a walk. Kayaking is a must; the Dordogne River is lazily paced and it's a wonderful adventure for your kids (life jackets provided) as you pass wildlife and fairy-tale chateaux.

FOOD AND DRINK The Cosy Nook Café turns out tasty salads (Natalie's dressing is a closely guarded secret), home-made pizzas, and toasted sarnies, as well as a bevy of coffees and alcoholic drinks. Fifty per cent of the food on site is sourced locally. Breakfast is perfect here, but for lunch you'll want to head into Sarlat-la-Canéda, which takes its cuisine very seriously. Try Le Bistrot on place du Peyrou (00 33 5 53 28 28 40), which is intimate and very French, with its red-checked table cloths and *menu* featuring regional faves such as *magret de canard* (duck breast) and *pommes sarlardaises* (potatoes cooked in duck fat). The *menu* starts at €15. If you're stocking up on supplies there's a giant Intermarché supermarket on the outskirts of Sarlat.

GETTING THERE Get off the A20 at exit 55 and follow signs for Rouffillac. From there follow signs to Carlux and continue on to Ste-Nathalène and the diminutive hamlet of Les Mathévies.

OPEN April–September.

THE DAMAGE Cabins (sleep 6) per week, low/high season: €300/€595. Cabins (sleep 6) per night, low/high season: €50/€60. Tents (2 persons) per night €10. Child (under 7 years) €3.50. Electricity €4.

camping de l'ouysse

Camping de l'Ouysse, Le Bourgnou, 42600 Lacave   00 33 5 65 32 63 01   d.vincent4@wanadoo.fr

The languid owner of Camping de l'Ouysse is a bit like a character from an old French novel: furrowed face, bottle-bottom glasses, and a tang of pipe tobacco that follows him about like a redolent cloud. He's been running this former foie gras farm as a campsite for the last 15 years. The demeanour of his riverside site is much the same – relaxed in the extreme. There's little to do here but absorb the natural environment; no mod cons, just a couple of garden gnomes and a wobbly suspension bridge, for those who want to live out their Indiana Jones fantasies. Pitch up in a shady spot in the orchard, or in the arbour of poplars by the banks of the chalk-green River Ouysse. The huge meadow is your third option; when you consider that there can only be 12 tents at any one time, you have an infinity of room to yourself. Glamping this is not. Instead you're compensated with pure nature; take in the colossal rock face towering over one side, then cast your eye along the river, meandering through lush valleys. Fall asleep listening to the babble of water, then in the morning borrow a kayak to explore the waterways.

COOL FACTOR Rustic, back to basics, no-frills camping in a beautiful meadow fringed by a sleepy river, fabulous nearby caves, and a halo of pipe smoke.

WHO'S IN? Tents, campervans, dogs – yes.

ON SITE Basic wash-block, washing machine, and self-catering area. BBQ pit. Free kayak and rowing boat. No electricity points.

OFF SITE Nearby Lacave has a world-famous grotto with trippy geological formations. The gallery by the entrance, Helg'Art, rotates surrealist work, and the owner is so bubbly her charm should be bottled and exported to melancholic corners of the world.

FOOD AND DRINK A bargain 5-course meal at the Ferme-Auberge Calvel in Le Bougayrou (00 33 5 65 37 87 20) starts at €13. The Friday market at Souillac sells local favourites, including foie gras, walnut oil, and seasonal veg.

GETTING THERE At Port de Souillac, just south of where A20 joins D804, is the turn-off for the D43 to Lacave. Before you reach the village you'll see signs on your right for Calès. The site is on the left-hand side at the foot of the hill.

OPEN April–September.

THE DAMAGE Tent (2 people) per night €8.60, child €2.50, campervan €10 per night.

le masvidal

Camping Le Masvidal, La Ferme du Masvidal, 19120 Bilhac   00 33 5 55 91 53 14   www.masvidal.fr

This really is *camping à la ferme* – French farmers' innovative idea of renting spare meadows out to nature-lovers while operating their working farms at the same time. Pitches are usually no more than half a dozen in number, with basic facilities in beautiful countryside. Well, Le Masvidal is no exception. Poised on the gentle hills of the southern Limousin and skirts of the Dordogne and Quercy, this site is charmingly laid-back and rustic. The pitches are dotted around a grassed lawn in front of owner Marielle's picturesque cottage, but their wild meadow might be preferred for its undiluted rusticity. Your companions are grass-munching sheep, who provide gentle percussion to the sound of crickets. Come morning you'll be woken by the call of the local shepherd and the sun turning the meadow russet gold. Food is available in the evenings from the industrious kitchen, though if you feel like it there are self-catering facilities in a separate barn. There's a petting zoo with more rabbits (as big as your toddlers) than you could fit in a magician's hat, as well as chickens, geese, and kittens.

COOL FACTOR Delightful meadows to pitch in, warm host and divine French aromas drifting from the farmhouse kitchen make this a real *camping à la ferme* experience.
WHO'S IN? Tents, campervans, rabbit-friendly dogs (on leads) – yes.
ON SITE Shower block basic and clean. No disabled access or nappy-changing. Room for 6 pitches (one electricity point) in meadow. Petting zoo and swings. No campfires.
OFF SITE Nearby is picturesque medieval town Beaulieu-sur-Dordogne. Canoeing in nearby Souillac at Copeyre Canoë (00 33 5 65 32 72 61; www.copeyre.com).
FOOD AND DRINK For tasty omelettes at prices that won't melt your wallet try Brasserie des Voyageurs in Beaulieu-sur-Dordogne (00 33 5 55 91 18 34). Rustic dishes available on site. Grocers in Bretoneux and Beaulieu-sur-Dordogne, but don't forget home-made farm products for sale back at base, including wine and pastries.
GETTING THERE From Brive-la-Gaillarde head south-east along D38, then south (right) along D940 through Beaulieu-sur-Dordogne towards Bretenoux. Watch for signs to Bilhac and La Ferme du Masvidal.
OPEN April–September.
THE DAMAGE Tent (2 persons) per night €6.

central france

l'étang du camp

L'Étang du Camp, 12320 Sénergues   00 33 5 65 46 01 95   www.etangducamp.fr

Situated on a mountain plateau beside a lake ornamented by a Monet-style bridge is L'Étang du Camp, a once-neglected municipal site, which, in 2006, was lucky enough to be rescued. The views are serene, but there are a couple of quirks you might want to prepare yourself for – you'll be shaking your head to be sure you've not been teleported to the equator. Imagine camping by a reed-fringed lakeside, honeyed African light dappling the canvas of your safari tent. Sneak a look outside for lions and, in the elephant grass, spy the hulking form of water buffaloes. Check your GPS and you're actually in Aveyron, home to ten of France's *plus beaux villages* (most beautiful villages). As to the buffaloes, they belong to a neighbour. But the lake and the safari tents, they're all real and very alluring. There's a fleet of mountain bikes you can freewheel to the valley floor on and there are evenings dedicated to story-telling around the fire, enjoyed with a glass of vino and *aligot-saucisse* (local-style sausage and mash).

Stuart and Christine are great hosts and an excellent source of knowledge on how to make the best of the area. Medieval Conques looks as if it's stepped straight from *In the Name of the Rose*; the cliff-huddling town is unforgettable. Sit in the peaceful Abbaye de Ste-Foy (best visited in early evening as the light is fading) and listen to choral music before walking the labyrinthine streets. You'll be following in the footsteps of thousands of Santiago de Compostela pilgrims, who've been coming through here since the 11th century.

COOL FACTOR An exotic-tinged mountain-top retreat with views, walks, and medieval towns to die for.

WHO'S IN? Tents, campervans, dogs – yes.

ON SITE The site has mature shaded areas and a maximum of 60 pitches. Clean wash-block catering for babies and disabled campers. There's also a washing machine (€5). Games room with table tennis, board games, and satellite TV. Play area. Lake home to pike, carp, and perch. Fishing €4. Campfires allowed.

OFF SITE Aveyron's wooded valleys, poppy-flecked mountain meadows, honey vendors, and pottery workshops. One of the loveliest walks is the 4-mile (7-km) ramble to La Vinzelle (ask Christine for details and a map). Views of the valley and glittering River Lot are life-affirming. Pick up a kayak and float down the Lot from Entraygues-sur-Truyère.

FOOD AND DRINK Christine serves up continental/full English breakfasts (€5.50–€6.50) with fresh bread. In July and August there are evening markets in Valady. The nearest town is St-Cyprien-sur-Dourdou, which has plenty of cafés and grocery shops. Hervé Busset (00 33 5 65 72 84 77) is a 1-star Michelin restaurant in a magnificent historic setting. Dishes range from €35–€95. Auberge St-Jacques (00 33 5 65 72 86 36) is also in the old town and is great value with 3-course meals starting at €18.

GETTING THERE By car from Brive-la-Gaillarde, head to Figeac on D840, then to Decazeville. From here it's easy to reach St-Cyprien-sur-Dourdou, then follow signs to Sénergues (D502 then D46) and L'Étang du Camp is signed.

OPEN April–September.

THE DAMAGE Safari tent (2–4 people) low/high season €182/€210 per week. Tent (2 people, electricity) €18.50 per night. Campervan (electricity) €19.50 per night.

les quatre saisons

Les Quatre Saisons, Chignat, nr Bourganeuf, 23250 Soubrebost   00 33 5 55 64 23 35   www.les-4-saisons.com

Ah yes, the Four Seasons. Great Motown band. No? The hotel chain? No. The Vivaldi concertos then? No. The pizza? No, no, no. Les Quatre Saisons campsite, of course. There's been a campsite on this classic *aire naturelle* site for ages, but it's only in the last three years, since it was taken over by Andrew and Bernie Carnegie, that it's really taken off. The new owners dug flat pitches into the sloping field and turned one of the barns into a games room and campers' shelter for the occasional spells of inclement weather (ah, so that's why it's called the Four Seasons!).

And what they've produced is a great little getaway in the heart of the Creuse region of Limousin. It's plonked amid rolling hills just 2½ miles (4 km) east of the little town of Bourganeuf, which was supposedly founded by the Knights Templar and was one of their favourite French hang-outs, though you probably wouldn't guess this because it didn't feature in *The Da Vinci Code*.

The main camping area is fairly open and fringed with trees but with a couple of hidey-holes if you want to keep out of site of the neighbours.

Off to the side are a couple of smaller, more discrete, areas behind farm buildings for the Howard Hughes and Greta Garbos among you. But if you are happy to show your face, you could do worse than sign up for one of Bernie's evening meals. She's a qualified chef and when the weather's nice will serve up a four-courser on the lawn. Just don't ask for a *quattro stagioni*.

COOL FACTOR Discreet, serene hideaway.

WHO'S IN? Tents, campervans, caravans, dogs (for a fee and notified in advance) – yes. Large motorhomes – no (they get stuck on the steep drive).

ON SITE There's one central facilities block with 3 showers/WCs, and 1 disabled toilet and shower. There's also a washing machine (€4) and electricity can be made available at every pitch. Elsewhere there's a barn with games for the kids, a fridge for campers' use, and free wi-fi.

OFF SITE The site's on the GR4 walking trail and there are over 93 miles (150 km) of trails around the region. There's also horse-riding, biking, and fishing and slightly further afield is the huge Lac de Vassivière; one of France's top water-sports venues.

FOOD AND DRINK Evening meals available on site at €20 per person for 4 courses, wine €6 a bottle. Home-made bread and croissants in the morning (order the night before). Nearest places off site are in Bourganeuf, where there are 2 small brasseries in the square opposite the church: Le Central (00 33 5 55 64 05 67) and La Mezzanine (00 33 5 55 64 31 17), which both serve standard fare.

GETTING THERE From N145 between Guéret and La Souterraine take D912 for Bourganeuf. Follow D8 towards Lac de Vassivière. After 2 miles (3.5 km) turn left on to D37 and follow the road down the hill and then turn right (there's a site sign). Carry on up the hill and the site is dead ahead, though the camping entrance is off to the left and up a steep climb.

OPEN Officially April–September, but by arrangement you can probably stay any old time.

THE DAMAGE Adult €4 per night, child up to 6 years €2, tent, caravan €3, campervan €5, car €2, dog €2.

Not far to the east of this site, the little town of Treignat claims to be the geographical centre of France. It's not the only place to make the claim as there are dozens of villages, fields, and hilltops bearing plaques and flags making the same claim. Quite how you calculate the centre point is complicated and all to do with how you define the borders of France and whether you include Corsica, and so on. Anyway, staying at Nigel and Sheila Harding's tipis in the hamlet of Folbeix is as close as makes any difference to staying right in the heart of France.

For centuries this heartland region was so dark and dense that it was virtually bypassed by roads, commerce, modernity – you name it. No one since the Romans had really ventured in. During the Second World War even the occupying Germans knew better than to try to police such a difficult area. They simply threw a cordon around it and tried to stop people from getting in and out, though this didn't prevent a couple of plucky British agents parachuting into a nearby field to make contact with the Résistance. What they got up to after that has never been really clear, but Nigel found an old service revolver in the attic of the farmhouse, so they must have come here for more than a walk in the woods and to check out the local cheese.

tipis at folbeix

Tipis at Folbeix, Folbeix   00 33 5 55 80 90 26   www.vacanesdetipienfrance.com

When the first edition of *Cool Camping France* was published, the site was ending its first season and Nigel was busy up ladders with a hammer in his hand, still building the facilities. Now that it's all complete it's even more impressive than it was first time around.

Beside a picture-book, ivy-clad old farmhouse is a piece of ancient natural woodland, which houses the six tipis, each one situated in a different part of the wood. They sleep up to five people (two adults and three pre-teen kids), though there's one tipi, the one furthest from the others, which is reserved for couples (where two's company and three's a crowd).

Such is the charm of the place that it's become a huge hit with families. The natural boundaries of the site make it an ideal spot for the kids to roam around and get mucky. Nigel can provide bows and arrows if you want to play cowboys and Indians and he organises midnight walks, where he leads a gaggle of petrified children through the dark woods.

Despite the greater emphasis on family fun, the site remains a haven of environmental consciousness. Solar power and candles provide the lighting, waste is composted and recyclable, and biodegradable products are used wherever possible; all good things to teach your kids.

Meanwhile Sheila's a dab hand at table d'hôte and serves a mean dinner in the restored barn. And just so that you're ready for it, in addition to the three courses plus wine, plus a fantastic cheese board, you'll be offered one of Sheila's home-made liqueurs. So make sure you've left room for one because they're delicious. Particular favourites are the strawberry and the walnut, described by Sheila as 'tasting like Christmas in a glass'. And if you could distil the essence of a great campsite into a single dinky liqueur, you can bet the result would taste something like this.

COOL FACTOR Peaceful and natural woodland site with an environmental conscience.

WHO'S IN? People under 7 feet tall – yes. Campervans, caravans, dogs – no.

ON SITE Bedding is provided, but you need to bring your own towels. Outside the sanctuary of your tipi there are male and female facilities with a couple of hot showers and a couple of WCs. There's also a handy kitchen (with a fridge and cool box with ice packs, plus everything else you'd need) and the day room in the restored barn, which doubles as the breakfast and dining room; *une salle de réunion,* as they say. There are herbs for picking in the garden and various jams, chutneys, and home brews available from the house. There's one communal fire pit and BBQs off the ground are allowed.

OFF SITE This area's pretty remote, making for some great walks and cycle trails. You can hire bikes from the site or Nigel and Sheila can point you in the right direction if you fancy a walk. Nearby is the area known as Pays de Trois Lacs, a collection of three lakes, and further afield is Lac de Vassivière, a huge man-made lake that's one of France's top water-sports centres. Check out www.lelacdevassiviere.com.

FOOD AND DRINK In this remote spot it's best to come prepared to cook for yourselves or to partake of Sheila's table d'hôte (which is €15 for adults and €10 for kids, with under 3s eating for free). Meals are usually on Fridays and Sundays, though you can make a special request. There are plenty of herbal pickings at the site and drinks available from the house and a local market every Friday in Châtelus-Malvaleix, along with a *boulangerie* and *pâtisserie*. Further afield there are plenty of restaurants in the medieval part of Montluçon, particularly on the rue Grande, which goes up to the castle. Try L'Eau de la Bouche (00 33 4 70 03 82 92), whose owner also runs a saucy cabaret review bar called Le Royal Avenue (www.leroyalavenue.com) if you fancy it. It's cheaper than the Moulin Rouge.

GETTING THERE The site is discreet so pay attention. Heading east from Guéret on N145, turn on to D11 at the sign for Ajain, and follow it to Ladapeyre. If you're coming west from Montluçon via Gouzon then turn on to D990 to Ladapeyre. From Ladapeyre take D990 towards Châtelus-Malvaleix and you'll pass through Folbeix, which is little more than a few houses on either side of the road. One of the first is an ivy-covered house on the right. Pull in there and shout 'Bonjour'. If you're coming from the north on D940, take D990 just past Genouillac, through Châtelus-Malvaleix and the ivy house is on your left in Folbeix. You should still shout 'Bonjour', though.

PUBLIC TRANSPORT The nearest railway station is at Guéret (with services from Paris) and you can arrange for the Hardings to pick you up.

OPEN May–end August.

THE DAMAGE Three-night breaks are around €150/€170/€200 in low, mid, and high season and full weeks are €300/€350/€400. Prices are based on 2 adults and 2 kids and additional kids are €15 for a 3-night break and €35 for a full week. Breakfast in the barn is included.

Don't you just hate it when you turn up at a campsite and the owner whips out a red marker pen and a site map of numbered pitches and plonks a big fat cross on No.127? It's usually way down the far end, between the fence and the bins and with a long, desperate walk if nature calls. It's really not what you want.

How much nicer when, instead of that kind of welcome, a campsite owner stands in front of a green field, opens his arms out wide and says 'Anywhere you like. Just don't scare the donkeys.'

Thankfully that's more the kind of welcome you'll find at Mathonière, a complex of buildings and a campsite set amid the forests and lakes in the heartland of the old Dukes of Bourbon. Behind the fine old rustic farmhouse there's an expanse of green field, broken up here and there with the odd hedge and tree, but essentially an open area, where you can pick a pitch to suit your mood. There's a large tree in the middle, which usually has some kind of makeshift wooden fort the kids have cobbled together, and there's a pool, too; one of those freestanding things that looks like the kind of giant cooking pot cannibals use.

Elsewhere, closer to the farmhouse, there's a great little café-cum-bar with a sheltered seating area. Here you can enjoy a *café au lait* or something stronger, if you prefer, and there's a *menu* with a

mathonière

Mathonière, 03350 Louroux-Bourbonnais   00 33 4 70 07 23 06   www.mathoniere.nl

range of meals. The best bit, though, is a covered cooking area with a huge paella pan where the owners throw together communal meals for everyone to enjoy.

It's a tried-and-trusted French formula, this. A few old farm buildings converted into a lovely owners' home, some *gîte* accommodation, an open field for the camping, and the cooking of communal meals, if you want. No worries if you'd rather do your own thing, but it's good to meet the neighbours. There's also another common feature of these kinds of places; a large pre-erected tent that sleeps six and comes complete with gas and electricity.

This may make Mathonière sound a little formulaic, but honestly, it's not. It's a simple, wholesome, unpretentious site that's a great place to bring the kids to, but with enough space to stretch out if you don't want to be pestered.

Round and about, this region is dotted with forests and copses and has loads of interesting old towns and villages to explore. While it is possible to get to places on foot, by bike, or by donkey, the farther-flung destinations are really only accessible by car. If the cooking-pot pool doesn't tickle your fancy, there's a sandy beach in the vicinity and loads of forest trails that are great either on foot or by bike. Just don't get lost. Perhaps it's best to lay

a trail of breadcrumbs behind you and hope that you manage to find your way back before the birds eat them. Because you'll want to find your way back to Mathonière, and probably more than once. It may be based on a simple formula, but then all the best formulae are simple. Like $E=mc^2$; and it doesn't come much simpler than that. At least in theory it doesn't. But then, when you think about it, in practice, making things look as effortless and simple as this is often the hardest trick in the book. And you really don't need to be Einstein to figure that out.

COOL FACTOR Middle-of-nowhere peace and quiet and a great safe haven for the kids.

WHO'S IN? Tents, campervans, caravans, dogs – yes.

ON SITE There are all sorts of goodies. In addition to the usual facilities of hot showers, WCs, and washing facilities, there's a great little café-cum-bar with a sheltered outdoor seating area, where the communal meals are served and where you can sit and play some of the games available, from chess to dicey board games. Next to it is the area with the huge paella cooking pan. Then there are the animals, the pool, and the home-made fort to keep the kids happy. And if none of that works then the site is big and secluded enough just to let the kids run amok on their own.

OFF SITE Where to start? There are some great little towns and villages in the vicinity, such as Hérisson and La Salle. In the former, for example, there's a wonderful ruined 14th-century castle with a crumbling keep. For something a little more adventurous head to the Plan d'Eau de Vieure (00 33 4 70 02 04 46). It's a T-shaped lake just off D11, north of Les Magnoux, that boasts a small section of sandy beach, but also offers kayaks, canoes, and pedalos for hire. In the opposite direction is the 27,182-acre (11,000-hectare) Forêt de Tronçais. It's so old that Julius Caesar is said to have passed through it. Today it contains oaks that are hundreds of years old. Just don't get lost. Or take some breadcrumbs.

FOOD AND DRINK If you don't fancy partaking of a pan of paella at the pleasant café-cum-bar on site, head into Cosne-d'Allier, where you'll find a large Carrefour supermarket with everything you need to cater for yourselves, including garden furniture if you've forgotten to bring your own. Just remember, when you go, that French supermarkets don't offer plastic carrier bags, so make sure you take something to put your baguettes and bottles of wine in. Unfortunately the town's not that hot on restaurants or bars. For those you'd be better off going the extra miles to Montluçon, where there's a much better choice on rue Grande in the medieval part of town.

GETTING THERE The site is off D16 north of Cosne-d'Allier. Come off D16 for eastbound D251 and go through Louroux-Bourbonnais, keeping left and heading along D57 for Theneuille. About 1 mile (2 km) beyond the village, turn left at the crossroads. There's a small sign for the site, but if you're coming south you can't see it. Follow the road up the hill and the site is on your right. Parking is past the house. If you go to the Mathonière website there's also a handy link to Google Maps with a pin right on the site.

OPEN May–October.

THE DAMAGE It's €6/€7 per person per night in low and high season and €4/€5 for kids up to 12 years. Dogs, too, have their seasons and are charged €1/€2. The pre-erected tent is €250/€270 and includes water, electricity, and gas. There's also a €30 cleaning charge at the end of your stay, which seems a bit steep for changing the linen and running around with the hoover. High season is from 1 July to 31 August, as you'd expect.

domaine les gandins

Domaine Les Gandins, 1 allée des Gandins, 03140 St-Germain-de-Salles   00 33 4 70 56 80 75   www.domainelesgandins.com

Un gandin, you may or may not have known, is a dandy, an aristo, the kind of guy who lost his head to the guillotine when the French Revolution rolled into town. There were loads of them who lived lives of quiet luxury on little estates, just like this one, until the Revolution came along and recommended that that kind of thing ought to come to a stop.

The estates, of course, remained, even though their owners went the way of Louis XVI and Marie Antoinette. Of course, once the dust had settled and the cobbles hosed down, most of them eventually found their way back into the hands of a new aristocracy, as is the way with so many revolutions, but thankfully many of them are now little hotels, B&Bs, *gîtes*, and campsites, open to the *sans coulottes* – like us lot. And of all the similar domaine-style campsites in France, this one, at Domaine les Gandins, is surely the dandiest of the lot. A magnificent house, dating back to long before the Revolution, sits at the centre of a glorious little estate comprising various *gîtes* (including one in a converted pigeon loft), a stretch of sleepy river, a fantastic tree house and – this is where you come in – a spacious and leafy camping field.

The main house, with its red-tiled roof and deep-green shutters is postcard-perfect, and the grounds are all immaculately kept by the friendly Dutch family who own and run the site. With all its attendant facilities, Domaine les Gandins is really something of a one-stop shop of a campsite,

so much so that you might be forgiven for pitching your tent one day and staying for a whole week without ever venturing beyond the confines of the site.

For a start, the river of La Sioule is a minute's stroll through the meadow behind the complex of buildings and past the tree house. It's not the raciest of rivers, so it's perfect for a paddle or just for cooling off on a hot summer's day, and there are plenty of shady places in which to lounge around and listen to the birds or the gentle sound of the water. That's assuming you can block out the sound of the kids. Then there's the busy kitchen, which is at the heart of the site and always seems to have steam and smells emanating from inside. Whether you just want a morning cuppa to go with your croissant or fancy taking part in the communal table d'hôte meal in the evening, you'll find that the kitchen is the social hub around which everything else revolves.

Given its Dutch owners, the site is obviously especially popular with Dutch campers, but it gets its fair share of Brits, Belgians, and various breeds of our other continental cousins, too. Curiously, though, if you come here in the high season of July and August you won't find a single French person. They tend to feel a little out of place amid all those people speaking Nederlands and Eeengleesh and cooking sausages for breakfast.

If you do venture off the site while you're here you could do worse than head down to Vichy. This old sulphur spa town gained notoriety during the

Second World War, when it became the seat of Marshal Pétain's government. Thankfully now it's reverted to being a thermal spa town next to the wide Allier River, where folk come to take the waters in search of a cure for rheumatism or gout, or just for a stroll through the leafy riverside parks.

However there's no reason why you can't do much the same thing by the quiet waters of La Sioule at the campsite. It might not have the same kind of sulphurous healing powers, but the peace and tranquillity will surely have much the same restorative effect on the mind.

COOL FACTOR Really dandy camping in upper-class surroundings by a sleepy river.

WHO'S IN? Tents, campervans, caravans, groups, dogs (on leads) – yes.

ON SITE There's one large chalet-style accommodation block tucked off to the side of the site, with a row of WCs and hot showers, which is perfectly serviceable. There are also laundry facilities. There's a great tree house between the estate and the river, and down at the bank there's a communal fire pit and some wooden furniture for lazing about by the water. BBQs off the ground are permitted on the camping field.

OFF SITE The site is rather out in the boonies, and the nearest town of any note is Vichy, which is worth a visit if you're a fan of thermal waters. Unsurprisingly, perhaps, there are few reminders of the town's collaborationist past under Marshal Pétain. Otherwise, if you're looking for inspiration, you could do worse than check out Les Gandins' website, where you'll find suggestions of things to do in the local area listed under 24, yep 24, separate headings, ranging from parachuting and where to browse the best bric-a-brac shops, to thermal bathing in Vichy and bike hire. It's an impressive list – it even has a volcano in there – so if you can't find something useful to do with yourself after browsing that, then take a walk along the river and give yourself a stern talking to.

FOOD AND DRINK You can pick up bread from the van that visits the site and there are coffees and ice creams available from the kitchen during the day. You can get a 4-course table d'hôte meal in the evenings, which is €25 for adults, including wine and coffee. There's also a 2-course kids' dinner at €7.85, including lemonade. These meals are available every night during high season (July and August), but not on Mondays and Thursdays outside those months. If you want to self-cater, there's a small Proxi convenience store a couple of miles away in Étroussat, but it's only good for the basics. The town of Gannat has a better range of shops. For a real treat, though, head into Vichy to Maison Decoret (00 33 4 70 97 65 06; www.jacquesdecoret.com); a kind of French-fusion restaurant with set *menus* from €40, for whatever the chef chooses to give you, to €165 for a multi-course meal with selected wines for each course.

GETTING THERE Midway between Gannat and St-Pourçain-sur-Sioule on N7/D2009 turn left on to D36 heading for Étrousset. Just over the bridge, and before the large agricultural building that looks like a metal cathedral, turn left at the red and white houses. There's a signpost saying Les Perrets. Follow the road straight and over the old railway track and eventually the site entrance is on your left.

OPEN April–September.

THE DAMAGE A pitch for a tent, caravan, or campervan is €7.50/€3.75 in high and low season. Then it's €6.50/€3.75 per person per night and €3.95/€2.70 for kids between 2 and 10 years. High season is 3 July to 28 August. A dog is €1.50 whatever the season.

les voisins

Les Voisins, 03150 Montaigu-le-Blin   00 33 4 70 43 73 99   www.lesvoisins.info

There's a marvellously ramshackle feel to Les Voisins; what the French would call *délabré*. The site's only a short stroll from the bijou village of Montaigu-le-Blin, with its neat, shady green, posh artisto's house and lovely little church. But Les Voisins is a bit different from that. It's a collection of old farm buildings, some turned into modest *gîtes*, some into a facilities block, one into a bar/restaurant, and another left derelict for the goats to live in. Scattered about are reminders of the site's agricultural past, mainly old tractors and ploughs.

It may all be a bit down-at-heel, but the place carries it off with *élan*. Round the back there are a few pitches by the pool and the bar/restaurant. But beyond the buildings there's a spacious field with several pre-erected *tentes de savanes* (square, white tents that would look more at home at a medieval tournament than on safari) and plenty of pitches away from the jousting and carousing, with views across the smooth fields to Château de Montaigu. This must surely be the perfect place to sit out and enjoy a glass of wine as the sun sinks slowly through the trees.

COOL FACTOR Wide open space with views.

WHO'S IN? Tents, campervans, caravans, dogs – yes.

ON SITE Four hot showers and WCs in 2 separate areas (both unisex). Covered area for washing dishes.

OFF SITE It's well worth a wander around the village of Montaigu-le-Blin, but check out Vichy, the old sulphurous spa town, home of Marshal Pétain's collaborationist government.

FOOD AND DRINK Bar/restaurant on site selling beers, wines, and evening meals (around €18 per person) plus bread in the mornings. In the village there's Auberge des Tureaux (00 33 4 70 43 74 66).

GETTING THERE Come off N7 just south of Varennes-sur-Alliers and head for Boucé. Turn right at the main junction in town to Montaigu-le-Blin. In the village turn left for D32 (signposted Servilly and Lapalisse) and follow the road up the hill. Site entrance is on your left.

PUBLIC TRANSPORT The closest you can get to the site is the railway station at Varennes-sur-Alliers.

OPEN May–October.

THE DAMAGE In high season €9.50 for a pitch and €4.75 per person, €3.75 for a child under 8 years. Electricity €3. In low season €15 per night for 2 plus tent. *Tentes de savanes* €265–€425 per week, plus a cleaning fee of €20.

la ferme des maziers

La Ferme des Maziers, 490 route des Maziers, 71480 Varennes-St-Sauveur   00 33 3 85 74 67 14   www.lafermedesmaziers.com

Now this is what you call *camping à la ferme*. Sixteen pitches amid trees and wild flowers on a small plot of land next to an old single-storey farmhouse owned by…wait for it…French people. It's not possible. *Mais oui*, real French folk, whose forebears have seen every revolution and republic French history has to offer (if you're counting, it's at least two revolutions and five republics).

Best to bring your phrase book when you come here because there's only a smattering of English spoken. In fact, given the ubiquity of English-speaking campsite owners in these parts, you should really welcome the opportunity to *parler un peu* of the local lingo. You'll certainly want to brush up on vocab for eggs, bread, milk, and honey because they're all for sale from the farmhouse. Whether you then go on to slam EU farm subsidies and suchlike depends on how good your French is. Other than a bit of bartering for your morning bread there's not much to do around here but sit back and listen to the birds because this place is pretty much out in the sticks. Or *dans la brousse*, perhaps you should say.

COOL FACTOR Real farm camping with real French hosts.

WHO'S IN? Tents, campervans, caravans – yes. Dogs – no.

ON SITE Facilities are pretty limited. A couple of showers with hot water and 2 WCs. That's it.

OFF SITE Mâcon's worth a visit to do the wine thing. There's the Maison Mâconnaise des Vins (www.maison-des-vins.com) in town on ave du Maréchal de Lattre de Tassigny, or follow a 'wine road' (www.bourgogne-tourisme.com).

FOOD AND DRINK Basic supplies from the farmhouse. In Varennes there's a butcher, a baker, no candlestick-maker, but a Proxi store and, for a treat, try Le Saint Sauveur (00 33 3 85 74 65 59; www.le-saint-sauveur.fr), a little restaurant specialising in local grub. Set *menus* €25–€40.

GETTING THERE Leave A39 at exit 10 and head for Cormoz on D56. Go through the town on D996 heading for Varennes-St-Sauveur. About 1 mile (2 km) beyond Varennes turn left at sign to Bellanoiset. At the T-junction turn left again, then first right and turn right again at the old barn. Right fork after a couple of hundred yards/metres (there's a Camping à la Ferme sign) and the site's on your right.

OPEN 15 April–15 October.

THE DAMAGE €2.50 per person per night and €2 for a tent, caravan, or campervan and/or €1.50 for a car.

auvergne naturelle

Camping Auvergne Naturelle, Le Cros, 43440 Laval-sur-Doulon   00 33 4 71 76 38 53   www.yurtholidaysfrance.co.uk

Deep in the heart of the protected Parc Naturel Régional Livradois Forez, hidden from view up the pine-clad slopes of Laval-sur-Doulon, Camping Auvergne Naturelle is earthy and magical. The sound of the babbling brook at the bottom of the wild-flower meadow here conspires with birdsong and wind chimes to create a symphony of peace.

Imagine leaving the majesty of your Genghis Khan yurt in the brilliant-blue dawn to gaze down the valley, birds of prey circling overhead. This campsite is truly off the beaten track, in the same region as the famed 18th-century Beast of Gévaudan; a wolf-like creature of the forests that claimed over 100 lives.

With its alpine feel, the area reminds one more of Switzerland than France. A campfire burns throughout the night, inviting story-telling and bread-making for nocturnal kids, plus the chance for you to get to know your fellow guests. That's easily done, for though the site has its own natural forest and is anything but small, the facilities themselves are within close proximity of one another. They include a funky wood shower block, which has been designed to maximise the mountain view; between soaping yourself down you can look out of the open-slat shower on to the woods beyond, as if you're in a Timotei ad.

The kids love it here, perhaps because the owners have their own child and set about enriching the site with as many child-friendly enchantments as they could think of. For a start

there are child-only trails; one such route leads into a little glade strung with bells, hammocks, and fairies. (Your kids can even email the fairies on return to the UK.) Children particularly love whittling their own walking sticks in the morning bushcraft sessions and they can also learn how to build a fire. For the adults, there are a few colourful pastimes to throw yourself into on site, from yoga to axe-throwing. The days stretch out lazily here. After your morning croissant and *café au lait*, you'll feel those wildman genes firing up so that apart from exploring the forest and surrounding meadows for the Beast of Gévaudan you might want to have a crack at exploring your inner bushman, along with the kids. There are courses for both age groups.

The yurts themselves, of which there are four, have been subtly positioned to create maximum privacy and give you the finest views. Inside they look like a summer shoot from an edition of *Homes & Gardens*, with cream throws, wood floors, fresh wild flowers, and rustic furniture.

And did we mention the owners? Rob and Katherine, a young couple from Manchester, make for perfect hosts: he's a joiner by trade who also studied bushcraft under Ray Mears, while Katherine turns her eye for detail to the interiors of the yurts, and is also a great cook.

The communal barn, charmingly tumbledown, is magical, with fairy lights, candles, and a huge beamed ceiling and long dining table, giving it the impression of a Viking longhouse. The space

also doubles as a playroom for kids on stormy days – there are creative materials and stacks of board games to have a go at. The self-catering kitchen and fridge are also here. A favourite aspect of this place, apart from the wonderful continental breakfasts, comfy yurts, killer views, and soporific pace of life, is the owners themselves and all the thought they put into ensuring that their guests never forget their stay here. Camping Auvergne Naturelle is intimate, amazing value for money, and destined to become one of the best sites in France for making your great escape to.

COOL FACTOR Natural heaven. This is one of the most relaxing and beautifully isolated campsites in central France.

WHO'S IN? This is a yurt-only site, so you can't turn up with your tent. And because of the steep gradient on which the site is situated, campervans cannot be admitted. Dogs are welcome so long as they're on a lead.

ON SITE The site has 4 deliciously decorated yurts. Each one with solar-powered lighting and a luxury en suite toilet, plus a washbasin outside. The yurts are also family-friendly, with 2 extra camp beds per yurt for the kids. Campfires are tended by Rob, who, according to his dad has been building fires ever since he was a little 'un. The shower block is simple, sparkling clean, perfectly located just a short walk from your yurt, and close to the communal barn. Each yurt is allotted its own personal shower. The water is lovely and warm (it needs to be as it can be chilly in the mornings). For babies there's ample room for nappy-changing in the yurts. The toilets and facilities don't lend themselves to wheelchairs, nor do the grassy slopes of the grounds. Other facilities include: self-catering kitchen, fridge, fairy trail, swings, wild meadow, and 20 acres (8 hectares) of woodland to lose yourself in. Morning bushcraft courses are available (adults €20 and kids under 12 years €10).

OFF SITE Donkey walks and horse-riding can be organised. There are markets in Brioude every Saturday morning (8am–1pm). The magnificent countryside is begging for you to hire a mountain bike from Oléon Motoculture, Brioude (00 33 4 71 50 10 07) and ride around like the Von Trapps.

Half an hour up the mountain, La Chaise Dieu is famed for its beautiful abbey (1043 BC) and bijou antique shops, cafés, and restaurants. A world-famous classical music festival takes place here in August. An hour-and-a-half away are 80-odd dormant volcanoes, the most dramatic of which is Puy de Dôme, a mecca for hiking and paragliding.

FOOD AND DRINK Katherine makes homely grub every evening including dishes like *boeuf bourgignon*, chicken chasseur, and sausage and mash local-style. Dinner costs €18 and includes delicious homemade desserts like *tarte aux pommes* (apple tart). For supplies there's a supermarket in nearby Brioude (half-an-hour away). If you fancy exploring the local area for foodie delights why not try Le Vieil Auzon at Brioude (00 33 4 71 50 10 07), a favourite for its authentic Auvergne cuisine.

GETTING THERE The closest major towns are Clermont-Ferrand and Le Puy-en-Velay, about 1 hour away. Get off A75 at exit 22 and head for Brioude, from where D588 wiggles to Laval-sur-Doulon – follow signs for La Chaise Dieu. From here take N122 to Brioude, from where you'll head up into hills following signs for La Chaise Dieu and Laval-sur-Doulon on D588. Finding the place can be tricky, so a satnav is useful. Check the website for coordinates.

OPEN April–September, though Rob and Katherine are looking to keep the site open year-round, so check their website for updates.

THE DAMAGE Yurt (maximum 4 people) €130 per night, €315 for 3 nights, €700 per week.

This is Beaujolais country around here, home of the first wines of the season. It's a bit like those MPs' constituencies that rush through the vote count on election night in the UK in order to be the first to declare a result; the wine in these parts is famous for being the first to be cracked open after the harvest.

The grapes are picked and the wine is made, but it's fermented for only a few weeks before the Beaujolais Nouveau officially goes on sale on the third Thursday in the month of November. And there's just as much of a race to get the first few cases of wine out and into the tasting salons as there is to declare Sir

Winthrop Cattlebray or Arwyn Jones the duly elected MP for Camperstown Central. It's strange, then, with all this emphasis on speed, that the Beaujolais vineyards are one of the few in France (Champagne and Châteauneuf-du-Pape are other examples) where grapes have to be harvested by hand. Bet you didn't know that. Quite why is anyone's guess, but it's nice to know that it's not all squish-squash and away you go.

Thankfully there's been no rush to put together the collection of gypsy caravans, here, at Les Roulottes de la Serve. The first one came courtesy of the owner of a local merry-go-round and looked so good that Pat and Pascaline Pain,

les roulottes de la serve

Les Roulottes de la Serve, La Serve, 69860 Ouroux   00 33 4 74 04 76 40   www.lesroulottes.com

owners of what was then a derelict 19th-century farmhouse, decided they'd like some more. So as they renovated their home they added a couple more authentic roulottes and decorated the whole place with trinkets they had garnered from their travels in India and Africa. And the result of this process, which has come together over the years, is really worth coming to see.

The site is up in the wooded hills, above all the south-east-facing slopes, where Beaujolais grapes are grown. Found down the end of a long shadowy track, it is well away from what is anyway a pretty quiet road, so there's little to breach the peace. There are the roulottes and a marvellously restored complex of farm buildings, which looks a bit like a Spanish finca, with a small, quiet pond, ideal for sitting about and pond-ering.

You have three roulottes to choose from; not quite one for every mood, particularly if you've got a teenager in tow, but with enough variety to make deciding which one you fancy a bit of a tester. La Roulotte des Amoureux is, as the name suggests, one for lovers, and is decked out in nostalgic 1950s style with beautifully carved wood and mirrors. La Roulotte des Ménages, the riding masters, began life plying the trade fairs of northern France and is more reminiscent of the 1920s, while the largest of the three is La Roulotte

des Étoiles, which comes with sequinned cushions and a variety of decorations collected from those travels through the Orient.

All the roulottes are tastefully kitted out and have the added bonus of en suite facilities. You can even have your breakfast delivered to your front door if you feel like really kicking back and enjoying the peace and quiet. If you want to crack open a bottle of the local *vin*, though, it's probably best to wait until later in the day. After all, it might have been made in a hurry, but that's no reason for you to rush.

COOL FACTOR Characterful caravans in an idyllic and flowery setting.

WHO'S IN? Wannabe gypsies, dogs (€5 per night) – yes. However, you should note that a night's rental of the caravans is from 4pm–11am the following day, which it has to be said, seems a little on the stingy side. By the time you've settled in and cracked open a bottle of wine, the afternoon's nearly over.

ON SITE The facilities are en suite for each roulotte, so there's no traipsing through the morning dew in your flip-flops to have a shower. Inside, the bedding is provided, but you need to bring your own towels. There's a breakfast room in one of the restored buildings and a reasonably stocked kitchen, but you can build a fire if you fancy cooking *en plein air*, so that you can enjoy the beauty of the gardens and the views over the red-tiled roof of the farmhouse into the valley beyond.

OFF SITE You really have to travel back down the slopes and stop off at one or two of the vineyards that offer tastings. Try the organic option at the 7th-generation Domaine du Crêt de Ruyère (00 33 4 74 69 92 39; www.cretderuyere.com). The site is also handily placed not far from the Burgundy sections of the *voies vertes*, France's network of cycling and roller-blading routes. Check out the details at www.voiesvertes.com. For something a little loftier, you can take a hot-air balloon ride and view the vineyards at a snail's pace from on high with Montgolfière Air Escargot (00 33 3 85 87 12 30; www.air-escargot.com).

FOOD AND DRINK Breakfast is included in the price of the roulotte and is served up each morning in the farmhouse. With 48 hours' notice you can order yourself a cold picnic to take with you for the day's activities. It costs €30 for 2 people. Otherwise you'll find local markets in Cluny (Saturdays), Villefranche-sur-Saône (Mondays), and Belleville (Tuesdays). If you feel the need to dine out, try the Auberge du Fût d'Avenas (00 33 4 74 69 90 76). It's housed in an old farmhouse and serves up set *menus* (€10–€20) made from local ingredients. Note that it's closed on Tuesdays during the summer.

GETTING THERE From A6, exit 30 to Belleville then D18 to Avenas. In Avenas, where D18 turns sharp left to Ouroux, continue straight along D18e towards the Col de la Serve. Eventually in La Serve, turn right at T-junction and site entrance is just down the hill on your right. There is a small signpost to guide you.

PUBLIC TRANSPORT Although there are regular trains to Belleville, you would need to take a taxi from there, which would be roughly €40 for the return journey.

OPEN April–October.

THE DAMAGE The 3 roulottes are available at €60 per night for 2 people, including breakfast, plus €0.40 per person per night for local tax. Heating is an extra €3–€5 per night. In the 2 larger roulottes there's a supplement of €8 for a child in their own sleeping bag or €11 with bedding provided.

The owners of Terre Ferme, Matthijs and Renske Witmans (yep, they're Dutch), bought this place years ago while they were still living in the Netherlands and over years of long-distance commuting have slowly and painstakingly turned what was an old maize farm into a new and stunning campsite.

They restored the magnificent long farmhouse and designed and built a facilities block in the local rustic style. Eventually, a few years back, the place was finally ready to make the big move south and it was so-long Holland and *bonjour La France*. Now that all the works are complete Matthijs and Renske can sit back and admire what they've achieved, which is a really charming little *aire naturelle* campsite.

Terre Ferme's situated in Le Petit Condal, a tiny *hameau* in rural Burgundy that is as small as the name implies. Condal's pretty small, but this place is so tiny that it hardly features on the map at all. Mind you, the property here is 17 acres (seven hectares), of which one has been cleared to make the camping field, some have been penned off to keep donkeys, sheep, and chickens, and the others have been left as natural woodland and a spring-fed pond. The two-and-a-half-acre (one-hectare) camping field has only 14 pitches and cars are kept off the grass, so you can imagine how much space

terre ferme

Terre Ferme, Le Petit Condal, 71480 Condal   00 33 3 85 76 62 57   www.terreferme.eu

there is to stretch out. The one slight downside of the site, a consequence of its recent conversion from a field growing maize, is that there's little or no shade to be found. Some trees have been planted, but it's going to take a few years for them to offer any relief from the summer sun. So, in the meantime, if you ask nicely, you can get a tarp set up to offer you some temporary cover if the sun (or the rain) is particularly fierce.

And if you don't fancy sticking up canvas yourself you can always hire a pre-erected safari-style tent in the field. This sleeps four and has its own cooking facilities and fridge. Or there's a compact wooden chalet, which sleeps four in a double and two bunks, which is set off to the side behind the facilities block.

Most of this area's given over to maize farming and its quiet back roads are a maze, too, and perfect for idling around on a bike. These are available to hire from the farmhouse, including a tandem, if you're that way inclined. But this is also the *terroir* which breeds the famous *poulet de Bresse*, the most famous chicken in the world. These beauties are reared outdoors on small, dedicated farms and are protected by the same kind of *Appellation d'Origine Controllée* that governs the production of wines. They don't come cheap, but let's face it, half the reason you come to France is for the food and

drink (the other half's probably a combination of the weather and the scenery), so it's worth giving one of these especially edible chooks a spin around the rotisserie. They are to your standard cellophane-wrapped supermarket chicken on its little plastic tray what a filet mignon is to a burger.

And much the same can be said for the delicious little site at Terre Ferme. This place is to your standard French campsite what a boutique hotel is to a Blackpool B&B. It's a class apart and you can't go far wrong with that.

COOL FACTOR Blissfully quiet rural hideaway – all just a couple of miles from the autoroute.

WHO'S IN? Tents, campervans, caravans, dogs (for a fee) – yes.

ON SITE There's one new central facilities block, built in the local rustic style, with free good hot showers and WCs (both unisex) and there's a urinal tucked discreetly round the back for the chaps. There are outdoor, but covered, washing-up sinks and a washing machine (€3.50), while round the front is a covered terrace with tables and chairs, which is great for mealtimes or just for general loafing around. All pitches have 6-amp electric hook-ups if you can't live without your hairdryer or electric toaster. A minute's stroll down the hill from the main camping field is a quiet pond fed by a spring and surrounded by trees, and there are various domesticated animals if you or the kids fancy a bit of heavy petting.

OFF SITE This is a fairly remote farming area and there isn't a decent-sized town for miles around. Neither is there a huge number of activities available. You can hire bicycles from the site at €18 per day. If you can make it that far (it's about 6 miles/10 km away) it's worth visiting St-Amour, a little town of narrow, colourful streets, ivy-clad houses, and an impressive old church. But then if you have a car exit 10 off the A39 could be the gateway to a whole other world.

FOOD AND DRINK There are various facilities (fridge, coffee-maker, for example) on the terrace, and all kinds of goodies for sale from the farmhouse in the egg and cheese line, along with wine and beer, and you can order up fresh bread and croissants for the morning if you ask before 6.30pm the night before. You can also order a continental breakfast for €6. The owners cook up a communal BBQ on Saturdays at €10 per person or there's a table d'hôte option at €15. In Varennes there's a *boulangerie* and butcher and a small Proxi supermarket plus a decent little restaurant, Le St-Saveur (00 33 3 85 74 65 59) specialising in local grub and with a range of set menus from €25 to €40. For better choice, though, head to St-Amour, which has a Casino supermarket and several small *tabacs*.

GETTING THERE The site is situated off the stretch of A39 autoroute that runs between Lons-le-Saunier and Bourge-en-Bresse. Come off at exit 10, and just after the *péage* booths, take the first right at the roundabout. Follow the road towards Petit Condal. Just before the village turn left and the campsite entrance is a few hundred metres on your left.

PUBLIC TRANSPORT The closest public transport hub is the railway station at St-Amour. You can arrange for the campsite owners to pick you up from here.

OPEN May–October.

THE DAMAGE A pitch is €5 and it's €4 per person over 6 years. A dog is €1. The safari tent is €190 per week and the wooden chalet is €100 for 2 nights or €300–€350 per week, depending on the season.

alps

le pelly

Camping Municipal Le Pelly, 74740 Sixt-Fer-à-Cheval,   00 33 4 50 34 12 17   www.sixtferacheval.com

Contrary to what you might think, Le Cirque du Fer à Cheval isn't a fancy post-modern circus troupe. You know, those guys who juggle chainsaws and tumble from the top of the Big Top on long silk sheets? Instead Le Cirque du Fer à Cheval is one of France's *Grands Sites Nationaux*; a kind of national park.

Un fer à cheval, in case you were wondering, is a horseshoe, and you'll see where the name comes from as you head further and further up the dead-end road from Sixt, which terminates at the campsite Le Pelly. Surrounding the site is a vast semicircle of soaring limestone rock with waterfalls cascading down its face, all topped off with La Corne du Chamois, the Goat's Horn, a point of rock that tops out at 2,500 metres, and Le Tenneverge, which towers to just shy of 3,000 metres. It's a pretty grand amphitheatre, with the site as the stage, so you'd better be prepared to put on a good show. There are over a hundred pitches at the site, with plenty of trees to shade you in midsummer. Not that you'll be lounging around. This is prime walking and climbing territory, with walks and waterfalls a-plenty, including the one known as the Queen of the Alps (*La Reine des Alpes*), all set in 9,000 hectares of glorious *réserve naturelle*. The most accessible walk of the cirque itself starts from just opposite the site and heads up the valley on the other side of the river. Due to the height of the rocks, it's a three-and-a-half-hour trip up the valley and back down again, rather than a circuit, but it's still well worth a crack.

COOL FACTOR End-of-the road camping surrounded by a soaring horseshoe of rock.

WHO'S IN? Tents, campervans, caravans, dogs on leads (allowed on the site, but not in the national park) – yes.

ON SITE Central chalet-style facilities block with hot showers and WCs and a separate refuge (*gîte d'étape*) for walkers that includes bunked sleeping areas.

OFF SITE Check Guides de Sixt-Fer-à-Cheval for advice on guided walks and climbs (00 33 6 30 07 66 63; www.guidesixt.com).

FOOD AND DRINK Small café at the entrance. It's nothing fancy, but it has a terrace and seating inside. In Sixt-Fer-à-Cheval, 3½ miles (6 km) down the track, you'll find a *boulangerie/pâtisserie*, pizzeria, and a couple of small bars.

GETTING THERE Come off A40 from Geneva to Chamonix at Cluses (exit 18) and follow signs for D902 to Châtillon-sur-Cluses then D907 to Samoëns and Sixt-Fer-à-Cheval. Just past the village there's a hut, where there's a €2.50 per person charge to enter the Cirque du Fer à Cheval. If you're going to the campsite you don't have to pay. The site is 3½ miles (6 km) beyond the village.

PUBLIC TRANSPORT Trains to Cluses and a bus from the station to Sixt-Fer-à-Cheval. It's usually only once a day and costs €8 one way/€16 return. Details from www.altibus.com.

OPEN 1 June–mid September.

THE DAMAGE 2 adults €5.10 plus €0.30 *taxe de séjour* per person. Tent/caravan €3.00, campervan €5.90, car €1.20. Additional adults €2.50, kids 2–12 years €1.50, under-2s free, dog €1.70. *Gîte d'étape* €9.00 per person per night.

le grand champ

Camping Le Grand Champ, 167 chemin du Glacier de Taconnaz, 74400 Les Bossons, Chamonix   00 33 4 50 53 04 83
campinggrandchamp@hotmail.com

Horace Benedict de Saussure may not have been the first man to conquer Mont Blanc, Europe's highest peak. That accolade fell to Jacques Balmat in 1786. But de Saussure surely did it in greater style. He assembled a prodigious team of guides and porters, took a bed and mattress with him, and made sure he had plenty of wine and fine cuisine. When rain made climbing impossible he passed the time learning passages of *The Iliad* by heart.

Of course, in those days the high snowy mountains were to budding Alpinists what the Moon was to the Apollo astronauts: a whole new world. No one had any idea what to expect up there, but popular legend had it that dragons roamed above the snowline, that there were caves full of fairy gold guarded by a black goat, and so on, so it was important to carry a blunderbuss along with your ropes and ice axe and keep an open mind. Safe to say, de Saussure encountered none of this and had to contend more with altitude sickness, which the wine wouldn't have helped, and some bad luck with the weather. On reaching the summit of the mighty mountain on the morning of 3 August 1787, he took out his telescope and picked out his wife waving to him from the town of Chamonix 12,000 feet below.

Sadly you can't see the summit from the campsite at Le Grand Champ. It looks out from the slopes of the Mont Blanc massif, across the other side of the Chamonix Valley, to the crags and peaks opposite. But you can sense its presence looming over you (and often feel the effects of the weather systems it generates) even as you settle down into one of the campsite's ample pitches. They're arranged discreetly between the hedges and trees that divide the site up into private parcels, so it can come as a surprise to discover that the place has 100 pitches. Where have they put them all? Here, there, and everywhere is the answer. However, all that greenery can mean that the majestic scenery around you is rather hidden from view, which is a shame. So when you arrive, it's worth asking the genial owner, Françoise Dudas, for a room with a view, and hope that you can soak in the expansive vistas as well as breathing in the crystal Alpine air. Even in summer the peaks are covered in snow and you can sit and marvel at the great glaciers that lie like cracked tongues of ice in the valleys. Catch them soon, though, because they're receding at an alarming rate.

The Chamonix Valley is a jam pot to the waspy swarms of tourists who've been clustering here ever since the late 18th century. The town of Chamonix, a favourite of the Romantics, who were in turns fascinated and horrified by the towering rocks, was a hangout of Turner and Ruskin and it also played host to the 1924 Winter Olympics. It's still a great ski resort today, though not for the faint-hearted, but is probably busier now in summer than it is in winter. It's estimated that 40,000 people a day pass through the valley in the height of summer. The majority of them are here for the walking, climbing, mountain-biking, paragliding, and rafting. Yes, OK, some

people come to play golf, but they're very much in the minority and tend to keep themselves to themselves. Nowadays you can hire a guide to get you to the top of Mont Blanc, if you're reasonably fit and up for the challenge, though be warned that the mountain can still bear its teeth and sadly climbers do perish on its slopes. Better, perhaps, to order a coffee and sit in the town square looking up… And then there are those who come to stand in the square looking up at Mont Blanc, waving in the hope that someone on the summit remembered to take their telescope.

COOL FACTOR Leafy camping in the shadow of Mont Blanc and the Aiguille du Midi.

WHO'S IN? Tents, campervans, caravans, dogs – yes.

ON SITE The facilities, while decent enough, are a little tired. It's not often you find squat toilets in France these days, but there are still some here (plus sit-down ones, too). There's hot water and hot showers, though, and a washing machine. A basic but amenable campers' room is pretty handy, too, and there are disabled facilities.

OFF SITE If you have a head for heights, like a real head for heights, you simply have to take the cable car up to the top of L'Aiguille du Midi. It rises in 2 stages from Chamonix town, which is at about 3,000 ft (900 m) to over 12,000 ft (3,600 m) in a matter of 10 minutes or so. It's expensive, though, at €25/€42.50 per person return summer/winter (though for some reason they also sell singles) and, once up there, it's an extra €3 to take the lift up to the very top. But the views across to the summit of Mont Blanc, just another 3,000 ft (900 m) above you, are second to none and, if you're lucky, you'll be able to pick out some climbers. For a more sedate ride, take the Mont Blanc Express up through Argentière and over the Col de Montet into Switzerland: it's a lovely Alpine ride. Details at www.tmrsa.ch.

FOOD AND DRINK There are basic provisions available at the site, including fresh bread and croissants in the mornings, but not much else in the immediate vicinity, so it's best either to stock up in Chamonix (where there's a decent-sized Super-U on rue Joseph Vallot) or just hang it all and eat out in Chamonix. The cheap option is Mojo's Sandwich Café on place Jacques Balmat, where you can sit out, or there's mid-priced Munchies, a Chamonix institution, down narrow rue de Moulins, which serves great modern international cuisine (00 33 4 50 53 45 41). Finally there's the restaurant at the Hameau Albert 1er (00 33 4 50 53 05 09; www. hameaualbert.fr). It has set *menus* from a mouth-watering €56 to an eye-popping €138. But then again, it does have 2 Michelin stars.

GETTING THERE For the past few years there have been extensive roadworks on N205 leading out of Chamonix, which means various exits are sometimes closed. However, the site is signposted just past Taconnaz on route Blanche, a few miles short of Chamonix. Once off the main road follow route de Vers le Nant to chemin du Glacier de Taconnez and turn left up the hill. The site entrance is on your left.

PUBLIC TRANSPORT There are good mainline rail links into the Chamonix Valley and a regular railway service on the Martigny–St Gervais Mont Blanc Express, which stops at Les Bossons and Taconnaz (a request stop). It's then a 10–15-minute walk to the site. There are also regular buses from Chamonix that stop at the shops about 875 yards (800 m) from the site.

OPEN 1 May–15 October.

THE DAMAGE A standard pitch is €5 and a large one is €7 (and large means large). Then it's €4.50 per person per night and €2.30 for kids up to 7 years.

ferme noemie

Ferme Noemie, Les Sables, 38520 Bourg d'Oisans   00 33 4 76 11 06 14   www.fermenoemie.com

Mention Bourg d'Oisans and most travellers will think of Alpe d'Huez, the world-famous ski resort that sits 21 hairpins atop of the bustling town. Advanced cyclists are likely to froth with excitement; they view these mountain bends the same way that Catholics view Lourdes, religiously, harbouring lifelong desires to visit their Mecca. Not for the actively-challenged, the climb is steep: it can take three hours to pedal to the top (or under an hour for the pros), but once there you can buy a certificate testifying that you've conquered what was the first alpine climb introduced to the Tour de France, in 1911.

Alpe d'Huez may boast the longest black run in the world, the 10-mile (16-km) 'La Sarenne', but as thrilling as the snow-covered mountain range is, summers here are truly special. Regardless of whether cycling is your bag or not, time spent sprawled out on the lawns of Bourg d'Oisans' outdoor swimming pool will do wonders for your limbs. It will bronze them at the very least. The scenery is delightful, engulfed by magnificent Rhône-Alpes, and the toddlers' pool and fun slide will entertain tiny tots for hours.

After a *tartiflette* lunch in town, march off the frighteningly calorific potato, cream, and cheese dish among the 425 miles (680 km) of walking trails at Ecrins National Park. It is the largest of France's six national parks, created purely to protect the environment. Mountains loom from all angles, cutting into the landscape like a helter skelter of peaks and valleys, visible, in all their glory, from the campsite at Les Sables, just up the road from Le Bourg d'Oisans.

Ferme Noemie has around 20 numbered pitches, in homage to the Alpe d'Huez hairpins. The owners Melanie and Jeremy are great skiers. They met working for a UK ski-holiday company in the late 1980s and basically never returned home. He's good with his hands; the chalet shower block and loft apartments are all his own work. And Melanie is a consummate hostess. Should the nights turn chilly at this high altitude, warm blankets are handed out. An office reception is crammed with information leaflets, a coffee-making machine, microwave, and fridge. If you've run out of beer, the couple will lend you theirs; they won't want anyone to go dry. In fact, they'll give away cider made from their own apples, gratis. Plastic tables and chairs are allocated to most pitches, so you can picnic under the gaze of the national park.

The adjoining cliff face is striking and majestic. Caravans have to park on the right of the driveway, so that they don't spoil the alpine serenity. 'Camping for softies' is the couple's latest project: bell tents with beds, duvets, wine glasses, plus a sheltered cooking stove. So successful are these tents that there are now four on site, cosy and contemporary-cool in green and cream.

Whenever you need a break from nature or sport (really?) the nearest places of interest are pretty niche; various museums celebrate minerals, fauna, hydro-electricity, and crystals. Or spend

a day perusing Domaine de Vizille's exhibitions dedicated to the French Revolution, set in a stunning deer park. Then, perhaps, you could try varying your itinerary. As well as walking, cycling and swimming, how about trying out rock-climbing, rafting, canoeing, horse-riding, fishing, golf, or parapenting. The latter basically involves running off the side of one of the gorgeous mountains with a large gliding canopy attached to you. This certainly isn't a campsite for the bone idle – you'll be fighting fit and ready to tackle those hairpins yourself by the end of your stay.

COOL FACTOR Everything about the site is cool: the location, the view, the British owners, the fresh air.

WHO'S IN? Tents, campervans, caravans, dogs, large groups, young groups – yes.

ON SITE Sixteen *emplacements*, plus 4 for caravans/mobile homes. Park next to a field of grazing, ageing horses, who are living out their twilight years in the most beautiful spot imaginable. The owners' wooden chalet house blends in with the various apartments for hire that the couple have built on to their property. The camping field is triangular in shape, with lush green grass, a few dainty blossoms, and the national park towering sky high in the background. Four 'camping for softies' bell tents can fit up to 4 beds (all singles), with solar lamp, kettle, wine glasses, and portable gas-hob stoves kept in an outside dining shelter. Two mobile homes (Apr–Oct) sleep 6, 4 chalet apartments including 1 loft conversion sleep 6, with cot and baby bath. One wash-block, gorgeous inside and out (looks like a mountain chalet), with hot showers, disabled WC. In reception coffee machine (honesty pot), fridge, freezer, microwave, and PC. Breakfast bread and croissants can be delivered right to your pitch in high season. Washing machine and drier €4. Play area. Badminton net. Free wi-fi. Communal BBQ next to the kids' play area. No campfires.

OFF SITE Cycle the Alpe d'Huez 9-mile (13-km) climb from Bourg d'Oisans to Alpe d'Huez, renting a bike from any of the town's cycle hire shops (they don't take advance bookings) from €25 for 1 day, €125 for 6. For information on the Domaine de Vizille 11-mile (18-km) drive call 00 33 4 76 68 07 35 or visit www.domaine-vizille.fr.

FOOD AND DRINK Make a detour to the right to stop off at the kind of bonkers art-deco restaurant that you'd expect to see on a film set. Hôtel de La Poste in Corps-la-Salette (00 33 4 76 30 00 03; www.hotel-restaurant-delas.com) serves a 5-course set lunch that you'll not forget in a hurry. Chintzy decorations fill every inch of space inside and huge serving plates of oysters, pastry canapés, sweet roulades, and shell fish are served on the balcony terrace or indoors.

GETTING THERE Plane or TGV train to Grenoble. The 'Romans' route is very easy, most of it is a long, straight, fast road that leads you on to the Grenoble bypass, the Rocade Sud, and up to the Oisans Valley. Follow A48, A41, or A51 into the region and you will finally find the town lying on D91/D1091. More windy, but with spectacular scenery, is the route de Napoléon that runs via Corps-la-Salette.

PUBLIC TRANSPORT From Grenoble and Lyon buses run to Bourg d'Oisans (€15). Pick-ups can be arranged if the owners are available, otherwise take a taxi the 2½ miles (4 km) to Les Sables.

OPEN April–October.

THE DAMAGE 2 adults and tent (or caravan or mobile home) €22–€44. Bell tents from €400–€450 per week, dogs free. Hook-ups €3.50. Mobile home weekend/week €90–€400. Children €2.50.

la source

Camping La Source, 05140 St-Pierre-d'Argençon   00 33 4 92 58 67 81   www.lasource-hautesalpes.com

There's something very wholesome about Camping La Source. Firstly, there's the air. Clean, pure breezes roll off the mountains and filter through the trees to fill every inch of expansive sky that dominates this charming campsite. Secondly, with only ten plots, it's never crowded, which explains the tranquillity. Birdsong and crickets provide a steady background chatter, adding to the all-natural ambience. A walk through the campsite's woods reveals a surprising variety of trees, including pine, cherry, lime, and walnut, but the stars of this woodland show are the giant sequoias. These towering trees are genuinely impressive; their thick trunks rising from the pine-needle-strewn ground so high that you have to crane your neck to follow them.

The purified atmosphere extends to the nightlife. You'll struggle to find many bars in the locality, but the sleepiness of the nearby villages perpetuates the calm back at La Source. There's no light pollution in the skies above, so the campsite is the perfect place to enjoy a little post-dinner stargazing with a glass or two of wine.

Whether you're just relaxing or using the campsite as a base for hiking from one picturesque village to the next, and fishing or swimming in the lakes, the wholesome hat trick that greets you every morning is the view. Whichever plot you pick, you'll be overlooked by mountains close enough to glide from – a fact that some hang-gliding regulars take advantage of by flying from the peak and landing right back at their tents.

COOL FACTOR Peaceful, spacious tranquillity with a spectacular backdrop. You half expect Julie Andrews to come running out of the woods in a habit.

WHO'S IN? Tents, campervans, caravans, young families, dogs (under control) – yes. Groups – by prior arrangement only. There is a no-noise policy from 11pm to 7.30am.

ON SITE There are 10 pitches, while a cute washblock has 2 hot showers with sinks, 4 WCs, 3 bathroom sinks, 3 washing-up sinks, all cleaned twice a day. Two washing machines from €3. Badminton court and *boules* pitches for sporty moments. A kids' play area and communal BBQs. No campfires or charcoal BBQs allowed. Five B&B rooms are for hire, also.

OFF SITE It's all about the Great Outdoors. Nearly 4,350 miles (7,000 km) of walking trails cover the Hautes-Alpes region, so pack your hiking boots.

FOOD AND DRINK At Aspres-sur-Buëch, Christian Breton sells everything from creamy local cheeses to spicy sausages. Large supermarkets are located in Veynes and Serres, both about 15 minutes' drive away. For eating out, try the Auberge de la Tour (highly recommended), Pont La Barque, Café de la Place or Les Tilleues, all of which offer local cuisine featuring regional specialities and are just a 10-minute drive away.

GETTING THERE Head south to A51, turn off to Sisteron/Aix-en-Provence/Nice, follow the signs right, to St-Pierre-d'Argençon, turn left and you'll see the sign.

PUBLIC TRANSPORT La Source is one of the best for carless campers. Fly to Grenoble. Trains to Aspres-sur-Buëch.

OPEN Mid April–mid October.

THE DAMAGE Tent, 2 adults €9.90. Extra adult €2.75, child under 7 years €1.50. Electricity €3 per night. Dogs €1 per night. *Chambre d'hôte*, including breakfast, €31–€54 for 1–3 people per night, depending on season.

riviera

orion tree houses

Orion B&B, Impasse des Peupliers, 2436 chemin du Malvan, F-06570 St-Paul de Vence   www.orionbb.com

There is no point beating around the bush – Orion's bedrooms are in the trees. However, this isn't a Heath Robinson job. The wooden huts (named after characters in *The Jungle Book*) are firmly built and are decked out with the finest of furnishings. The forest is tamed through porthole-shaped windows or shutters with oak leaves carved into them.

Instead of a rope ladder, a solid staircase leads you to your door. And rather than a nearby murky, steamy swamp, there's an eco swimming pool with gravel and plants working on the cleaning process instead of chlorine. Orion isn't battling against nature, but working with it.

Diane van der Berg, with the assistance of her two daughters, Aina and Maike, are here to help you harmonise. Diane is also a part-time life coach and conversation around the informal, Dutch-style breakfast table can often turn to a life-evaluation session. This is one of the main reasons why the family insists that you stay for a minimum of three days, so as not to upset the natural balance. Karma is a big thing here, too. Take the house's name, for example – it's called Orion because the previous owner planted trees in the shape of the star constellation.

But if you want to venture out of this idyllic world, St-Paul de Vence is a 20-minute walk away or there's snorkelling and diving off the Cap d'Antibes. But really, at Orion, with this life of a jungle VIP in the trees, why would you ever want to come down?

COOL FACTOR Tree-house living, being at one with nature with all creature comforts taken into consideration.

WHO'S IN? Small groups, families, or couples, ecologically aware people, with a taste for something better – yes.

ON SITE Four tree houses: Bagheera sleeps 2, Shere Khan sleeps 2–3, King Louie is for a family, while Colonel Hathi sleeps 2 adults and 3 children. All have en-suite facilities, wi-fi, and power. Eco pool, cool hammocks, and places to chill. No campfires.

OFF SITE Antibes is an excellent place to snorkel and there are plenty of diving schools, including Côté Plongée (00 33 6 72 74 34 94; www.cote.plongee.free.fr). Indulge your inner child, even if you don't have kids, and visit Confiserie Florian in Pont du Loup (00 33 4 93 59 32 91; www.confiserieflorian.com) because there's no such thing as being sweet enough.

FOOD AND DRINK There's plenty of restaurants in St-Paul including Le Tilleul (00 33 4 93 32 80 36; www.restaurant-letilleul.com), which specialises in French dishes made with seasonal produce. Le Relais des Coches (00 33 4 93 24 31 24; www.lerelaisdescoches.com) combines great local food with a log-fire-cosy ambience, plus it doubles up as a jazz and blues bar at weekends.

GETTING THERE Take exit 48 off A8 and take D336 towards St-Paul de Vence. At the third roundabout is chemin des Presses. Orion is signposted on the right as it turns into chemin du Malvan.

PUBLIC TRANSPORT Regular buses from Nice to St-Paul de Vence, then a 20-minute walk downhill to the site.

OPEN All year.

THE DAMAGE Prices vary from €650 for a 3-day stretch to €2,400 for a week.

It's not the sharp menthol smell of eucalyptus leaves that hits you when you turn off D93 on to chemin des Moulins, but the earthy acidity of rows of bountiful grapevines. Husband and wife Philippe and Florence Lamon have wine running through their veins after inheriting the farm from Florence's father in 1994. The Lamons also belong to a co-operative, Les Vignerons de Grimaud, which produces Les Grimaldines wines. The hard-working Lamon's enterprise doesn't stop with grapes. The industrious couple renovated part of the farmhouse at the turn of the millennium and converted it into holiday apartments. But the pièce de résistance of Les Eucalyptus is their site,

Camping à la Ferme, which is as close to St-Tropez's most famous beach as you want to be.

Just a short moped ride away from the farmhouse, the site is beyond the vines and near the working part of the farm, although the grapes are mushed offsite at the co-operative. The occasional sound of a putting tractor is drowned out by the comforting and inviting roar of waves beyond the bamboo plantation backing onto Moorea Plage, part of St-Tropez's legendary Pampelonne sands. The more discerning camper can sunbathe on the *plage privé*, with sunloungers reasonably priced for the area, however the public beach is equally delightful. Boutiques selling cool

les eucalyptus

Les Eucalyptus, chemin des Moulins, plages de Pampelonne, 83350 Ramatuelle   00 33 4 94 97 16 74   www.leseucalyptus.fr

clothes are fringed around the restaurants, which offer bar snacks with a French-Reggae vibe at the end of the beach. Or if you're into a little more comfort and delicacy, there's a finer-dining area that wouldn't look out of place in nearby St-Tropez. Even further, towards Pampelonne's world-famous Plage de Tahiti, is a larger campsite with its own supermarket. Perfect for stocking up before retreating to the privacy of Camping à la Ferme. But if you crave the glitzy limelight then you could walk to the ultra-exclusive Kon Tiki beach huts and Club 55, famous since Brigitte Bardot's first sashay and where megastars such as George Clooney have been spotted more recently.

Although you may occasionally spot a yacht on the horizon, the seclusion of Les Eucalyptus is miles from the mass camping holiday sites at Port Grimaud. The grounds host around 30 pitches and you're more likely to see a vintage Citroën van than a four-by-four parked up alongside the tent. The campsite is well spaced with a well-appointed, though basic, shower block. The Lamons promise to update the facilities soon and have added it to their never-ending to-do list.

Foodwise, a brick-built BBQ is available mid-season, when there is less wind and not so much risk of fire, but if you're looking for something smarter, inland there is Les Moulins de Ramatuelle,

a hotel-restaurant with style, just a seven-minute bicycle ride away. A visit to nearby Ramatuelle, a quaint medieval town in the mountains with a traditional museum and a nocturnal market every Wednesday, is heartily recommended. You can also stop by Les Vignerons de Grimaud to pick up wine made from your local vineyard. And, of course, you're only a short drive from St-Tropez and Port Grimaud, where if you want to live the life of the rich and famous you can always splash out on a yacht for as little as 2,000 euros a week.

COOL FACTOR The proximity to a beautiful beach, the privacy amid bamboo. The wry humour of Philippe Lamon.

WHO'S IN? Tents, campervans, caravans, dogs, small groups, young families – yes.

ON SITE Around 30 pitches with hook-ups, wash-rooms clean but basic, 4 sinks, 2 cold showers, 2 hot showers for €1, 2 women's toilets, 2 men's toilets, 2 outdoor urinals, washing machine (€5). Kids have the beach and bike rides. BBQ facilities in peak season. No campfires.

OFF SITE Pampelonne beach stretches over several miles, so it's well worth wandering along. The most famous area is Tahiti, where Brigitte Bardot used to hang around in the 1950s. There are also quite a lot of naturist beaches due to deregulation from St-Tropez. Exceptional views along the St-Tropez Peninsula. The town is only 3 miles (5 km) away, so if you want to rub shoulders with the rich and famous by night then a visit to Le Caves du Roy (00 33 4 94 56 68 00; www.byblos.com) in Hôtel Byblos is essential, but be sure to get out of those campsite clothes first. If the budget can stretch even further, then Madraco Yachting (00 33 4 94 56 48 00; www.madraco.fr) offers the perfect St-Trop posing-machine. Prices vary according to sail, speed, or motor power, season and, of course, length. Port Grimaud offers cheaper thrills, particularly Azur Park Gassin, with its mini-golf and fairground attractions. For the more adventurous, Pep's Spirit (00 33 4 94 96 88 04; www.peps-spirit.fr) in nearby Grimaud offers guided tours by mountain bike and facilities for outdoor sports, including anything from kayaking to mountain-climbing. Grimaud's Musée des Arts et Traditions (00 33 4 94 43 26 98) tells the remarkable story of the town's restoration, actually making it the richest town in the area in terms of desirable property prices. Musée du Phonograph et de la Musique des Maures (00 33 4 94 96 50 53) is a real treat for sound geeks or really old-school DJs, home to a personal collection of old record players and early Edison recording equipment. A local diving school is just down Kon Tiki Beach on the right (00 33 4 94 79 90 37; www.europeandiving.com).

FOOD AND DRINK Les Moulins de Ramatuelle at the nearby hotel of the same name is a good place for Tahiti-style glamour, so go for French cooking such as roast lobster with basil for €38 (00 33 4 94 97 17 22; www.christophe-leroy.com). St-Tropez has plenty to choose from, including Petit Joseph, offering contemporary Asian-style food cooked up by the same kitchen as the swisher Grand Joseph next door (00 33 4 94 97 01 66; www.grand-joseph-saint-tropez. com). The market at Grimaud is on Thursday with a bigger one at Port Grimaud the same day and Sunday. St-Tropez's famous place des Lices market happens Tuesday and Saturday morning; daily fish market near the old port.

GETTING THERE D93 runs down the coast from St-Tropez to Ramatuelle. Les Eucalyptus is on chemin des Moulins – follow signs for Moorea Plage.

OPEN End May–mid September.

THE DAMAGE 2 people and 1 tent €17–€27, 2 people and 1 campervan €21–€31.

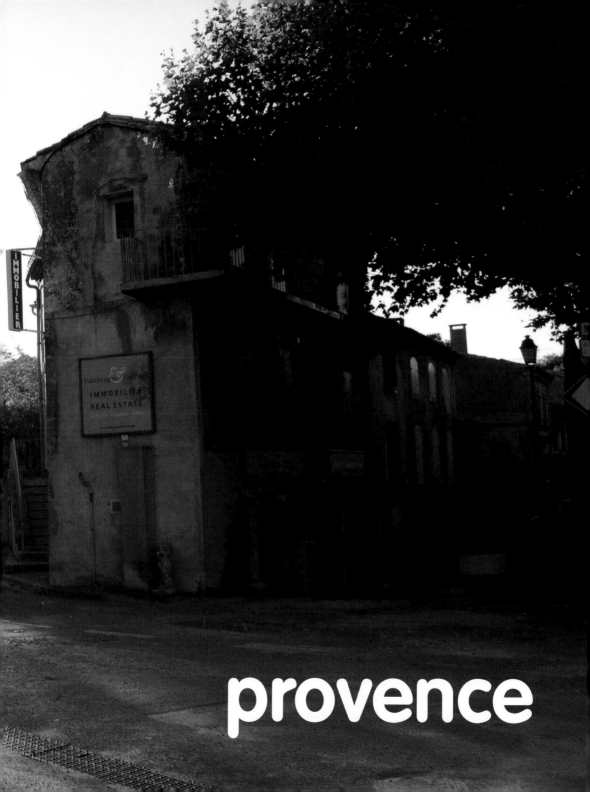

provence

les gorges du loup

Les Gorges du Loup, 965 chemin des Vergers, 06620 Le Bar-sur-Loup   00 33 4 93 42 45 06   www.lesgorgesduloup.com

With around 70 pitches this site is pretty big. Add to this the fact that there are also mobile homes, chalets, fixed caravans, and even a couple of TV rooms, and it makes for a veritable holiday village. Yet, due to Les Gorges du Loup's layout, staggered up the mountainside and camouflaged by shade-giving trees, the site holds on to its air of intimacy.

Quite why you'd want to sit in a dark TV room when this campsite offers excellent views of both the Vallée du Loup below and Le Bar-sur-Loup above is anyone's guess. Actually, despite the site's excellent facilities, including an impressive pool (making the site extremely child-friendly), the real benefit is its location. Le Bar-sur-Loup is a cluster of medieval beauty with a handful of houses gathered around a chateau. Nearby Tourrettes-sur-Loup has violets, artists' studios, chapels, and the Florian confectionary factory, which is sure to tear the kids away from the pool. Then there's the *plus beau* village of Gourdon, as seen in Hitchcock's *To Catch a Thief*. And for film buffs you're only a 30-minute drive from Cannes – but why you'd want to sit in a dark cinema…

COOL FACTOR Great location, perfect for children.

WHO'S IN? Tents, campervans, caravans, dogs, large groups, young groups, families, cycling enthusiasts – yes.

ON SITE Free hook-ups, 2 wash-blocks, playground, TV rooms, restaurant, fridges, pool. No campfires.

OFF SITE Hang-gliding facilities at Auberge du Gordoun (00 33 4 93 09 69 69), with Funtrip in Pont du Loup offering adventure sports (00 33 6 19 66 03 65; www.funtrip.fr).

FOOD AND DRINK Restaurant on site, but a real treat is La Jarrerie in Le Bar-sur-Loup (00 33 4 93 42 92 92; www.restaurant-la-jarrerie.com). Les Bacchanales in Tourrettes-sur-Loup (00 33 4 93 24 19 19) serves traditional dishes.

GETTING THERE From Nice take A8 and follow the sign for Cagnes-sur-Mer. At exit 48 merge on to D336 and follow signs to Le Bar-sur-Loup. The campsite is ½ mile (1 km) outside the village, clearly signed.

PUBLIC TRANSPORT Regular buses from Grasse and Cannes to Le Bar-sur-Loup. Local buses pass the site.

OPEN Early April–late September.

THE DAMAGE 1 person off-peak and peak season €8.50/€11.50, motorcycle €10/€13 or car €11/€15, 1 car plus 2 people €15/€21, caravan €15.20/€23.50. Mobile homes, static caravans, chalets €200–€670 per week.

camping rural

We stumbled across Camping Rural after spotting a wooden sign by the side of the D21. Five miles (8 km) further down a single road is Blieux and facing its only shop and bar is a field you can pitch up in for the night. Overseen by Madame Collomp, who doesn't speak English, Camping Rural has no website, no email, and is no-frills. The site has a single toilet block with one shower – and chickens. Simplicity is truly its strength. It is decorated with flowers and terracotta geranium pots line the steps up to the bar – a stone's throw from your tent. The view of the Gorges du Verdon at the end of the field, with its mountain background, is simply stunning.

Camping Rural is a genuine French experience. Madame also owns the shop and will open and close the bar at any time. The well-stocked *magasin* sells fresh baguettes each morning and the promise of beer or wine at the ring of a bell is delightful. Of course, there are the further-afield experiences of Castellane and Majastres, but Camping Rural is really about staying rural; the only nightlife is the amazing stars in the sky.

COOL FACTOR A genuine French experience; a campsite how they used to be, perfectly preserved.

WHO'S IN? Tents, campervans, caravans, dogs – yes. Large groups, young groups – no.

ON SITE Roughly 30 pitches, hook-ups €2.50. One toilet, sink and shower (€1 for 15 mins) very clean. Wrap up warmly, you're in the mountains. No campfires.

OFF SITE Blieux is halfway between Majastres and Castellane. Base Sport & Nature run adventurous water sports (00 33 4 92 83 11 42; contact@basesportnature.com).

FOOD AND DRINK Market days in Castellane are Wednesday and Saturday. The rather sweet eaterie Auberge de Teillon (00 33 4 92 83 60 88; www.auberge-teillon.com), a family-run place on route de Grasse in Le Garde, near Castellane, makes lovely meals, set *menus* from €22.

GETTING THERE From Castellane, D4085 north to La Tuilière then left onto D21 to Majastres. Look for a sign on the right and keep going up the track.

OPEN April–September.

THE DAMAGE Adults €2.50, children €1.20. Big tent, caravan, campervan €2 per night. Small tent, car, motorbike €1 per night.

As you turn off the tarmacked route Napoléon on to Ancienne Route Napoléon, there's a dramatic change in the road surface. This aged track stretches back to Roman times and once provided an escape route for Napoléon and his army. The 1-mile (2-km) trek up the mountainside by car (let alone foot) is hard work – but reassuring signposts remind you that you're on the right path just when you might contemplate turning around.

Ironically, Pierre and Olivia found Terre d'Arômes when their car broke down by the side of the mountain four years ago. Then, the site was little more than a tumble-down farm building, scrubland, and a wild forest. And so professional builder Pierre set to work, dragging 12 Mongolian yurts up the mountainside, erecting a log cabin and restoring the old farm building into rooms for guests who need a little more comfort – and a lot less bugs. If you've spent most of your holiday in a tent, then the yurts are comfort enough. With soft beds and low lighting it's like sleeping in a warm heartwood womb – and you'll sleep well here, only to be stirred by the braying of family donkeys, Brad Pitt and Tom Cruise, waking you up in time for breakfast. You'd be a fool to miss out on the fig or rosehip jam.

Suitably refreshed from a great night's sleep, you'll be ready for the day's activities and to be

ferme terre d'arômes

Ferme Terre d'Arômes, Ancienne Route Napoléon, 06750 Séranon   00 33 6 23 32 78 07   www.terre-d-aromes.fr

worn out again. There are lots of walks in the area and if you're feeling athletic you can trek to Parc de la Moulière on the north side of the mountain in Caille – or it's just 20 minutes by car. It's a ski slope in winter and a playground for outdoor pursuits in summer. When the chair lift's not carrying skiers up the piste, it's depositing mountain-bikers on the summit. Elsewhere in the park, there's tree-climbing with one of the longest zip wires in France, and an underground Via Ferrata course, cleverly known as Via Souterrata.

Nearby Gorges du Verdon offers water sports from rafting to canyoning, and only an hour from Terre d'Arômes are Nice and Cannes – nice for a spot of lunch. You won't catch Pierre or Olivia there, though; they came to the mountains to escape the city.

The real delight of Terre d'Arômes is that you're accepted into Pierre and Olivia's extended family. Email them in advance and they'll include you for dinner. This removes the pretence of some luxury campsites by being rough around the edges – something we like to call 'rustique boutique'. Reinforced by the fact that Pierre has seemingly created this mountain getaway with his bare hands.

While Olivia never stops smiling or being the perfect hostess, Pierre never keeps still and is permanently on the go. Plans are in place to take

Romany caravans up the mountainside and Pierre wants to build a zip wire across the valley. He also wants to clear scrub for tent pitches, ready for the hardiest of campers, and finish off the jacuzzi and sauna for those who want to be pampered. Olivia used to own an aromatherapy shop in Antibes and she brings her experience of essential oils to harness the nearby resources (including lavender, St John's wort, yarrow, Scots pine, and juniper).

Whether you like it rough and rugged or reclined and refined, Ferme Terre d'Arômes has got it covered.

COOL FACTOR Luxurious mountainside chilling, but plenty to keep you active.

WHO'S IN? Yurts, dogs, families, big groups, thrill-seekers, retreaters – yes.

ON SITE Twelve yurts, 4 rooms, 2 wash-huts with lovely warm showers, toilets, and 3 extra toilets, en suite bathrooms with rooms, baby-changing in rooms, playground with own mini zip wire, ice packs, fully equipped kitchen, shop selling oils, honey, wine, and jam. Water and heating mostly solar-powered; generator in the winter. No campfires.

OFF SITE For everything horse-based visit Ferme Équestre St-Pierre in Bargème (00 33 4 94 84 21 55; www. fermesaintpierre.net). Azur Canyonning runs canyonning courses for beginners along the Gorges du Loup; Planet Rivière runs every imagineable white-water activity out of the Var, Verdon, Vésubie, Roya, and Tinée Rivers. La Moulière has bike or ski runs, depending on the state of the slopes (00 33 4 93 60 45 39; www.ville-caille.com). There's also plenty of other *accrobranche* (tree-climbing) activities in the region, but the one at La Moulière is the best (00 33 4 93 36 60 57; www.parcours-aventure06.com) and the Via Souterrata is a unique experience (00 33 4 93 60 34 51). If you don't want to get quite so physical with rocks, there's always the 6-million-year-old grottos in and around Gorges du Verdon.

FOOD AND DRINK As we mentioned, if you email nicely you can sort out a light mountain-food supper or larger meal in advance. It's going to be a more authentic experience than in a lot of nearby restaurants. There isn't much in terms of fine dining around the activity areas. Much of the food is fuel for people in a rush who are seeking that next thrill. Snack des 3 Vallées (00 33 4 93 66 39 87) is a decent place to visit for a quick bite and also has a certain American diner chic to it. Strangely, more than French restaurants you'll see quite a lot of pizzerias on route Napoléon. A pretty good close option is Le St-Louis (00 33 4 93 60 30 86) – head to the bottom of the ancient track and turn left – with proper Italian-style pizzas at around €15. Real foodies should visit Le Moulin de Mougins (00 33 4 93 75 78 24; www. moulindemougins.com) in the small village of the same name on the way to Cannes. This is top-flight stuff with Chef Sébastien Chambru serving up gourmet works of art. Or you could venture even further into Cannes to sample the ecstatic delights of La Villa des Lys (00 33 4 92 98 77 41; www.lucienbarriere.com) or La Palme d'Or (00 33 4 92 98 73 00; www.hotel-martinez.com).

GETTING THERE From Castellane south on D4085 and D6095. From Grasse, D6085 north until you see signs for D79. Don't join D79 but stay on the Ancienne Route Napoloén – *ferme* signposted at this junction. Continue up rugged road. Have faith in the signs.

OPEN All year.

THE DAMAGE Yurts €25 per person per night, €5 for breakfast, rooms €55.

Nora and Michel met and fell in love while working in Paris; she was a web designer, he a documentary cameraman. They both wanted to escape the bustle of inner-city life and so began their three-year search for the perfect site. Les Olivettes was a winner for such a visually acute couple; this staggering mountainside vista, in the heart of Provence, bursts with colour all year.

The site is over 50 years old, but Nora and Michel took up the reins in 2009, bringing a touch of Parisian chic to its rural setting, giving it a boutique but bohemian vibe. The most recent additions are a solar-powered pool with a meditation area, a stylish BBQ spot with tables and chairs, and tastefully painted cornflower-blue amenities – in the modern mode. Michel, whose other love affair is with wood, has further plans for bespoke fixed tents and naturally sympathetic, but architecturally sophisticated, cabins. Yet there will always be a place in this olive grove for campers, as Michel admits they like their 'temperament'. Each camping and caravan pitch has been carefully considered and levelled, offering a variety of east- and west-facing pitches, with some olive trees totally shading you from the Provençal sun.

Ecology is important to Nora and Michel; both the showers and pool are solar-powered and all rubbish can be separated. The only additional

les olivettes

Les Olivettes, Hameau les Pourcelles, 04190 Les Mées   00 33 4 92 34 18 97   www.campinglesolivettes.com

lighting comes in the shape of small solar lights, which are only light enough to guide your way through the site at night. They certainly don't pollute the incredible view of the staggering star-flecked sky – which is said to be the clearest in Europe. If you need more proof, then from July to mid-September scrutinise the night sky further at the astronomical observatory in nearby Puimichel.

This star-crossed couple left life in the fast lane – and they believe that you should change down a gear, too. Nora and Michel want you to empty your mind and breathe in the natural surroundings. Inevitably teenagers may find this a *nul*, but Les Olivettes is perfect for young families. The site

is dotted with wooden toys, including a mini kitchen, perhaps to prepare little ones for future Provençal cooking. Keith Floyd would have raised a glass of *vin rouge*, too.

Although there is a supermarket in nearby Les Mées in summertime fresh bread and croissants are delivered and potatoes can be collected directly from the farmer. Twice a week baked delights such as Quiche Lorraine and home-made *confiture* are brought back from the bountiful local markets: at some point you'll want to experience these treats first hand.

Nora's little office at the entrance is stocked full of suggestions of what to do further afield

and Les Olivettes is quite perfectly placed. Just a 20-minute drive to the A51 means a great distance can be covered and so a wide range of activities are on offer – from gliding and ballooning in the east to swimming and water sports in the west.

Just down the road from Les Olivettes is the *moulin*, where Michel and Nora press their olives into oil in March. There's also a small museum that celebrates this special 'elixir of Provence'. Which, of course, is locally sourced and lovingly made.

COOL FACTOR Superb view, boutique chic, personal, loving touch.

WHO'S IN? Tents, campervans, caravans, mobile homes, young families, couples, dogs (upon presentation of rabies license) – yes.

ON SITE Forty pitches, all with hook-ups, 2 excellent amenities blocks with wash-rooms, coin-operated washing machine, 4 solar-powered showers (free), baby-changing, disabled toilet/shower, playground, swimming pool. Baguettes and croissants must be pre-ordered (available June–August). Information point run by Nora. You're in the mountains, so it can be cold at night. Great BBQ area with tables, chairs, and sculptures. No campfires.

OFF SITE From 1 July to 15 September you can visit the Observatoire de l'Alifant (www.lalunetteduperejosset.com) in Puimichel. Ecomusée l'Oliver is the place to go to find out everything about the history of the precious fruit (00 33 4 92 72 66 91; www.ecomusee-olivier.com). Les Olivettes is great if you love heights. Paragliding school Haut les Mains often does flights around Oraison (00 33 4 92 34 34 00; www.haut-les-mains.fr). Some days you might also see a hot air balloon drift your way. Hot Air Balloons Provence (00 33 4 90 05 76 77; www.montgolfiere-provence-ballooning.com) are based 35 miles (55 km) away as the balloon flies; €245 long flight, €175 short trip. For kids there's *accrobranche* at Jungle Parc in St Pons (00 33 6 86 73 37 57; www.jungle-parc.fr), though parents will have to venture further to Maillemoisson's Forêt Domaniale (00 33 4

92 35 29 79; www.arbre-aventure.com) for adult-orientated versions. Further north there's rock-climbing (www.ceuse. fr), or for those who like to climb a mountain and jump off it there's Fusion Paragliding near Gap (00 33 6 80 02 54 39; www.fusion-parapente.com).

FOOD AND DRINK Plenty of restaurants in Les Mées. The best is Le Marmite du Pecheur (00 33 4 92 34 35 56), specialising in seafood and, in case you're wondering, *marmite* is the name for the cooking pot. The local baker delivers in July/August, but La Boulangerie de Lurs (00 33 4 92 79 17 68) is worth visiting for the wide variety of specialist regional breads. Puimichel's Chez Jules (00 33 4 92 74 98 10) offers a changing menu based on seasonal availability. Further into the mountains, 9 miles (13 km) from the site, in Entrevennes, is Le Paradiso (00 33 4 92 77 25 92; www.bistrotdepays.com) a very reasonable bistro with an extensive vegetarian menu/seasonal delights. Regional specialities at the markets in Oraison (Tuesday morning) and Gréoux-les-Bains (Thursdays). Provence celebrates different produce every week from end of August until mid October (00 33 4 92 73 02 57; www.semaine-senteurs-saveurs.fr).

GETTING THERE Halfway between 2 junctions of A51 follow signs to D4. Campsite signposted from Les Mées, but make sure you're following signs for Les Olivettes not L'Olivettes.

OPEN 15 April–15 October (site partially closes September to ready the olive crop).

THE DAMAGE Tent plus 2 people €16.

le moulin de cost

Le Moulin de Cost, 26170 Buis-les-Baronnies   00 33 4 75 28 09 82   www.camping-moulindecost.com

Welcome to Baronnies; a remote, rugged land of olive and lime trees, lavender fields, vineyards, and apricot groves in the heart of the Drôme Provençale. Fields of purple, yellow, olive green, red, and pink paint a beautiful landscape. The town, Buis-les-Baronnies, attracts visitors for its brightly painted façades, medieval town walls, and gothic and Renaissance architecture. Nearby is the unique, protruding limestone rock, St-Julien, which, along with the Gorges d'Ubrieux, is an internationally renowned rock-climbing haunt. If scaling vertical heights doesn't appeal, market-browsing might. Markets take place daily in most villages; twice a week in Buis-les-Baronnies.

These site-owners are so welcoming you'll feel as though family friends have invited you round to use their pool: a trickling river runs along the foot of a track. Be prepared for farmhouse-envy; the grand abode, with huge blue shutters, is the kind of home most of us dream of owning. A cavernous dining room is tucked inside, a hop and skip from the courtyard bar. Camping Le Moulin de Cost is the genuine – French and uncommercial – article.

COOL FACTOR A small river and a swimming pool; we're sold. Nature-lovers will love the countryside vibe.

WHO'S IN? Tents, campervans, caravans, dogs, large groups, young groups – yes.

ON SITE Fifty pitches, 29 of which can be mobile homes and caravans. Tents only by the water. Twelve WCs, 6 showers, 1 disabled WC/shower. Dish- and clothes-washing sinks. Washing machine €5. Pool. Restaurant and bar sells ice creams, soft drinks, breakfasts, salads, main meals. Volleyball, water polo. Bread service. Wi-fi. No campfires.

OFF SITE Beginner/intermediate rock-climbing or introduction to canyoning with guides (www.guides-baronnies.com).

FOOD AND DRINK Auberge de la Clue in Plaisians (00 33 4 75 28 01 17) has an excellent reputation, so book ahead.

GETTING THERE From A9 exit at Orange. Head east along D23 and D977 to Vaison-la-Romaine, then east towards D5 to Buis-les-Baronnies. Turn right into Eygaliers. Farmhouse signposted on the left.

OPEN 1 May–15 September.

THE DAMAGE July/August 2 adults with tent €13 per night (25% less May/June). Electricity €3. 4 statics €390–€490 per week and caravan €240–€300. Breakfast €6.

le grand bois

Le Grand Bois, Col de Boutière, 26460 Le Poët-Célard   00 33 4 75 53 33 72   www.legrandbois.nl

Peek through the trees of this nature reserve woodland and, behold, a cluster of humungous safari-lodge tents loom into view. Near the Parc Régional du Vercors limestone scenery this settlement pioneers next-level glamping. Sturdy canvas homes perched on wooden decks are hidden in woodland behind an 18th-century inn.

These constructions are simply huge; you'll stretch your legs just fetching a glass of water and families can hang out here all day without feeling claustrophobic. Choose between a covered or uncovered terrace porch, then tie back the front flaps to create an open-plan abode filled with double and bunk beds and full-sized wardrobes. Look outwards towards a view of arboreal wilderness. A cheaper camping option is to book a tunnel tent sleeping five, with awning, bedding, towels, and gas stove. Or pitch a tent in the camping meadow near the pool, snack bar, dining patio, and wash-block. Once acclimatised, book a hiking, cycling, or motorcycling package to explore the park. Otherwise enjoy your house in the woods; it's too special to leave for too long.

COOL FACTOR Taking camping in the woods to a whole new level in this mini-town of safari tents.

WHO'S IN? Campervans, caravans, dogs, large groups, young groups (all low season only) – yes.

ON SITE Twenty-five tent pitches, 6 caravans, 5 safari-lodge tents increasing to 10 for 2011, and 2 tunnel tents. Forty electric hook-ups. Table d'hôte dinners, pizzas, breakfasts available. Swimming pool, playground, volleyball, wi-fi, bread service. Bar 4pm–10pm. No BBQs or campfires.

OFF SITE Mountain-bikers can take on the challenge of Mont Ventoux and the Vercors. Bike storage on site.

FOOD AND DRINK Stuffed ravioli is a local speciality. Auberge de l'Estang in Saoû is a good place to start.

GETTING THERE From A7 take exit 18 to Montélimar Sud and follow D540 to Dieulefit, then Bourdeaux. Follow signs Vers Pascalin and Le Grand Bois.

OPEN 30 April–30 September.

THE DAMAGE 2 adults with tent €21.50. Child under 2 years free, 2–7 years €5, 8+ €6.75. Tunnel tent €400–€575 per week. Safari lodge €550–€775 per week, €75–€95 per night (not July/Aug). Dogs €3.50. Hook-ups €3.50. B&B €52–€80 including breakfast. Breakfast €5–€8. *Gîte* €525–€725 per week, €95 per day. Table d'hôte dinner €25.

les oliviers

Les Oliviers, avenue Jean Jaurès, 13810 Eygalières   00 33 4 90 95 91 86   www.camping-les-oliviers.com

With just 33 pitches for tents and caravans, Les Oliviers isn't stuffed full of resources, but this campsite makes a very good job of looking after the small details. From the comfortable benches you sit on waiting for a hot large-headed shower, and the attentively cleaned toilet block, through to the beautiful flowers and manicured olive trees.

The key appeal of this small, wonderfully presented site is its proximity to the listed village of Eygalières. On the cusp of the Alpilles, it is postcard-perfection of what a small town in Provence should look like, complete with a *pâtisserie*, food shop, a florist and, of course, a *pétanque* pitch thrown in for good measure.

If you want to venture further afield you can walk down GR6 or rent a bike from the campsite and head out of Eygalières through the Alpilles. By car you can visit St-Rémy-de-Provence only 6 miles (10 km) away, which reveals classic fountains, chic boutiques, and vivid van Gogh-inspired art shops around every well-preserved corner. Or if you can beat the crowds, head to the mountains for Les Baux-de-Provence, although it might be best to buy your olive oil, red, rosé, or white wine, and honey from one of the farms as prices are pushed up in the labyrinthine town. Back in Eygalières for an evening's entertainment, there are both chic and typical Provençal bars to enjoy a drink in. For such a small town the food options are bountiful, ranging from simple bar/bistro affairs, to a crêperie and a handful of Michelin-mentioned restaurants.

COOL FACTOR Closeness to the town. Lovingly cared for.

WHO'S IN? Tents, campervans, caravans, dogs – yes. Large groups, young groups – no.

ON SITE Thirty-three pitches and hook-ups, clean, well-maintained wash-rooms, 4 showers, 3 good washing-up sinks, disabled access, playground, caravan hire, mountain-bike rental, boulodrome. No great view or mind-blowing activities, but well looked after and located. No campfires.

OFF SITE Horse-riding lessons and treks arranged at Eygalières Riding Centre (00 33 6 16 17 03 68). For climbing, canyoning, and up-mountain pursuits in Les Alpilles contact Muratti Adventures (00 33 6 63 89 05 16; http://muratti. adventures.free.fr).

FOOD AND DRINK Market days are Friday mornings in Eygalières and Wednesday and Saturday at St-Rémy-de-Provence. Wine buffs can visit Domaine de Costebonne at Cave du Mas de Longchamp (00 33 4 90 95 23 54). La Ferme d'Eygalières (00 33 4 90 90 62 14; www.laferme-eygalieres. com) offers a memorable set-price lunch. Bar Le Progress (00 33 4 90 95 91 16) has a set-price evening meal from around €15. More upmarket bistro fare can be found at l'Aubergine (00 33 4 90 95 98 89; www.laubergine-eygalieres.com). Chez Bru (00 33 4 90 90 60 34; www.chezbru.com) is top notch; if you're a foodie the chef's surprise (€135) won't disappoint.

GETTING THERE Halfway between St-Rémy-de-Provence and Cavaillon. Take exit 25 for Cavaillon from A7 on to D99. In the village follow the green signs to Les Oliviers.

PUBLIC TRANSPORT Trains run to Cavaillon 6 miles (10 km) away from the site. Buses run from Cavaillon a few days a week and stop in the high street in Eygalières.

OPEN April–November.

THE DAMAGE Tent plus 2 people from €13.

The listed village of Eygalières

pegomas

Camping Pegomas, avenue Jean Moulin, 13210 St-Rémy-de-Provence   00 33 4 90 92 01 21   www.campingpegomas.com

St-Rémy-de-Provence has evolved from its small, ancient Provençal beginnings into a buzzy town with 11,000 inhabitants. Gallo-Roman stone buildings with sky-blue shutters line cobbled streets enclosed by the remnants of a 14th-century wall. Café patios swarm with couples, day-trippers, and city folk. Big bowls of shiny olives grace the tables and wafts of garlic and *herbes de Provence* fill the air. The campsite is a short stroll away. It's not quiet; the pool borders a busy road and a snack bar and communal BBQ are focal points. But the owners are friendly and the town is charming. People-watch while sitting outside Café des Arts before hunting down a traditional lunch of codfish with garlic mayonnaise or anything *à la Provençal* (with tomatoes, olive oil, and garlic).

Art buffs can make a beeline for St-Paul de Mausole, the psychiatric hospital where Vincent van Gogh confined himself after cutting off his ear. He produced more than 150 paintings of his surroundings, including some of his most famous works – many are exhibited here along with his actual bedroom, depicted in 'Bedroom in Arles'.

COOL FACTOR The campsite is a pleasantly practical base for exploring one of the oldest towns in France.

WHO'S IN? Campervans, caravans, dogs, large groups, young groups – yes.

ON SITE Hook-ups €3.50 per day. Three heated wash-blocks have 18 hot, powerful showers, 17 WCs and sink cubicles, 2 disabled showers/WCs, 2 baby-changing areas. Dog shower. Swimming pool. Snack bar. Playground. Communal BBQ. Baguette service €0.85, order before 7pm, pick up 8am. Wi-fi at pitch. No campfires.

OFF SITE St-Paul de Mausole (00 33 4 90 92 77 00) is walkable from the site, or it's a 5-minute drive.

FOOD AND DRINK On Fridays codfish and vegetables are eaten with garlic and chilli mayonnaise.

GETTING THERE Take E80 towards Alès. Continue on N572 and N113, then exit 7 to Avignon. At third roundabout take D99, keep right and the campsite is on the right.

PUBLIC TRANSPORT Buses from Avignon (€25 cab ride from airport), drop off at place de la République.

OPEN 12 March–29 October.

THE DAMAGE 2 people with tent or caravan/campervan €17–€23, kids under 3 free. Dogs free except July/Aug €1.70 per day. €17 reservation fee July/Aug.

la pierre verte

La Pierre Verte, Quartier As Codes, Arpaillargues, 30700 Uzès   00 33 4 66 22 56 31   www.lapierreverte.eu

Simple yet comprehensive, affordable yet classy, this glamping site is hidden among olive trees in peaceful Languedoc countryside a half-hour's drive from Nîmes airport. You'll probably arrive to find the young owners in their vegetable nursery, pitchforks in hand, sowing the seeds of a life of self-sufficiency. Funding their dream are two chic and cheery encampments, secluded and nestled snuggly among bushy trees.

The bell tent is an explosion of bright primary colours with sprawling double bed, but leaving ample room to move freely about. Outside is your very own outdoor, open-plan camp with solar-powered shower, basins, and camp kitchen featuring shelves, a cooker, and sinks. Through the bushes sits the smaller, unfussy yurt. It can hot up under canvas inside, but a small swimming pool across the meadow and an abundance of shady trees will both help to keep you cool. However, you can break up the long spells spent at your own private camp with a day at the Roman Pont du Gard (the three-tiered aquaduct you see in school textbooks) or mooching around medieval Uzès.

THE COOL FACTOR Affordable private glamping for couples, groups, and young families.

WHO'S IN? Large groups, young groups – yes. Tents, campervans, caravans, dogs – no.

ON SITE One yurt and 1 bell tent, each sleeps 4. One-bedroom stone Mazet sleeps 1 couple. Each camp has a kitchen. One compost loo, 1 solar-powered shower. Honesty bar. Two bikes €10 per day. Four 2-man tents for hire in addition to bell or yurt. 'Dipping' pool. Massages from €50.

OFF SITE Arpaillargues is a 15-minute walk away with shop, bakery, restaurant, bar, and pharmacy.

FOOD AND DRINK Truffles available year round in Uzès at Maison de la Truffe (00 33 4 66 63 86 45).

GETTING THERE From Uzès follow one-way system direction Arpaillargues-et-Aureillac. Turn left on D22 to Dions. After bend note fence on right with sign to nursery.

PUBLIC TRANSPORT Buses daily from Nîmes and Avignon, then €10 taxi ride.

OPEN June–October.

THE DAMAGE Weekly hires only; no set days. Yurt €550, bell €450 for 2, and can include 2 extra beds €15 per week. Four 2-man tents €70 single, €120 double per person per week includes bedding. Travel cot free. Bikes €10 per day.

ardèche

les roulottes de campagne

Les Roulottes de Campagne, Domaine de St-Cerice, 07200 Vogüé   00 33 4 75 37 08 66   www.saintcerice.com

To know France is to know roulottes: wooden units modelled on old-fashioned Romany wagons, with painted wheels and verandas, they are hugely popular. Les Roulottes de Campagne now have over 50 sites and this hillside location rents out 12 roulottes. Each sleeps five, with a shower, kitchen and, for a little extra, they'll throw in a TV. What the sun-dried/baked site lacks in wow-factor the Ardèche more than compensates for. For an even more unusual abode check into one of the Carré d'Étoiles. Wood-panelled, cubed booths with lime-green porthole windows, they resemble funky garden sheds, but they contain a kitchenette, shower, two-seater sofa folding out to accommodate two small children, and the star attraction, a telescope. Climb the ladder on to a raised double bed, snuggle under duvets, flip the roof open, and stargaze all night long. Of course, should it rain, then there's barely room for two people to dry off inside, let alone their mucky offspring. Couples and lone travellers would, literally, fit right in, then. A long weekend should suffice, unless you're seeking a romantic retreat.

COOL FACTOR Stargazing through an open roof, or accommodation in Ardèche roulottes: take your pick.
WHO'S IN? Families, couples, solo travellers, astronomers – yes. Dogs, tents, caravans, campervans – no.
ON SITE Twelve roulottes, 1 with disabled access, and 2 Carré d'Étoiles. Breakfast hampers included. Kitchens fully equipped. A tiny swimming pool keeps the heat off. Surcharges add up: cot €4, €35 for end-of-week cleaning (€18 for a weekend). Book table d'hôte evening meals, €24 adult, €14 child, picnics from €35. No BBQs. No campfires.
OFF SITE Vogüé is good for canoeing or kayaking (00 33 4 75 39 79 96; www.descente-ardeche-canoe.fr).
FOOD AND DRINK Picodon is a delicious, local goats' cheese. Find plenty at Aubenas market (Sundays), along with sausages, hams, and chestnuts.
GETTING THERE Directions sent on booking. From Vogüé, follow sign to St-Cerice, up a hill and turn right at the top.
PUBLIC TRANSPORT Fly to Lyon or Nîmes, then train to Montélimar or Aubenas, then taxi.
OPEN All year.
THE DAMAGE Carré d'Étoiles: 2 adults, 2 kids €92.60 per night. €90 per night for 2. Roulottes €74–€160 per night for 2 adults and 2 children (5th person €10).

ardèche détente

Ardèche Détente, route de Vallon Pont d'Arc, La Villette, 30430 Barjac   00 33 4 66 24 54 77   www.ardeche-detente.com

Finding this site isn't easy. In a scene straight from *The Chronicles of Narnia*, once you've located the obscure entrance and pushed open the creaking door a fairy-tale land awaits. Tucked behind the thick farmhouse walls and traditional cobbled courtyard are all manner of fancy camping abodes, as well as a hamman boudoir, bright kitchen/diner, five *gîte* B&B rooms, and an inviting pool with sunloungers. Squawking bantams aside, resident talking animals are thin on the ground. Narnia this isn't, then, but camping nirvana it is. An Indonesian bamboo hut sleeping two points to two yurts at the end of decking pathways. The interior glass candleholders, patchwork throws, and wooden chests the handiwork of the architect-owners.

A second field is more private and fancier still, with wide skies and hill views. Lolloping lawns roll gently downwards. At the top are self-catering cottages, at the bottom two tree houses sitting regally on stilts. In between are two more yurts, a well-stocked 'summer kitchen' yurt, and a larger pool with space for sunbathing. This is a perfect spot to indulge in some truly enchanted escapism.

COOL FACTOR Self-contained beautiful, luxury camping.

WHO'S IN? Large groups, young groups – yes. Tents, campervans, caravans, dogs – no.

ON SITE Four yurts sleep 2, 3, or 4. Two chalet bathrooms with enamel sinks, loos. Two tree huts sleep up to 6 in 3 bedrooms, 2 bathrooms. Sauna, dining room, table tennis.

OFF SITE Pont d'Arc is 7½ miles (12 km) away. Canoeing is the main activity. Parc National de Cévennes (www.cevennes-parcnational.fr), Parc Naturel Régional des Monts d'Ardèche, and Uzès should all be on the itinerary.

FOOD AND DRINK Make the most of the table d'hôte. Local, organic food served by candlelight outside your abode. Bio gourmet baskets (tablecloth, silver cutlery).

GETTING THERE From Barjac village heading to the route de Vallon Pont d'Arc, on the right are a few roadside houses.

PUBLIC TRANSPORT Fly or train to Avignon/Nîmes or Montélimar. Buses between Avignon and Barjac and from Montélimar to Gare de Vallon Pont d'Arc.

OPEN Mid March–end October.

THE DAMAGE Yurts 1 person €55 per night, €270 per week, more for 3/4 people. Table d'hote €22 (kids €12), gourmet baskets €18–€30. Bamboo hut €60/€80 for 1/2 people. Sauna €10 per hour for 2.

mille étoiles

Mille Étoiles, Mas de Serret, 07150 Labastide de Virac   00 33 4 75 38 42 77/00 33 6 10 85 04 98   www.campingmilletoiles.com

Pushing his heavily pregnant partner 1,000 feet (300 m) up a steep valley-side track from the Ardèche River bank can't have been an easy feat, but you get the feeling that Luds van den Belt and Ruth Lawson probably used the opportunity to hatch their next plan. Since meeting in London and roaming Europe in a campervan, their second summer spent running and living in a shack bar by the river's edge was drawing to an end. Their customers had been children seeking sugar rushes to speed their ascent back to camp and the occasional surprised canoeist passing downstream. Now it was home time.

Used to the Massif Central's Mediterranean climes, the prospect of a British winter wasn't appealing. When land on this nature reserve came up for sale, the couple pounced. Fast-forward the best part of a decade and with two daughters now at school, their beautiful campsite Mille Étoiles, overlooking the Ardèche River, is easily one of France's loveliest.

The forested land, sitting high above a canyon of sparkling, turquoise waters, is so fairy-tale-perfect, in fact, that weddings aplenty have taken place here. Stylish touches, creative design, all those little comforts catered for – lanterns at night, posh toiletries in the wash-rooms – and, of course, the close proximity to the gorge means you could book in for a fortnight and still not be ready to go home at the end. Experienced campers who celebrate the great outdoors, who like being active, and who can always opt for a little luxury

(a proper bed to sleep on) get the most out of a stay here. Mille Étoiles test-drove a few yurts in 2003, with no electricity or water, way before the glamping boom, and cite nature as their star attraction. Although one look at these nomadic Mongolian yurts and fancy family bathrooms suggests that there's a lot more to the campsite than the enchanting surroundings.

Coming in from Barjac, the village is signposted. Head down a country track shadowed by ancient oaks and olive trees and park on the gravel drive. Introductions are made in the couple's handcrafted camp café – a fantastic oak-framed tunnel tent with a cream canvas over chaises longues, a fashionable terrace, patio tables, and chairs. Outside, the stillness of the Ardéchois woodland is calling the world to run feral and free.

Five natural canvas forest yurts on pine platforms are scattered decent distances apart. Sumptuous double beds with thick duvets are draped with mosquito nets. Each one is themed (for example boudoir, Edwardian safari, Indian, Thai) and furnished with chunky wooden chests or canvas wardrobes, ethnic pictures, and recycled bedside tables. Starched, comfortable hammocks swing outside and self-catering yurts with cooking facilities are shared among the guests.

The Village, a tent-only camping field, is a recent development to encourage more campers. Situated on the other side of the café, the field is near a facilities block and all guests share the kids' playground, camp café, and paddling pool. If

wildlife is the luxury you need, bag one of the 20 pitches there or in the woods.

Mille Étoiles is a 20-minute scramble down a steep decline to the water and, once on the river bed, walkers can follow the river the length of the gorge. With no electricity on site, the stars shine brightly after dark. If all the splashing about on the river hasn't worn you out then counting those Mille Étoiles will get you well on your way to a good night's sleep. 1, 2, 3… [*At time of going to press the site had been sold, but we trust the new owners maintain the standards set by the last ones.*]

COOL FACTOR Camping right next to the Gorges de l'Ardèche, a camping field, luxury yurts, a forest, beautiful river, and welcoming young Brit hosts.

WHO'S IN? Tents, canoeists, nature-lovers – yes. Campervans, caravans, dogs – no.

ON SITE A giant communal yurt (pictured) in the middle of the woods was built by Luds and is available for group-occasion hire or for general use (yoga routines, story-telling, hide-and-seek). Twenty tent pitches in the woods and in a field with water points, a few electric hook-ups, picnic tables, and hammocks. Five self-catering yurts comfortably fit a family of 4, a young family of 5 at a squeeze. Breakfast can be taken in the camp café 8.30am–10.30am. Dinners available in high season on Saturdays (arrival buffet) and Tuesdays (BBQ). Two shower blocks, one by the yurts with 6 family bathrooms (sink, shower) and a block with 4 shower cubicles and 5 loos. Bath towel hire €15 for 2. Bar opens mornings and evenings selling local wines, beers, fresh juices, water, and ice creams. Playground, paddling pool.

OFF SITE Canoe on the Ardèche or Cèze. Hire boats and instructors from www.aigue-vive.com to take a 2-hour or 2-day excursion. Park at Sauze and a shuttle bus runs to Vallon Pont d'Arc, so you can pick up your vehicle at the end of the day. Join the throngs at the iconic sandy beach of Vallon Pont d'Arc, or view it from the road above. This stone 'bridge' is one of France's best-known landmarks and epitimises all that is great about the country (throwing off your clothes for a swim in a river sounds appealing to us). Barjac is a short drive away – worth a visit on Friday mornings for market day.

FOOD AND DRINK The Ardèche is famous for its chestnuts. For a special occasion dine at La Petite Auberge (00 33 4 75 38 61 94; www.lapetiteaubergelabastide.com) in Labastide de Virac, with its enchanting terrace and wonderful view of the vineyards. It's so near it's walkable (no more than half an hour). Service is efficient, the restaurant small, the portions huge, and the food scrummy. One visit might not be enough. There is a small farm shop near the campsite; ask for directions.

GETTING THERE From Nîmes airport follow A54 to Nîmes, turning on to A9 to Avignon/Lyon. Follow signs for Bollène/Montélimar, take exit 19 at Bollène and follow D994, D6086, and D901. Then turn right on D979 into Barjac. Follow signs to Labastide, look for a sign on the left to Les Crottes, then Mille Étoiles signs direct you in.

PUBLIC TRANSPORT Avignon or Montélimar are the nearest TGV stations, from where buses run to either Barjac or Vallon Pont d'Arc, then take a taxi. Nîmes, Avignon, and Lyon are the nearest airports, 90 minutes away.

OPEN June–September.

THE DAMAGE Tent campers €21–€28 a night for 2 people. Extra person €10.50, child 3–12 years €8, and under-3s free. Self-catering yurts from €85 for 2 people, minimum 2 nights' stay and in high season weekly bookings €650 for 2 people, price includes bed linen, and bath towels. €15 for 2 people per tent max. Dinners €20 adult, €10 kids.

Nestled at the end of a narrow lane and found by following home-made signs, just outside the village of Goudargues in Provence, Haut Toupian is exclusive by design. The accommodation is limited – there are only two pitches on the 11-acre (4.5-hectare) site and they come pre-filled with tents. But what spectacular tents.

Both of the large, rectangular safari constructions are set on raised timber decks with a terrace out front. From one of the terraces the panorama of trees and mountains is spectacular. The other terrace enjoys a more rustic view, taking in the traditional stone farmhouse, *gîte*, and surrounding woods.

There are no busy roads within earshot, so birdsong and wind rustling through trees forms the soundtrack – with the occasional rustle of a nearby boar. Fungus growing on oak trees is testament to the purity of the air (fungus can't grow in polluted air), as is the crystal-clear view across the Cèze Valley's woods, vineyards, and lavender fields. The calm tranquillity is genuinely overwhelming and it really takes your breath away.

Having taken in the view, you need to prepare for more delights as you step into the tent. For a start there's a double bed: a real bed, draped with a thick duvet and soft, furry chocolate-brown throws. There are sofa chairs that open into

haut toupian

Haut Toupian, 30630 Goudargues   00 33 4 66 50 40 71   http://web.me.com/pollycrichton/Luxury_Tents

single beds, a wine-and-cheese fridge, an espresso machine... taking the term 'all mod cons' to a whole new level. The bathroom, tucked away at the back of the tent, has a porcelain loo and basin, jet shower, fluffy towels and dressing gowns, and a range of organic toiletries.

Already this is 5-star camping, but there's more. Haut Toupian's owners are Polly and Hans. Polly is a great cook, who, with a little notice, will prepare a four-course feast using fresh, local produce. Your dinner might well be the highlight of the whole trip. Perfectly griddled scallops served with local peach wine, neat stacks of goats' cheese, aubergine, courgette, tomato and Parmesan, *confit* of duck

with sautéed veg, cherries poached in Merlot, cheeses, and bread. All bursting with local flavour and accompanied by local red and white wines. Polly also prepares traditional continental breakfast; all buttery, melt-in-the-mouth croissants and local jams and cheeses.

In keeping with the lazy mood so easily brought on by good food, great wine, sunshine, and a pool, the countryside around Haut Toupian is sleepy. Horse-riding, cycling, canoeing, and walking are recommended for active types, and for everyone else the region's plentiful wine-tasting tours combine agriculture, history and, of course, regular swigs of velvety reds and crisp whites.

The canal at Goudargues

Adventurous foodies will enjoy exploring the culinary treats in Goudargues, also known as 'Venice of the Gard' – an exaggerated title for somewhere with just one canal. The weekly market (on Wednesdays) is well worth a visit for its cheeses, wines, and sausages in particular. Between Polly's kitchen talents and the village, a stay at Haut Toupian is a treat for the tastebuds, if not the waistline. This is certainly not a cheap camping break, but Haut Toupian's luxurious tents, idyllic location, and sublime food have set a new standard at the very top of the glamping scale.

COOL FACTOR Luxurious accommodation, fantastic food, beautiful scenery – this isn't a campsite it's a sublime, alfresco hotel. The remote country location provides the ultimate escape, but the quality of the accommodation is excellent and Polly's 4-course dinner seals the deal. This site is a rural glamping superstar.

WHO'S IN? Couples, young families, groups (by arrangement) – yes. Tents, campervans, dogs, large groups, young groups – no.

ON SITE Two safari tents with en suite bathrooms. King-sized bed with bedding, bath towels, and dressing gowns, 2 single sofabed chairs that fold out to beds for children, a wine-and-cheese fridge, espresso machine, kettle, lighting, power sockets, a safe, and wi-fi. Bathrooms have loo, basin, and excellent jet shower. No cooking facilities on site. All detergents must be organic as waste water is reused on the land. Each tent is on a platform with terrace out front plus table and chairs. A few steps from the tents there's an unheated pool (shared with the *gîte*) with a resident plastic duck, half a dozen sunloungers, plus chairs and tables.

OFF SITE The tourist office in Goudargues is a great starting point for any local adventures. From there, find information on wine tours and tastings, olive-oil mill tours, horse-riding (a huge paddock with riding tuition is just left as you leave the drive – www.laballade-val-de-ceze.fr), canoeing, golf, climbing, cycling, and walking routes. Culture vultures will enjoy exploring Avignon, Châteauneuf-du-Pape, Orange, and other nearby towns, and for sun worshippers the Med is 2 hours away (but why bother when you've got the pool plus view?). Coincide visits to towns with market days.

FOOD AND DRINK Included are continental breakfast with local cheeses and preserves, and a bottle of wine on arrival. Picnic hampers with local produce available (€22) – great for day trips. Some evenings a 4-course 'tent service' dinner is available. Cooked in her kitchen, using fresh local produce, Polly's table d'hôte rivals the best local restaurants. Off site a local vineyard, Domaine La Rémejeanne, hosts Thursday-morning tours followed by wine-tasting and lunch buffet, €17 per person (00 33 4 66 89 44 51; www.remejeanne.com).

GETTING THERE Train or flight to Avignon or Nîmes. Collection by arrangement, but to explore the area a car is almost essential. By road, as you leave Goudargues, take the left marked Uzès and after 160 yards (150 m) you'll pass Café des Sources. Follow the road for 1¾ miles (3 km) then look for the right turn signed Haut Toupian. From there follow the lane, taking heed of the signs marked Polly-Hans.

PUBLIC TRANSPORT Nîmes and Avignon are each a couple of hours from Goudargues by bus (www.edgard-transport.fr). Local public transport is limited, so bikes or a car are best to make the most of exploring the area.

OPEN End February–end March 2 nights minimum, then end March–end October weekly.

THE DAMAGE Per tent (2 adults and 2 children) from €110 per night to €960 per week June to August, otherwise €785 per week.

languedoc

You'd better take a jaw-sling with you when driving to La Cascade along the Gorges de la Jonte. Because if the views along this scenic chasm (especially the part between Le Rozier and Meyrueis) don't make the lower half of your face succumb to the force of awe-inspired gravity, then the fantastic atmosphere at the campsite will.

While the area around the gorge brims with campsites, the majority are large, commercial and – dare we say – *déclassé*. La Cascade deftly sidesteps any such negative associations by virtue of its location, slightly away from the gorge itself, positioned at an altitude of 2,460 feet (750 m) at the foot of the majestic Causse Méjean.

There's no denying it's big – but big in a large, open, and friendly way, rather than a packed-with-caravans-God-I-can't-breathe-properly way. Rather than welcoming motorhomes and building loud discos, La Cascade's hospitable French owners, Marie-Hélène and Eric Marilou, have kept it deliberately natural, with just a smattering of wooden chalets (13 to be exact) and a huge amount of space for campers.

There are 50 pitches in total, split between two main fields (plus a couple in a delightful little hidden area next to a stream). Wherever you throw up your tent you'll get lots of space and lovely open-sky views, either of the handsome Causse

la cascade

Camping La Cascade, Salvinsac, 48150 Meyrueis   00 33 4 66 45 45 45   www.camping-la-cascade.com

Méjean or the fresh, towering pines on the other side. In the morning the first sounds you're likely to hear are bells and sheep.

Both Marie-Hélène and Eric grew up in the area. Eric's family have long owned the land that La Cascade was built on and, in fact, he can trace his ancestry back an impressive 1,500 years – talk about carrying on the family business. The couple take their environment seriously, which is reflected in the ardent eco-policy of the site (they were awarded the Clef Verte in 2005): 60 per cent of the energy needed to heat the domestic water is solar, two-thirds of the lightbulbs are low-energy consumption, and there's an emphasis on recycling.

There's a fair amount to do on site. A sizeable *boules* court, small library with documentation about the surrounding region, a playground for kids, and a badminton net stretched across one field. You can splash around in the spring and waterfall right next door (which is connected to the River Jonte), hire a bike from the site, or take one of their guided hikes during summer. There's no restaurant on site, but the shop sells lots of excellent local produce.

Since the site is located within the Parc National des Cévennes, there's an abundance of activities off site, too. You have direct access, of course, to the nearby Gorges de la Jonte, which

Canoeing in the
Gorges de la Jonte

offers plenty of climbing, hiking, and cycling opportunities; but the even more spectacular Gorges du Tarn, formed by the Tarn River between the Causse Méjean and the Causse de Sauveterre, is also just a half-hour drive away.

Here you can take walks and drives, enjoy kayak trips or rafting, go fishing, caving, or canyoning… all you'll need are some wheels, a desire for adventure, and your very durable jaw-sling.

COOL FACTOR Spacious and peaceful eco-camping in the Parc National des Cévennes.

WHO'S IN? Tents, campervans, caravans – yes. Dogs, groups – by arrangement in low season only.

ON SITE No campfires allowed, but BBQs okay (if they are raised off the ground); 50 camping pitches; a clean and well-maintained shower and toilet block with 5 showers, 6 toilets, and a dry toilet (all free); washing machine available (€4). *Boules* pitch, kids' playground, free bikes, and table tennis. The onsite shop sells local delicatessen goods and you can also access wi-fi if you need to. Binoculars are available to observe the copious birdlife – vultures, short toad eagles, and more – from the site and on walks.

OFF SITE Hiking in the Cévennes National Park (www.cevennes-parcnational.fr) is a hugely popular activity and there are hikes available for all levels, such as the breezy 3-hour climb up to the Corniches du Causse Méjean, or a hike up to Le Puech Pounchut (also 3 hours), where fabulous 360-degree views of Mont Aigoual and Causse Méjean await. Reception has details on these walks and many more. The Dargilan caves in Meyrueis (00 33 4 66 45 60 20; www.grotte-dargilan.com), discovered in 1880 by a shepherd who was hunting a fox, are a beautiful riot of ochres, yellows, saffron, and pinks, and well worth a visit; La Barbote (00 33 5 65 62 66 26; www.canoekayak-gorgesdutarn.com) is a great place to organise canoeing and rafting in the Gorges du Tarn and de la Jonte, as well as other activities such as via ferrata and climbing. Les Arts du Vide, run by Géraud Fanguin

(00 33 6 81 06 34 96) is also recommended for organising canyoning, climbing, and bird-watching trips in Jonte Gorge. If you'd like to paraglide over the Gorges du Tarn, try Antipodes Millau (00 33 5 65 60 72 03; www.antipodes-millau.com), who are open all year round and organise trips from €70 per person.

FOOD AND DRINK The site serves fresh bread (croissants, pains au chocolat) each morning and has a deli shop selling local produce. Meyrueis has lots of pleasant cafés and restaurants such as Le Jardin des Glaces (00 33 4 66 45 43 75), which serves a delicious *aligot* (potatoes, crème fraîche, Cantal cheese); Hôtel du Mont Aigoual (00 33 4 66 45 65 61; www.hotel-mont-aigoual.com) is one of the best in the area – elegant but still good value, with a *terroir menu* for €20 and gourmet *menus* from €32. Slightly more down to earth, but with consistently good food, is the aptly named Hôtel Family (00 33 4 66 45 60 02; www.hotel-restaurant-family-48-12.com). There are also plenty of smaller restaurants along the river.

GETTING THERE Take A75 to Millau and exit 44/1. Pass through the Gorges du Tarn, Le Rozier, Meyrueis, and take the direction Florac on D996 until you see the sign for La Cascade at the town of Salvinsac. From A75 Marvejols, take N108 to Balsièges, then D986 Ste-Enimie – Meyrueis. Follow directions, as above, to Salvinsac on D996.

OPEN April–September.

THE DAMAGE Tent plus 2 people €11–€17.50, chalet €260–€505.

domaine de pradines

Domaine de Pradines, route de Millau, 30750 Lanuéjols   00 33 4 67 82 73 85   www.domaine-de-pradines.com

If you like your campsites to come with a healthy dose of history, check out Domaine de Pradines. According to official documents connected to the property, the site was once owned by a certain M. Cambacères, a key official in Napoléon's government. Indeed, Napoléon is said to have stayed here during the period of his Egyptian campaign, for which Cambacères planted some trees following the outline of the imperial eagle as a welcoming gesture.

Not impressed? Well, architectural evidence shows that the site harks back at least to the Knights Templar. Still not enough? Okay – how about the discovery of a 4th-century Roman coin on the grounds? (Yes, it really happened.)

Today's incarnation of the campsite is in the capable hands of Virginie (from France) and George (from Scotland), who have been in charge of the place, along with their respective families, since 2006.

Situated slap-bang in the middle of the Parc National des Cévennes and Parc Régional des Grands Causses, Pradines is as idiosyncratic as they come. It boasts Turkmen yurts, a series of vaulted buildings that date back to the 13th century, wooden chalets, and an almost unbelievably large tract of land (370 acres/150 hectares) that's mostly left wild. Almost. Seventy-four acres (30 hectares) have been reserved for the main camping site, a vast and fairly unruly space that has a touch of the savannah about it, helped by the African-style BBQ-eating area and tall, blonde grass.

Campers can choose to take one of the huge spaces around the periphery of the field, or lose themselves completely in the woods. Either way, it's unlikely you'll be disturbed by your neighbours unless they're shouting through a megaphone; and unless you have powerful binoculars, you won't be seeing many of them either.

While the owners admit that the rugged feel of the site isn't for everyone, it'll certainly suit anyone with a sense of adventure or with a yen for nature. Besides, it's not so rough really – the amenities include a shower block ensconced in a charming old vaulted stone barn, a kids' playground, a pool, a restaurant, a reception with a well-stocked shop… you can even get wi-fi here if you need to.

The real idea, though, is to get a bit closer to nature. To take a memorable hike or adrenalin-pumping raft trip through one of the nearby gorges – the Tarn, Jonte, and Dourbie are all within easy reach – outdoor playgrounds that offer a multitude of activities, from climbing and hiking to kayaking, rafting, and canyoning. You can even paraglide if you want to see the area from a bird's-eye perspective. Or explore the forests, granite hills, and magnificent caves of the Cévennes; a decidedly different landscape, also in close proximity. There are places like the charming holiday town of Meyrueis to visit. Or try Millau, once the largest pottery-production site for export throughout the Roman Empire and home to the marvellous Millau Viaduct, the highest bridge in

the world (designed by Sir Norman Foster).

Twice a week the site organises high-season outdoor activities for children, such as playing with bow and arrows or hut-building, and guided walks and maps are available from reception. Plus there's canoeing, climbing, parascending, horse-riding, potholing, and caving nearby, and, of course, the campsite's expansive terrain, which includes wild flowers (including 30 species of wild orchid among other rarities), birds, and butterflies. Maybe you'll find something older than a coin from the 4th century BC. A dinosaur footprint maybe?

COOL FACTOR Wild-style camping in the middle of 2 great national parks.

WHO'S IN? Tents, caravans, tents, cars – yes. Groups by arrangement.

ON SITE Three communal BBQ areas, 50 huge pitches, 48 of which have hook-ups, 9 hot and 2 cold showers (including a hot shower with disabled access), washbasins in cubicles, washing-up sinks, washing machine, and dryer. Swimming and paddling pool, 2 tennis courts, *boules* court, children's playground. Restaurant with a beautiful vaulted ceiling typical of the region, takeaway food options, shop, Internet access, volleyball and badminton courts. No campfires.

OFF SITE An embarrassment of riches awaits. There's the Grotte de Dargilan caves (00 33 4 66 45 60 20; www.grotte-dargilan.com) or the famous Roquefort cheese caves (00 33 5 65 58 56 00; www.roquefort.com); The Micropolis Insectarium will appeal to creepy-crawly lovers of all ages (00 33 5 65 58 50 50; www.micropolis-insectworld.com). Fremyc (00 33 6 58 13 48 48; www.nature-cevennes.com), in Meyrueis, organises rafting, canoeing, walks, bike rides, speleology tours, via ferrata, and more. Airzone Parapente (00 33 6 60 84 76 23; www.airzone-parapente.fr) can organise tandem rides over Millau and the Grands Causses. Randals Bison (00 33 4 67 82 73 74; www.randals-bison.com) offer cowboy-style riding on their bison farm.

FOOD AND DRINK Pradine's auberge serves food in July and August in an ancient building with an impressive stone vault (formerly a Templar chapel). It has a pleasant grassed terrace. The village of Lanuéjols has a hotel-restaurant and bar called Hôtel Bel Air (00 33 4 67 82 72 78; www.hotel-restaurant-belair.com), which is informal and family-run. Meyrueis has a number of different restaurants and bars such as Hôtel Family (00 33 4 66 45 60 02; www.hotel-restaurant-family-48-12.com), Hôtel du Mont Aigoual (00 33 4 66 45 65 61; www.hotel-mont-aigoual.com), which has good food and a down-to-earth atmosphere, and Le Jardin des Glaces (00 33 4 66 45 43 75), which serves up local specialities. For local restaurants, try Ferme Auberge de la Tindelle (00 33 5 65 59 18 39; http://latindelle.pagesperso-orange.fr) and the wonderful Lou Puech in St André de Vézines, which serves excellent hearty and rustic meals from home-grown and local produce. Farms in the region rear unique *brebis* sheep that produce rich milk and fine cheese. Try Au Marché Paysan – Magasin de Producteurs Fermiers in Millau (00 33 5 65 61 39 35).

GETTING THERE Pradines is 40 minutes' drive east of Millau, and 1½ hours north of Montpellier, 2 hours west of Nîmes, 3 hours' drive south of Clermont-Ferrand.

OPEN Camping officially 1 June–15 September, depending on the weather. Yurts can be rented 1 May–15 October. *Gîtes* and apartments open all year (reservation necessary).

THE DAMAGE Tents: 2 adults €10.20–€14 (electricity €3); large yurts (sleep 4) €500 per week (high season), €350 per week (mid season, June, September); small yurt (sleeps 2) €180 per week (high season) and €120 per week (mid-season), tipi €40 (sleeps 2), minimum 3 nights high season.

domaine de belaman

Domaine de Belaman, Belaman, 34330 Fraïsse-sur-Agoût   00 33 4 67 97 59 54   www.belaman.com

Belaman's history dates back to the beginning of the 17th century – maybe even earlier. The landlord De Belaman gave his name to this tiny hamlet, where in the 18th and 19th centuries about 100 people lived. The site is now right where the lord's castle was; built to give a commanding view over his land and people. Iris and Markus bought the *domaine* in 1999 and transformed part of the prairie into a campsite. It's a small but attractive place, a reflection of the couple's preferences for intimate, away-from-it-all campsites. And while Iris and Markus make no claim to being either lady or lord, their pitches still command views every bit as regal as they were centuries ago. In the heart of the Parc Naturel Régional du Haut-Languedoc, the site makes a good start point for hiking, biking, and horse-riding, and there are lots of pretty villages to look at. Before hurrying off, though, bear in mind that the last landlord of Belaman wrote in his will that he had buried gold on the land. The owners say they haven't tried looking for it yet. So we suggest you pack your metal detector, just in case…

COOL FACTOR A small site with big views in the Haut Languedoc regional park.

WHO'S IN? Tents, campervans, caravans (small) – yes. Dogs and groups – by arrangement.

ON SITE Six pitches, 2 toilets, 3 showers, 3 *urinoirs*, 5 basins (1 for laundry, 2 for dishes, 2 for hand-washing), all in a covered area (solar-heated). Free refrigerator. No playground. Campfires not allowed. BBQs okay.

OFF SITE Hiking, horse-riding, mountain-biking, hiking with a donkey (00 33 4 67 97 52 93; www.signoles.com). Canoe or kayak (00 33 4 67 89 52 90; www.canoe-france.com).

FOOD AND DRINK Order bread or breakfast and/or dinner (€18/€10) at the B&B. Best restaurants are Lou Castel in Nages (00 33 5 63 37 06 12) and La Petite Table Tranquille in La Salvetat-sur-Agoût (00 33 4 67 97 24 11).

GETTING THERE From Lyon, A7, then A9 direction Montpellier to Béziers, then direction St-Pons. Mazamet, Castres; D612 to St-Pons, then D907 direction La Salvetat. After 6 miles (10 km) take D169 to Fraisse. Take D14 to Belaman (after ¾ mile/1.5 km).

OPEN Mid May–mid September.

THE DAMAGE €8 per person; child (10–15 years) €4; (4–9 years) €2; electricity €2.

le martinet rouge

Le Martinet Rouge, 11390 Brousses-et-Villaret   00 33 4 68 26 51 98   www.camping-lemartinetrouge.com

Located between Carcassonne and the Montagne Noire, Martinet Rouge is a site of two halves. On the left are campervans and mobile homes, a scene that's generally quite unappealing to campers. But on the right you'll find 63 pitches arranged amid olive and oak trees – and a spread of distinctive boulders that date back to bygone eras. These features give the site its unique feel and will keep kids happy for a surprisingly long time. The excellent facilities will keep them entertained the rest of the time. The large pool (with water slide) is a popular feature, as is the excellently conceived play area, which cunningly combines a football pitch and a basketball court. Over at reception you can play pool or table tennis or slip inside and enjoy a coffee and snack. There's also a lot to lure you away – lovely villages like Aragon and Montolieu, lots of Cathar castles, abbeys, and churches. Nature-lovers will also enjoy the site's proximity to nature; the famous Canal du Midi, forests, lakes, rivers, and caverns. And if you're feeling like sand instead of stones, the beaches of Gruissan or Narbonne are only an hour away.

COOL FACTOR Great facilities and boulders.

WHO'S IN? Tents, campervans, caravans, dogs, large groups, young groups – yes.

ON SITE Sixty-three pitches. Large pool, baby pool. Basketball, football; café-bar, wi-fi, shop. Four wash-blocks.

OFF SITE Site surrounded by castles like majestic Saissac (00 33 4 68 24 46 01; www.saissac.fr). Caves at Limousis (www.showcaves.com), or hire a boat on the Canal du Midi (00 33 6 87 37 24 74; www.embarquement-immediat.net).

FOOD AND DRINK Freshly baked baguettes and croissants daily; snacks all day. Basic meals at the café-bar. Try L'Auberge in Aragon (00 33 4 94 47 71 65; www.fontaines-daragon.com) for great food.

GETTING THERE Site 9 miles (13 km) north of Carcassonne. From Toulouse, southbound A61 to exit 21 Castelnaudry, then wiggly D103 through St-Papoul and Saissac (scenic route); or exit 22, D4 to Bram, east along D6113 and just before Pezers left on to tiny D48 north to Brousses. Left at D103 and follow signs for campsite.

PUBLIC TRANSPORT Take the train to Carcassonne. Daily bus to the village.

OPEN March–September.

THE DAMAGE Tent, 2 people around €20.

solongo

Solongo, La Garrigue, 34360 Pardailhan   00 33 4 67 97 18 08   www.camping-solongo.com

High up in a nameless, south-facing valley, near the little hamlet of La Garrigue, is Solongo, a working farm and campsite that blends a rough-and-ready farming environment with a delightful 'boutique' aesthetic. The site has just three official spaces for tents, but all of them are set in lovely, leafy, quiet locations, with lots of natural shade and space for sunbathing. Since Solongo means 'rainbow' in Mongol, you might not be surprised to find a yurt, which joins the single Romany roulotte, hand-painted, 1920s caravan and a Tibetan tent that doubles as a children's play area, in creating the site's cute and colourful atmosphere.

You'll see chickens and horses roaming around and there's an extensive vegetable garden, the 'fruits' of which supply guests with tasty, home-made breakfasts, lunches, snacks, and evening meals. There's a dining room and a lovely terrace outside as well as a pool where you can take a dip and admire views that stretch right down to the sparkling Med on a clear day. And did we mention that owner Christine is trained in massage and qigong? Aaah. If you can tear yourself away from these delights, you'll find yourself at the gateway of the Parc Naturel Régional du Haut-Languedoc. You can explore the terrain on a site horse, or borrow a map and stroll through the valley to one of the surrounding churches or historical sites. The town of St Chinian is 10 miles (16 km) away; you can be in Béziers in 30 minutes, and at Narbonne and the Med in less than an hour. Peaceful valley peaks or sandy beaches: the choice is yours.

COOL FACTOR Authentic farm-camping with a delightful boutique aesthetic.

WHO'S IN? Tents, campervans, caravans – yes.

ON SITE Three camping pitches, swimming pool, hot showers, washing machine, a communal refrigerator. Yurt and caravans also available for hire. Reception with small shop and a lovely dedicated kids' play area. Campfires not allowed. BBQs okay if raised off the ground.

OFF SITE The site rents horses for rides into the surrounding countryside. The Santiago de Compostela walking trail can be picked up a short stroll away and the Gorges d'Héric Mons-La-Trivalle, accessed from the small village of Mon la Trivalle, has streams and waterfalls to admire and is a good place for a picnic. Canoeing and kayaking are possible in the area (see reception for details).

FOOD AND DRINK Breakfast (€5.50) and dinner (€17 adults, €10 kids) can be prepared on request from Thursday to Sunday. Organic products from the farm (eggs, lavender, fruit, and veg) are available for sale on site, and picnics can also be made for trips. A mobile *boulangerie* also attends the site on Wednesdays and Saturdays (10am). The towns of St Pons and St Chinian (both a 20-minute drive away) have plenty of cafés and restaurants.

GETTING THERE Take A9, turning off at Béziers Ouest. Then take N112 in the direction of St-Pons, turning off at St-Chinian. Take D177 in the direction of Assignan, continue via D178 to Coulouma. At Coulouma, follow the sign indicating La Garrigue via D176.

OPEN May–September.

THE DAMAGE €10 per pitch; €5 per adult, and €4 per child (under 12 years).

la serre

Camping La Serre, 09600 Aigues-Vives   00 33 5 61 03 06 16/00 33 6 81 96 04 23   www.camping-la-serre.com

Robert and Françoise have never been camping. Ask them about it and you'll get a double Gallic shrug, a pair of wry smiles, and the oft-repeated explanation that they've been far too busy running La Serre, the site they've put their hearts and souls into for 20 years. When they initially opened in 1990, the site was basically a large tract of land in the middle of nowhere. Curious visits turned into word-of-mouth recommendations, and the subsequent trickle, two decades later, has turned into a veritable flood. Little wonder: the site today is a fully fledged, award-winning work of wonder. The first impression is the sheer amount of space. This is no higgledy-piggledy campsite with people heaped on top of each other, but an orderly, manicured place with masses of trees, well-kept grass, views, and wide-open skies.

There are 14 wooden chalets on site as well as an area for caravans, but the high hedges mean they're generally unobtrusive. Plus the 46-pitch tent area is also separate and comes with similarly vast, enclosed terraces that are shaded by ancient oaks, thoughtfully placed so as not to obscure the views. The site is connected via large walkways that have their own names, underlining the impression that you're in a self-contained universe here. The reception area is fairly simple – a small cabin with an adjacent basic laundry room, a naturalist's library, and tourist information leaflets. The owners are always at hand to give out advice, maps, cycling circuits, and more.

Around the corner there's a decent-sized pool and an area with a badminton net, slides, and a football pitch. On the other side of the reception wall lies a huge warehouse filled with farming equipment – an eco-museum, no less, started by Robert a few years ago and expanded through donations from the local community to give a thorough picture of regional farming practices over the last century or so. In the summer months the site also organises weekly programmes that include slide shows, an eco-tourism day (Thursdays), where each family creates an activity to share with others, and a local (organic) product-tasting evening with local farmers, who bring their wines and goods to sample. Large and spacious as it is, the campsite only takes up a small portion of the total 170 acres (70 hectares). Some of this space is used by the 100 or so sheep the couple breeds, but another 15 acres (6 hectares) have been turned into a wild nature reserve that houses various species of orchids, birds, and butterflies. Campers have access to well-marked trails through the area, which has information points about the flora and fauna along the way.

As for those awards – the Clef Verte and Camping Quality hallmarks and involvement in La Via Natura and the French Federation for Ecotourism – they were earned for the campsite's ardent commitment to the environment. The black water pipes that run around the edge of the site are heated by the sun and generate hot water for the showers, and the predominant building materials are stone and wood.

The site is close to two towns. Lavelanet, the bigger, has a couple of cafés, but not much more. A ten-minute drive the other way is Mirepoix, a small but charming town. The surrounding countryside is a pleasure to explore, with plenty of peaks for cyclists to take on, pretty villages to discover, and larger cities, such as Toulouse, to visit. You can even be at the Mediterranean in an hour and a half. Most people just relax on site, soaking up the atmosphere. Robert and Françoise may have never been on a wonderful camping holiday themselves – but they sure know how to host one.

COOL FACTOR Giant pitches and an onsite nature reserve at this award-winning eco-campsite.

WHO'S IN? Caravans, campervans, tents, groups, dogs – yes.

ON SITE Forty-six very large pitches, protected by trees. Swimming pool, washing machine (€5), huge children's play area, 4 clean and decent lavatory and shower blocks (free), nature reserve and eco-museum on site (both free).

OFF SITE Bikes can be arranged through the site, or you can make a call to Vélomondo (00 33 6 31 94 24 91; www.velomondo.com), who deliver bikes and can advise on routes. Adults and kids alike will love the Parc de la Préhistoire (00 33 5 61 05 10 10; www.sesta.fr) in Tarascon, which has outdoor installations showing how caves are formed by water flowing over rock, examples of the types of shelters used in Magdalenian times, and replicas and photos of drawings and paintings found in other caves. There's also a restaurant and picnic area. If you enjoyed La Serre's eco-museum, the Forges de Pyrène in Montgailhard (00 33 5 34 09 30 60; www.sesta.fr) comprises several different areas in a pretty park that's set in some beautiful scenery. There are exhibitions on sabot-making, and horn-comb manufacture, plus an old forge and bakery. The beautiful 10th-century Château de Foix (00 33 5 34 09 83 83) is one of the key Cathar sights located near the town of Foix. Pre-history, in the shape of rock drawings, can be found in the Grotte du Mas d'Azil (00 33 5 61 69 97 71; www.grotte-masdazil.com), and the small prehistory museum in the nearby village of Mas-d'Azil. Castle-lovers will not want to miss the formidable Château de Montségur, which has been listed as a *monument historique* by the French Ministry of Culture since 1862.

FOOD AND DRINK The site sells fresh baguettes, croissants, and coffee in the morning, as well as excellent bio wines from local producer Coteaux d'Engraviès (00 33 5 61 68 68 68; www.coteauxdengravies.com). There are local food- and wine-tastings once a week on site during July and August. In the tiny town of Léran you'll find a very nice British-run bistro called Le Rendezvous (00 33 9 51 42 47 91), which has good lunches and evening meals as well as free wi-fi access and regular music nights. Mirepoix has several decent restaurants, the best perhaps being Le Comptoir Gourmand (00 33 5 61 68 19 19; www.lecomptoirgourmand.com), whose elegant meals are made from regional produce.

GETTING THERE The site is accessed via D625, between Mirepoix and Lavelanet. It is well signposted from both of these towns.

OPEN April–September.

THE DAMAGE Low season €14 for 2 people plus tent. July/August €21 for 2 people plus tent. €2 for dogs; extra person €7. Mobile homes €100 for 2 people for 2 nights, €330 for a week (low season), €380–€630 (high season).

belrepayre trailer park

BelRepayre Airstream & Retro Trailer Park, nr Mirepoix   00 33 5 61 68 11 99   www.airstreameurope.com

A couple of decades ago, Perry Balfour and his wife, Coline, set about transforming a beautiful part of the Ariège countryside into a themed trailer park. Locating an impressive collection of 15 Airstreams, the pair painstakingly restored each one to its former glory, then decked them out in 1970s-era fabrics and flea-market paraphernalia. Most of these glistening beauties have come all the way from America, although one, transformed into a distinctive, colourful diner called Apollo Lounge, was discovered sitting under the Eiffel Tower.

Though the exteriors look majestic – especially when winking simultaneously in the Ariège sunshine – the interiors look even better, with their tiny bathrooms and showers, funky bedrooms, and plethora of aptly psychedelic touches that includes floral curtains, retro crockery, black-and-white TVs and even an eight-track music system. Sliding in a scratchy Sly and the Family Stone cassette and putting your feet up on the sun lounger outside is a pretty cool experience, to say the least. There's not much else on site save for an activities field, a nearby wood to explore, and a small store at reception. In the evenings, all the action is centred around the neon playground known as the Apollo Lounge, where Coline serves up tasty French food and wine and Perry, cunningly disguised as DJ Bobby Lotion, lives out his pop-star fantasies, spinning everything from Motown to rock 'n' roll and disco on vinyl.

If ever there was a campsite to help you trip back in time – this is it..

COOL FACTOR Airstream trailers, vintage caravans, and campers (retro tents preferred). Europe's first retro Airstream trailer park, in the foothills of the Pyrénées.

WHO'S IN? Tents, vintage caravans, camping cars, groups – yes. Pets – not in the Airstreams.

ON SITE Retro Apollo Lounge; 10 Airstreams for rent, each equipped with furniture and kitchen; a slightly old-fashioned but well-maintained block with 3 toilets and 3 showers; field next to reception caters for tenters and, increasingly, VWs. Sauna, yoga room, table tennis, badminton, bike tracks, outdoor cinema screen, small shop. No campfires.

OFF SITE Hiking and mountain-biking; bikes rented on site or delivered (00 33 6 31 94 24 91; www.velomondo. com). Medieval castles close by, the marvellous Château de Montségur included. Discover Ariège by microlight with Partag'air (00 33 5 61 01 92 00) in Troye-d'Ariège.

FOOD AND DRINK Decent organic food on site in the evenings plus local produce. Apollo Lounge well stocked with beer and wine. The Airstreams have cooking facilities. Mirepoix has great cafés and restaurants, and a good farmers' market every Monday on place du Maréchal Leclerc. Try Le Comptoir Gourmand (00 33 5 61 68 19 19), where you can feast on mussels and monkfish in a converted barn.

GETTING THERE Near Mirepoix. Full directions on booking. Fly to Carcassonne, get to Pamiers or Toulouse by train, then hire a car or Perry may be able to pick you up. Or, arrive in your own classic car to get a 10 per cent discount.

OPEN End April–September.

THE DAMAGE Pitch and 2 people €20–€30 per night. Airstream €80 per night to €785 a week (sleeps 2 or 4). Three rates: 1 or 2 nights, 3 nights plus, 7 nights. Sheets, towels, cleaning extra (not for the 1- or 2-nighters).

roussillon

les criques de porteils

Les Criques de Porteils, Corniche de Collioure, 66700 Argelès-sur-Mer   00 33 4 68 81 12 73   www.lescriques.com

You'll find Les Criques de Porteils tucked away near the pretty university town of Collioure, around 15 miles (24 km) south of Perpignan. Shaded by an elegant spread of green trees, the site occupies a stellar location atop a winding clifftop, looking out on to the calm, coruscating waters of the Mediterranean. It's not the easiest place to find, but it is worth seeking out, even if the first thing that strikes is the deceptively sizeable and sprawling nature of the place. It's an undeniably commercial site, with mobile units and beach houses, a buzzing restaurant, and a large wash-block, but beyond these you'll find a run of sea-facing camping pitches and, at the other end of the site, a couple more sheltered camping areas that are among the best in this part of France. Inevitably, competition for the sea-facing pitches is high, and even if you do bag one (book ahead), the tents can feel slightly on top of one another. Therefore if it's privacy you seek, this place really might not be for you. But if you're willing to compromise a little bit of intimacy then the rewards are bountiful.

The site organises a lot of events, from wine-tasting to golf, adventure parks, and day-tripping to Spain. The aforementioned restaurant has wi-fi as well as decent food. And, best of all, you get access to the secluded pebble beaches at the foot of the cliffs, where you can swim, paddle, or even take scuba-diving lessons. Or you can sunbathe outside your tent, dozing gently to the sound of the lapping sea and the pleasantly distant echo of the more active folk below.

COOL FACTOR   Sun, sea, sand, and sangria.

WHO'S IN?   Tents, caravans, motorhomes, dogs (on leads), groups – yes.

ON SITE   A total of 250 tent pitches, 40 mobile homes (sleep 6), and 10 Bengali tents (sleep 5). There are 3 shower blocks, a launderette, recycling bins, Internet, a heated swimming pool, tennis, *boules*, restaurant/bar/takeaway, and a place for golf practice. Diving lessons available on site (starting at €10). No BBQs or campfires.

OFF SITE   The narrowest caves in the world, Gorges de la Fou (00 33 4 68 39 16 21; www.les-gorges-de-la-fou.com) are in Arles-sur-Tech and there are a number of fortresses to choose from, including the impressive Fortresse de Salses (00 33 4 68 38 60 13; www.salses.monuments-nationaux.fr).

FOOD AND DRINK   For Catalan fare (and for fish-lovers) try Collioure's Casa Léon (00 33 4 68 82 10 74); the Cinquième Péché (00 33 4 68 98 09 76), also in Collioure, offers French cuisine. For wine-tasting with a difference, try the Ferme Auberge Les Clos de Paulilles (00 33 4 68 98 07 58; www.clos-de-paulilles.com) at Port-Vendres.

GETTING THERE   From Perpignan airport, take the A9 turning off at exit 43 at Le Boulou. Follow signs to Argelès-sur-Mer, then follow D914 towards Collioure. Turn off at exit 13 and after 328 yards (300 m) on your right is Hôtel du Golfe. Follow the road and signposts for the site.

PUBLIC TRANSPORT   Take the train from Perpignan to Collioure; the campsite is just over 1 mile (2 km) away.

OPEN   Early April–end October.

THE DAMAGE   Prices €20.50–€38 for a tent and 2 people per night. Upgrading to a Bengali tent costs €169–€689 per week, depending on season. If you turn up without booking and there's space you can stay up to 3 nights.

mas de la fargassa

Mas de la Fargassa, Montalba, 66110 Amélie-les-Bains   00 33 4 68 39 01 15/00 33 6 16 93 02 73   www.fargassa.com

Mas de la Fargassa, high up in the Pyrénées and 20 minutes from the nearest town, is hidden away amid a dense wonderland of trees and farmland bisected by an atmospheric mountain creek.

It took owner, Madhu, several years of travelling down never-ending roads to find this dream location. One day, 11 years ago, she caught a glimpse of chimney smoke rising through a clearing in the trees. The owner of that particular home wasn't selling, but next door was: a dilapidated forge that had been uninhabited since the 1930s. Madhu and her partner snapped it up, along with the surrounding 600 acres (243 hectares), then set to work transforming rubbles of stone into fully functional, modern accommodation. Nowadays, they hire out a *gîte*, a chalet, and a pig sty, which in total sleep 18 people.

The camping area was inaugurated some seven years ago, with six Dutch-designed De Waard Albatros tents named after the trees they're next to (holly and plum, for example). They sit either by the stream or on a raised level overlooking the garden. The pitches are well spread out, meaning you have a lot of privacy. As well as a pre-erected tent (big enough for 4-5 people), you also receive home comforts such as mattresses, a cooking hob, a fridge, and picnic tables.

There's also an organic fruit farm connected to the property that sells plums, apples, strawberries, gooseberries, raspberries, pears, and organic bread, which is sold each week at the excellent Céret market on Saturdays. Madhu doesn't manage this all alone, of course: the farm offers work placements to WOOFers (World Wide Opportunities on Organic Farms) from all around the world in exchange for free accommodation and food. These volunteers are a big part of the atmosphere at Fargassa; arriving here is a bit like being welcomed into a family, thanks to the camaraderie of the workers and the fact that most people stay here for a week or two (at least). Because of this the site feels far less transitional than many, especially in the evenings when the campfire is lit and people eat at the communal table, which can hold up to 50 people.

There are plenty of things for kids to do: swing on the trees, swim, or splash about in the river. They can cook marshmallows over the fire, or even go for donkey rides. Outdoor enthusiasts will enjoy the many miles of well-marked trails – so many, in fact, that you'll rarely encounter another hiker. A long-distance, coast-to-coast footpath crosses the property and ancient paved mule trails lead to nearby villages, past abandoned farmhouses, chapels, and to Spain. There are two-hour and five-hour organised walks available. If you came in your own 4x4 you'll be able to make it over rocky terrain by car, maybe passing a few wild boars on the way. If you do mosey across the border, it might be worth checking out the 15th-century Fortresse de Salses, whose layout and architecture present a rare example of the transition between medieval castle and the fortresses of the modern period. Madhu also

arranges regular group outings, where you can hike to a Spanish restaurant for supper, after which cars will bring you back. Anyone who's trekked to far-fetched lands will be impressed with the journey to get here. The windy path that cuts through the mountains is certainly something to behold – some might avoid looking down, but others rate the precipitous view of the Gorges du Mondony as one of their holiday highlights. Either way, once you've climbed to the dizzying heights of Fargassa, you might never want to come back down again.

COOL FACTOR Chilled and sociable mountain camping.

WHO'S IN? Tents (selected times) – yes. Caravans, campervans, dogs, groups – no.

ON SITE Communal fire at night. Six pitches, with pre-erected tents. Internet connection in the kitchen (cable, but no wi-fi). Hot showers, kids' play area, site shop, and a shared BBQ area. No campfires allowed.

OFF SITE Plenty of mountain-hiking available (for all levels of fitness) accessible from Fargassa (ask at reception), and donkey rides can be arranged on site, too. Prats de Mollo la Preste (www.pratsdemollolapreste.com), a tiny, medieval maze, has lots of cafés and daily afternoon 'knight' shows at the Fort Lagarde (3.30pm). The lovely Gorges de la Fou (00 33 4 68 39 16 21), located in the Tech Valley, west of Céret, now have a 1-mile (2-km) walkway that's safe and good for families. History buffs will love the 8th-century Abbaye Ste-Marie (00 33 4 68 83 90 66; www.tourisme-haut-vallespir. com) or the remarkable 15th-century Fortresse de Salses (00 33 4 68 38 60 13; www.salses.monuments-nationaux.fr,) on the Spanish side of the mountains. Kids may get more of a kick from the Museum of Dinosaurs (00 33 4 68 74 26 88; www.dinosauria.org) in Espéraza. Céret is a pleasant day out with cafés, cobbled streets, and the excellent Musée d'Art Moderne (00 33 4 68 87 27 76; www.musee-ceret.com).

FOOD AND DRINK Site shop is fairly comprehensive, with basics such as bread, milk, coffee, and wine, but also pasta, sauces, bio-products, and more (no meat products). Home-baked bread, jams, chutneys, and organic vegetables and fruits. Vegetarian suppers served twice a week (€10 per person, €6 for kids). Regular communal 'pot luck' gatherings. Nearest and best restaurants are in Céret; La Praline (00 33 4 68 87 71 21 10) has not only great chocolates and sweet treats, but serves good lunches, too. For evening meals, try the simple, atmospheric La Fontaine (00 33 4 68 87 23 47), or Les Caves Mouragues in Arles-sur-Tech (00 33 4 68 54 97 72), where you can munch good pizza in the garden.

GETTING THERE From the A9 (Perpignan direction Barcelona) take the last exit before the Spanish border. Leave A9 and follow D115 direction Céret and Amélie-les-Bains-Palalda. Drive through Amélie-les-Bains until you see the 'end of Amélie-les-Bains' sign opposite a car park. Turn left, take D53 direction Montalbà and Mas Pagris. After 328 yards (300 m) go right (route Montalbà l'Église). Follow this road for about 2½ miles (4 km) until the road forks; keep to the right, direction Mas Pagris. After ½ mile (1 km) the road becomes narrow. After Mas Pagris cross the bridge over the River Therme. Go another 1 mile (2 km) until the first letterbox with a sign saying La Fargassa.

PUBLIC TRANSPORT Bus from Perpignan to Amélie-les-Bains. It's a 2-hour walk or they may be able to pick you up.

OPEN April–mid October; other accommodation open all year. May is a great time for cherry blossom.

THE DAMAGE 6 equipped tents €450 per week. Chalet (sleeps 5–6) €550 per week. 2 apartments (sleep 2 or 9) €350/€1025 per week. Campers with own tents €10 per person per night (no camping with own tents July/Aug).

la solane

La Solane, Mas de la Solane, 66260 St-Laurent-de-Cerdans   00 33 6 16 93 02 73   www.solane.info

La Solane means 'on the sunny side' in Spanish, which says a lot about this marvellous site hidden away in the French Pyrénées. Facing south towards the nearby Spanish border, it's perfectly placed to catch the sun as it rises behind the Spanish peaks. The simple pleasure of waking up to watch and feel the sun's golden rays as they filter through the site's chestnut, linden, and fruit trees and across the scenic mountain landscape is reason enough to stay here. And there's not a trace of civilisation to be seen.

Dutch couple Eva and Jeroen converted the site from an overgrown tangle of mountain vegetation and a couple of abandoned farmhouses into the beautiful place it is today. They cleared the area, carved terraces into the hillside, and converted one of the farmhouses into a reception. Being eco-minded, they built a hydro-ram pump to generate water from the local rivers and constructed solar panels for electricity. The six generously sized, atmospheric pitches are all well shaded and well spaced out. Except for the large, new swimming pool, there's just a reception area, a couple of hot showers, and a washing-up area (and a nice campfire area, where guests can mingle at night). There's no playground, as such, but the kids will love exploring surrounding woods and sploshing around in the nearby river. Tree houses are being built and one of the farmhouses is being sensitively transformed into *gîte*-style lodging. There's also an indoor pool and sauna complex planned, but the owners promise that it won't impinge on the site's sun-kissed, natural vibe.

COOL FACTOR Remote camping in the middle of the Pyrénées.

WHO'S IN? Tents, campervans, tent-trailers – yes. Caravans – no.

ON SITE Campfires allowed on the terrace and on site if weather permits. There are 6 tent pitches in total, plus a wooden family cabin; 2 new showers and 2 toilets; washing-up area with great views; a river with natural swimming pools and a waterfall. Tree houses and swimming pool. Indoor pool and sauna planned.

OFF SITE Hikers will enjoy the walks through the mountains, not least the GR10 – try the hike to the rocky peak of the Roc de San Salvador (4,050 feet/1,234 m). The lovely medieval Spanish town of Maçanet de Cabrenys is a 45-minute drive away (www.massanetdecabrenys.com).

FOOD AND DRINK Basics on site, and a well-stocked kitchen. Three-course evening meals available (€12.50; €7.50 for kids). Closest supermarket St-Laurent, a 25-minute drive. Best market in Céret (Saturdays). Nearby Tapis has a large restaurant (00 33 9 72 54 33 11; www.canmach.com) serving hearty cuisine for good prices. Maçanet de Cabrenys has several nice restaurants serving Catalan/Spanish food, the best being Hôtel Pirineus (00 33 9 72 54 40 00).

GETTING THERE Last exit 'Le Boulou' on A9 in France, then D115 into Vallespir Valley; after Arles-sur-Tech take road to St-Laurent-de-Cerdans. Follow the signs saying La Boadella and, after a while, La Solane.

PUBLIC TRANSPORT Train to Perpignan and bus (Courrier Catalan, Line 341, €1.5, 6 times daily) to Amélie-les-Bains or St-Laurent-de-Cerdans: pick-up can be arranged.

OPEN May–October (any other time of year on request).

THE DAMAGE Family of 4, own tent (summer) €30.

l'orri des planès

L'Orri des Planès, Cases del Mitg, 66210 Planès   00 33 4 68 04 29 47   www.orrideplanes.com

'Rustic boutique' is perhaps a good way to describe L'Orri des Planès; a small but perfectly formed campsite nestled atop the lovely Planès Valley. Owner Arif originally came here to transform a ruined farmhouse into a rustic 10-room lodge for nature-lovers. A few years on and he's added a lovely pool, dorm-style hiking lodge, and four yurt-style eco-tents, which come with circular wooden floors, futons, pillows, chill-boxes for food, cooking sets, and camping chairs.

There's also space for four tents if you want to bring your own, though short-term tenting is preferred as a courtesy to passing cyclists and hikers. There's a covered eating area for campers, with a BBQ grill and twin-burner stove; picnic tables are dotted around, and round the back you'll find a nice stream that the kids can play in.

As well as being impressively eco-friendly (solar installation, water-consumption limiters, and discounts for guests arriving by public transport), L'Orri's maison d'hôtes is one of the best places to eat in the area, by a long shot.

The site also works with around 30 local producers, who supply the place with everything from cheese and veal to honey and wine. You can buy their products from L'Orri's shop, but Arif will happily give you directions to the farms themselves.

With the GR10 Trans-Pyrénées walking trail, nearby hot springs, and a beautiful nature reserve within walking distance, as well as the entire Pyrénées region at your disposal, this is a great place to immerse yourself in nature – and food.

COOL FACTOR Eco-camping with a foodie twist.

WHO'S IN? Tent campers (backpackers and short stays only), large and young groups, well-behaved dogs – yes. Campervans, caravans – no

ON SITE Campfires are okay. Four eco-yurts, plus space for 4 tents; modern toilets and showers in the hiking lodge; pool access (solar-heated); bar service on poolside terrace; site shop selling hiking maps and regional products; meals in the lodge (booking essential); self-service laundry (€5 per load); wooden picnic shelter, washing-up area.

OFF SITE St-Thomas hot springs (00 33 4 68 97 03 13; www.bains-saint-thomas.fr) are an hour's walk (€2/€3 entrance). Mont-Louis (00 33 4 68 04 21 97; www.mont-louis.net) is the highest fortified citadel in France.

FOOD AND DRINK The best place to eat is at L'Orri, just below the campsite. If there's no space, visit surrounding farms for excellent meats, cheeses, and charcuterie. There's also a crêperie at Mont-Louis that does lunches and crêpes.

GETTING THERE From Perpignan highway N116 to Mont-Louis, then D32 through La Cabanasse to Planès. The town is at the end of this road and L'Orri is in the upper part of the town. Follow signs in town.

PUBLIC TRANSPORT Planès station is on the Yellow Train line, which connects Villefranche-de-Conflent (and Perpignan) with Latour-de-Carol (and Toulouse or Barcelona). Passengers must ask to stop at Planès station. To get to the town, follow the trail up the valley for about 20 minutes.

OPEN Campground June–September. Lodge June–September and December–March.

THE DAMAGE 4-person tents €60 per night, €50 per night for 2 plus nights; €300 per week (off season €50/€40/€200). Pitch your own tent €7.50 per person per night.

midi-pyrénées

la ferme de lacan

La Ferme de Lacan, Lacan, 12290 Ségur   00 33 5 65 70 64 21   www.lafermedelacan.com

Ostensibly a working farm that has turned some spare land into half a dozen terraced pitches, La Ferme de Lacan offers a splash of bucolic French farming life. Nathalie and Gilles Gaubert have been running the farm since 1989, employing a 'human-scale' style of agriculture and emphasising the links between rural and wider society to inspire people to eat locally. They have cattle and goats, have recently diversified into donkeys, and they grow their own vegetables, which they offer table d'hôte a couple of times a week to campers. Most of the pitches are shaded by trees and have lovely views of the surrounding hills.

You can also hire horses for rides around the paddock or donkeys for longer excursions into the woods. Other than that you're pretty much left to your own devices. Not that you'll be left twiddling your thumbs. There are lovely villages to explore and the farm offers excellent access to the nearby Gorges du Tarn and the Parc Naturel Régional des Grands Causses. Or spend the day watching the wildlife mooch around and the wind turbines twirl lazily as you breathe in some genuine countryside air.

COOL FACTOR Camp on an authentic working farm in lovely French countryside.

WHO'S IN? Tents and dogs – yes. Caravans and campervans – by arrangement.

ON SITE Six pitches, large garden with shaded areas and bathrooms (in a barn). Horse hire €7 an hour, or arrange donkey trips for 1–3 days (€30–€200). No campfires.

OFF SITE The Gorges du Tarn and the Parc Naturel Régional des Grands Causses are close by with lots of walking and cycling trails and kayaking and canoeing. Lake Lévezou is good for a picnic, and the town of Millau – which is famed for its nearby viaduct and water sports – is just a 30-minute drive.

FOOD AND DRINK Tasty home-made meals are served twice a week in the farmhouse (€17 adults; €12 kids).

GETTING THERE The closest airport to Ségur is Rodez-Marcillac Airport 19 miles (30 km) away. Lacan is halfway between Rodez and Millau. It's located 20 minutes from A75 motorway and the Millau Viaduct, which can be reached via D911. Keep following the camping signs to the tiny hamlet of Lacan.

OPEN April–October.

THE DAMAGE Adult €5, child (under 3 years) €3.

les chalets du tarn

Les Chalets du Tarn, Le Pont de Lincou, 12170 Réquista   00 33 5 65 72 34 84   www.leschaletsdutarn.com

Les Chalets du Tarn is a bit of a local camping secret. Cut into a gorge at Pont de Lincou, where the River Tarn idles gently by, the site is located right next to the Château de Lincou and enjoys a scenic, yet tucked away, feel.

Run by Valérie and Frédéric, who came here in a bid to escape Paris and find a good life in the countryside, it has 15 chalets and 21 pleasant pitches scattered among a thicket of forest trees. The feel of the site is slightly rambling and old-fashioned when compared to many modern French sites, but it's a homely and surprisingly cosmopolitan kind of place.

People tend to congregate around the reception area, where you can enjoy pizza, paella, chicken, and regional specialities a few days a week. You can relax in a hammock, or play *boules* or table tennis in one of the two play areas.

Local villages, such as Lincou, will charm you, as will other nearby attractions such as Brousse-le-Château, one of the most beautiful villages in all France, Roupeyrac's old mill and – one for the cheese-lovers – the Roquefort caves.

COOL FACTOR Tranquil, riverside site in hidden valley.

WHO'S IN Tents, caravans, campervans, groups, dogs – yes.

ON SITE Fifteen chalets and 21 pitches; reception, shop, and café. Small play area and *boules* court. Four cubicle toilets, 3 urinals, 4 showers, 4 sinks. Washing machine and dryer (€3.50 each). No campfires, but there are fixed BBQs.

OFF SITE Brousse-le-Château and its chateau is worth visiting (http://brousselechateau.free.fr), as is Château de Coupiac (00 33 5 65 99 79 45; www.chateaudecoupiac.com).

FOOD AND DRINK Onsite bar offers evening meals. Try La Planquette in Réquista (00 33 5 65 46 60 00; www.hotel-planquette-aveyron.com) for good regional food.

GETTING THERE A68 gets you to Albi. From there take D903 to Réquista, pass the church and turn left on D902 to River Tarn. Long drive from Clermont-Ferrand (exit Millau) on A75, then east on D908, then north on D902. Follow D2088 from Rodez on to D902, also south, to the river.

PUBLIC TRANSPORT Ryanair fly to Rodez from London Stansted, otherwise Toulouse is the nearest airport. Trains run to Rodez. Buses between Réquista and Rodez.

OPEN Mid June–mid September. Chalets available March.

THE DAMAGE Tent and 2 people €13–€16 per night. Chalets €270–€550.

le bourg de belcastel

Le Bourg de Belcastel, Le Bourg, 12390 Belcastel   00 33 5 65 64 52 25

In the words of Bjork, 'It's, oh, so quiet.' We're in the heart of the Aveyron, one of France's largest, least-populated, *départements* and, we might venture, one of its most beautiful, yet there's hardly a soul to be seen. It's high season, after all. A time when, at tourist hotspots the roads are choked with traffic and café tables permanently taken.

Here in Belcastel village, though, home to just 200 residents, you can enjoy a slice of France unspoilt by mass tourism and, crucially, pitch up at one of the most perfectly placed campsites ever. Your temporary home is right by the river, with the village's 11th-century chateau towering above. Next to it lies a spread of ancient houses, set on cobbled streets, nestling on wooded slopes along the river bank. The site also sits next to a hump-backed gothic bridge, which virtually demands an impromptu game of Pooh Sticks. It's easy to see why this has been officially voted one of the most beautiful villages in France.

Anna and Jean-Bernard took over the campsite in 2009, and it had previously been run by Jean-Bernard's grandmother for over 30 years. Their decision to take it on was based purely on quality of life. Even in July and August it feels very relaxed here. The peace and quiet attracts writers and painters and some stunning paintings have been produced by guests right here on the river bank. More active types can enjoy kayaking, world-class trekking, and mountain-biking in the area, but for many a bottle of decent local wine and the sound of silence suits just fine.

COOL FACTOR You're just a few feet from a crystal-clear river and in the shadow of a truly imposing chateau.

WHO'S IN? Tents, campervans, caravans, kids, large groups, young groups, dogs – yes.

ON SITE Thirty pitches for caravans, tents, and campervans plus 10 pitches at Camping Le Bourg, 328 yards (300 m) from the village entrance. Shower block with 4 shower rooms. Lots of hot water. Separate hand-washing, laundry room. Disabled access, shaded play area, tennis court (rackets for hire), table-tennis table (bats and balls for hire), mountain bikes for hire and wi-fi on the terrace. Store has local produce, including some decent wine from the region. Hand-made jewellery for sale. BBQs allowed in specified areas. No campfires.

OFF SITE Home to over a dozen villages officially listed as 'Les Plus Beaux Villages de France'. Cordes-sur-Ciel and Albi are also within an hour's drive.

FOOD AND DRINK Lovely picnic area across the bridge. Site-owner Anna also runs a small bistro (Chez Anna) next to the site, offering simple, home-cooked food. The village also boasts a 1-Michelin-starred restaurant Hôtel-Restaurant du Vieux Pont (00 33 5 65 64 52 29; www.hotelbelcastel. com). The prices are in 'special treat' territory. Better value is Restaurant 1909 (00 33 5 65 64 52 26) on the opposite side of the river, offering set-price menus (€19.50, €26, and €36).

GETTING THERE Belcastel is a 30–40-minute drive from Rodez-Marcillac airport, in the north-west of the Aveyron department. Sat-nav works pretty well and the village is well signposted.

OPEN April–October.

THE DAMAGE €7–€11 per night, depending on size of pitch and time of year. Dogs €1 per night.

le camp

Le Camp, 82330 Varen   00 33 6 11 94 33 68   www.lecamp.co.uk

If there's a better feeling than that of gliding smoothly through a crystal-clear 'natural' swimming pool, while eye to eye with frogs perched nonchalantly on rocks, then we've yet to experience it. The chirp of crickets, the buzz of dragonflies, birdsong, and, of course, the croaking chorus of those ubiquitous frogs provide the soundtrack to this wonderfully wild swim. It proves the perfect introduction to Le Camp, a secluded site in south-west France, set in leafy surroundings, which combines 5-star facilities with a truly relaxed atmosphere.

The site is owned and run by Sally and Stephen O'Hare, a British couple, who in 2007 gave up high-flying jobs as, respectively, a headhunter and a top exec at Google, to set up the sort of camp that they would want to stay at. They were looking to create something small, personal, comfortable, and natural, especially with kids in mind, as it's well known that kids don't like 5-star hotels, even if their parents do. Here, children can run around in a safe, beautiful setting while mums and dads can relax and feel treated.

These treats, as the visitor will discover, are many and varied. From the fluffy towels (John Lewis, natch) in each of the tents and yurts, to the large hand-made double beds, feather pillows, and clever in-room composting toilets (saving you a bleary late-night stroll to the toilet block), this is camping with the rough edges smoothed off. Take breakfast, for example. Where morning in most sites might see you struggling to fire up a primus stove and slowly rustle up something to start the day, Le Camp takes the strain out of *le petit dejeuner*. Head to the 'snug' from 7am onwards to enjoy proper lattes from a machine that wouldn't look out of place in Starbucks, fresh pastries, local cured meats, cheese, yogurt, and fantastic baguettes, all overseen by the tireless Sally. And all, crucially, included in the price of your stay.

Don't worry, though, the essential spirit of camping still remains. The central cooking area lets different visitors meet and chat while they prepare dinner, but there's none of that cringeworthy group activity action. Sure, there's a little court set up for an impromptu game of *pétanque* and a volleyball net hangs ready for the more energetically minded types to make use of, but there are no chalked-up league tables or (shudder) happy-camper types urging you to join in the fun. The vibe is as natural as the surroundings.

And what surroundings. Even an attempt to be blasé about them falls flat. Let's try. The view from your temporary home is just of standard lush countryside, surrounded by the requisite soaring mountains and flanked by the usual handsome French villages. See, it just doesn't work.

Sitting in the stunning Aveyron Valley, in the Midi-Pyrénées region, this formerly run-down, 38-pitch campsite, discovered while the owners were on holiday, now numbers just six tents. There are three safari-style ones, two woodland yurts, and one 'giant' yurt, with the latter boasting its own sandpit, firepit, and shaded seating area.

As you'd expect, this site's eco-credentials are impressive. The resident pig gobbles up the remains of breakfast, 'grey' water is recycled, and the pool is cleaned naturally by gravel and plants. Local products (such as bathroom toiletries) are used as much as possible and most of the furniture has been hand-made by Stephen himself. His transformation from high-flying Google exec to capable man-of-the-woods type is one that he clearly relishes. It's an incredible place to bring up children, he says, and every day is an outdoor adventure.

COOL FACTOR The most refreshing campsite pool you'll ever swim in, plus thoughtful touches of luxury throughout.
WHO'S IN? Kids, large groups, young groups – yes. Tents, campervans, caravans, dogs – no.
ON SITE Campfires allowed under supervision. Six tents on pitches picked for privacy and great views. All have wide beds, solar lighting and, in all but the 2 woodland yurts, dry composting toilets. Shower block houses 3 super-clean shower rooms, plus an additional shower in the disabled facility. Lots of hot water; organic, locally produced, bath products. Full range of kitchen appliances, crockery, utensils, condiments. Snug block offers complementary breakfast, selection of books, magazines and games, wood-burning stove. Recharging facilities, but no power sources in tents. There is wi-fi and a small office facility. Free laundry facility. BBQ and salad/herb garden to help yourself to. For kids, cot, sheet, blanket, or camp bed and duvet, baby bath, baby chair, high chair, changing station, steriliser, baby monitor, plastic cups, plates and cutlery, potty, microwave, bike-trailer, rucksack baby-carrier, spare pushchair, and plenty of toys. The natural fully fenced swimming pond does not have a lifeguard, but has a wristband-operated alarm system. There's a trampoline, sandpit, rope-swing, *boules* area, and volleyball court. No shop, though, so make sure you stock up at a local supermarket en route.
OFF SITE The Midi-Pyrénées region is home to over a dozen villages (officially listed as 'Les Plus Beaux Villages de France'). This is more than almost any other region in the country. There are over 1,000 climbing routes around the Gorges de l'Aveyron and the landscape is criss-crossed by way-marked walks. Head to the nearby St-Antonin-Noble-Val to enjoy a spot of kayaking, hiring your boat for the day from Location Canoe/Les Pieds dans l'Eau (00 33 5 63 68 24 80; www.locationcanoe.com). Alternatively, buy a fishing licence from a local newsagent and do some angling for trout from one of the area's many bridges. Further afield, the Forêt de la Grésigne offers the chance to experience the largest oak forest in Europe. If it rains, take a short drive to the UNESCO World Heritage town of Albi and check out its Toulouse-Lautrec museum (00 33 5 63 49 48 70; www.museetoulouselautrec.net).
FOOD AND DRINK In the nearby medieval town of Cordes-sur-Ciel, the Michelin-starred Hostellerie du Vieux Cordes (00 33 5 63 53 79 20; www.vieuxcordes.fr) is very good, if pricey. Or seek out La Falaise in nearby Cahuzac-sur-Vère (00 33 5 63 33 96 31; www.lafalaiserestaurant.com) where owner and chef, Guillaume, offers high-class cooking.
GETTING THERE Le Camp is a 1¼-hour drive from the airports of Toulouse and Rodez or a 9–10 hour drive from Calais. Follow directions, which are sent when you book.
OPEN June–September. Minimum stay of 7 nights in July and August and 4 nights in June and September.
THE DAMAGE Yurts and tents from €160–€235 per night. Price includes breakfast, parking, wi-fi, use of all facilities including washing machine, bed linen and towels, and a variety of kitchen provisions.

They say that when horses instead of cows were brought in to pull ploughs in the region surrounding Caudet Radha, the farmers refused to change over. Their reason? The horses would move too fast. The adage, apocryphal or not, gives an insight into this beautiful but understated region, which continues the same quiet, unhurried pace of life it's been nurturing for generations. Its gentle pull was strong enough to persuade Danuta and Steve, originally from Kent, England, to set up a yoga practice here in 2006. The couple had spent the previous six months shuffling around Spain and Portugal looking for a rural escape, but they'd found nothing. Only on the return trip, empty-handed and despondent, did they discover Caudet. Four years and a whole lot of elbow grease later, the place looks vastly different to how it was when they first saw it, and it's easier than ever to see just why the couple were bowled over. Nestled in the Gers countryside, Caudet is surrounded by the gently undulating patchworks of sunflowers, vineyards, and wheat, which along with the clusters of woodlands, beautiful farmhouses, and that unhurried pace of life, earned it the sobriquet 'French Tuscany'. This place has 'peaceful retreat' written all over it.

The couple have renovated the main farmhouse into a gorgeous home and yoga centre,

caudet radha yoga centre

Caudet Radha Yoga Centre, 32700 Marsolan, Gers   00 33 5 62 68 87 95   www.radhacaudet.com

where Danuta holds weekend and week-long retreats for international participants. But don't worry, you don't need to be able to wrap your legs behind your head or pass any circular breathing tests to stay at Caudet – just an appreciation of Nature, tranquillity, and simple living will do.

For, while the main *raison d'être* of the place is yoga instruction, the campsite has been built as a creative and sociable annexe to the site rather than an annexe to the yoga philosophy per se. There are just three pitches, all close to the house and garden or hidden away in a charming area of woodland. The site has open grassy areas on two levels, overlooking a valley that hosts wheat, melon, and sunflowers, and great views of the surrounding area. There's also a lovely little tipi perfectly poised beneath a chestnut tree, and a bell tent is further away, close to a little cave with a spring. At the time of writing an eco-cabin was being built, but if you fancy a bit of comfort in the meantime, make a bid for one of the gorgeous rooms in the main house. In fact, the campsite is usually closed when the centre is open, though owner and course instructor Danuta, being – ha ha – very flexible, would no doubt be happy to book a one-to-one or small-group course.

Otherwise there's plenty to do in the area, which is secluded but not isolated. The unspoilt

spa town of Lectoure is just five minutes away by car. It has small cafés, restaurants, a weekly market on Fridays, and a relaxing thermal spa, which offers a range of treatments and experiences.

The charming 'pink city' of Toulouse, with its abundant churches and cathedrals and quirky space and aeronautical attractions, is also only just over an hour away, and you can access the Mediterranean in three hours, the Atlantic in two and a half hours, as well as the Pyrénées in two hours. Nothing, in other words – and somewhat paradoxically – is too much of a 'stretch'.

COOL FACTOR A real chill-out option in the heart of 'French Tuscany'.

WHO'S IN? Tents, campervans, caravans (limited) – yes. Pets – no.

ON SITE Campfires in designated areas welcome. One superb bathroom using solar-heated water. Laundry facilities (€2). Compost and conventional toilets; washing-up area or dishwasher. No playground, but lots of woods and fields. No onsite shop.

OFF SITE The pilgrimage route of St Jacques de Compostelle (Santiago de Compostela) passes through Marsolan, which is also the route of the GR65 – the section from Marsolan to La Romieu is very pretty and drop-offs can be arranged. There is a spa in Lectoure (00 33 5 62 68 56 00; www.macurethermale.com) and a good outdoor swimming pool; also there you can visit Bleus de Pastel de Lectoure and witness the revival of the art of woad-dying (00 33 5 62 68 78 30; www.bleu-de-lectoure.com). Putting fanatics can find a nice 9-hole golf course in nearby Fleurance (00 33 5 62 06 26 26; www.golf-fleurance.com). En route, watch out for signs for the Pony Club. And the Lac des Trois Vallées, 5 miles (8 km) away, is lovely and big, perfect for family picnics. Also in Fleurance is an observatory, and, if your French is up to it, the Hameau des Étoiles runs courses in school holidays on astronomy and the origin of the universe (www.fermedesetoiles.com). This area has very little light pollution so is wonderful for star-gazing. Bicycles can be hired just outside Lectoure (ask on site for details). La Romieu, within cycling distance, has an inexpensive pottery, and is a world heritage site on account of the 14th-century cloisters.

FOOD AND DRINK The owners can provide breakfasts (€5). Off site, try Auberge des Bouviers on Lectoure's main street (00 33 5 62 68 95 13; http://aubergedesbouviers.e-monsite.com), which has a lovely ambience and good-quality seafood. For something special try Le Logis du Cordeliers in Condom (00 33 5 62 28 03 68; www.logisdescordeliers.com), which is listed in the Guide du Routard and Michelin, or head to Astaffort (20–30 minutes away) for the wonderful surprise menu at the Auberge en Gascogne (00 33 5 53 67 10 27; www.uneaubergeengascogne.com), one of the top 350 gourmet restaurants in France. In Agen, a 2,000-year-old city about half an hour away, is Le Mariottat (00 33 5 53 77 95 77; www.restaurant-mariottat.com).The area is well known for foie gras and Armagnac and the owners recommend shops, farms, and vineyards. Markets are in Lectoure (Friday), Fleurance (Thursdays), and Nérac (Saturdays).

GETTING THERE Quarter of a mile (½ km) south, off D7, about 5 minutes from Lectoure.

PUBLIC TRANSPORT You can get to Lectoure by bus from Agen railway station or ask the site for a pick-up.

OPEN All year, when courses are not running (they run every 1st and 4th weekend of the month, and every 2nd full week of the month).

THE DAMAGE Campervans and caravans €15 per night per person. Tent €10 per person. Tipi €25 per person (including breakfast).

la brouquère

Camping La Brouquère, Betbézé, 32330 Gondrin   00 33 5 62 29 19 44   www.brouquere.com

Located in Gers, which is midway between the Mediterranean and the Atlantic, in a deliciously untouristy region, La Brouquère was set up a few years ago by Sonja and Wouter, who came here from Switzerland to restore an old winery, using its original stone for the structure of their gorgeous bijou home: think bright-blue shutters, a view of rolling hills, and, from July, blossoming sunflowers.

There's a pleasant drive past vineyards, and an intimate camping vibe greets you on arrival. All of La Brouquère's USPs share equal pride of place: the little swimming pool (not much bigger than a hot tub, but it'll cool you down on sunny days), the terraced patio, the views, and the house are all vividly enchanting. The site's remoteness enables farm workers to travel freely about their daily business, which for many is the production of foie gras, the Côtes de Gascogne wines, and, of course, Armagnac. Talking of food, as well as the option of pre-ordering bread and croissants the day before, you can take advantage of the wonderful home-cooked fare. To walk off, or work up, an appetite, try one of the walking and cycling routes starting from the site or there's even a circular swimming pool a couple of miles away in Gondrin.

With vineyards visible from your tent in one direction and rolling hills in the other, it's little wonder Sonja and Wouter believe that the Gers is the best region in all France, that the locally produced wine is better than any Bordeaux, and that 'don't worry' is your password to a happy stay at La Brouquère.

COOL FACTOR Tiny, friendly campsite; wine and Armagnac brandy virtually on tap. Hic.

WHO'S IN? Everybody is welcome.

ON SITE Six pitches for tents and cars. Two showers, 4 toilets, and 1 private shower room with a toilet. If you have to stay in touch there's wi-fi, and you can re-freeze blocks for your cool box. Plus there's a children's playground, a small adventure forest, and a *boules* pitch. No campfires.

OFFSITE The tiny museum in Lupiac commemorates the birthplace of d'Artagnan (00 33 5 62 09 24 09; www.lemondededartagnan.fr), who fought alongside the three musketeers and is worth a look. The Thursday market at Eauze and the regular night markets in Vic-Fezensac are must-sees. A racing car circuit is 30 minutes away at Nogaro. One-day courses start at €340 (00 33 5 62 09 02 49; www.circuit-nogaro.com).

FOOD AND DRINK La Ferme du Cassou (00 33 5 62 29 15 22; www.fermeducassou.com) in Gondrin offers a tour of the production of pâté followed by a sampling session of duck omelettes, sausages, tarts, and jams. The best place to try brandy is Château de Cassaigne (00 33 5 62 28 04 02), offering free tours and tastings, then a decent bottle of Armagnac will set you back around €25. An excellent mid-priced restaurant with lots of Gersoix character is Les Caprices d'Antan (00 33 5 62 65 76 92) in Lannepax.

GETTING THERE The village is located on D931 between Condom and Eauze, 30 miles (50 km) from Auch and Agen.

OPEN May–September.

THE DAMAGE It costs €7–€9.20 per person per night (slightly less for children). You can rent your own bathroom for a small charge. The owners also rent a *gîte*, which sleeps 5 and is nestled among the vineyards, from €250 a week.

domaine les angeles

Camping Domaine Les Angeles, Les Angeles, 32410 Cézan   00 33 5 62 65 29 80   www.domainelesangeles.com

Though affable Franco-Dutch couple Guido and Clara have only been running Les Angeles since 2008, the campsite's history goes back to 1985, when it was first converted from an old Gasconian farmhouse, which doubtless explains the comfortable vibe you get when you first step on to the site. What Guido and Clara have brought to this site is an air of cosmopolitanism, and the option to let everyone enjoy its wonderful serenity and location in the middle of a Gascony valley, surrounded by glittering sunflower fields and bristling vineyards. Pitches are arranged around the periphery of the site – generous rectangles protected from the sun by lovely old trees, which help lend the site a cosy, leafy atmosphere. You'll find reception at the top of a gentle slope, next to the picnic tables and a sparkling blue pool. There's a sunny terrace and a paddling pool for smallies plus a playground with swings and a slide. If the weather forces you indoors there's a games room, pool table, library, and bar. And you'll find plenty of up-to-date brochures to help plan your stay.

A few times a week during high season the site arranges a table d'hôte, which helps guests to mingle and get to know each other. You can also sample the region's wonderful produce: everything from delicious wines, Floc and Armagnac, to that controversial French favourite, foie gras. As Guido and Clara point out, though, Les Angeles is also one of the best places they know to just relax and read a book. Like being at home, perhaps, but minus all the pesky distractions.

COOL FACTOR A lovely spot to relax and read your book in the middle of the Gascon countryside.

WHO'S IN? Tents, campervans, caravans – yes, to an extent, though numbers are limited. Dogs – no.

ON SITE Thirty-four pitches for tents or tent-trailers; 2 wash-blocks containing 6 showers, toilets, and washbasins. Mini-market. Washing machine (€5) and a couple of fridges for rent (€2 per day). *Boules* pitch, volleyball, small football pitch, table-tennis table, mountain bikes for rent. No campfires but BBQs allowed.

OFF SITE There are lots of cultural and religious spots around, like the Abbaye de Flaran in Valence-sur-Baïse (00 33 5 62 28 50 19) and Château de Lavardens (00 33 5 62 58 10 61; www.chateaulavardens.com).

FOOD AND DRINK Drinks, ice creams, snacks, chips, bread, and croissants (except Mondays) are available from the shop/bar. For a sociable drink, try La Légende Irlandaise in Jegun (00 33 5 62 64 55 13), while Chez Vous in St-Puy (00 33 5 62 68 98 52) also serves local dishes and has a relaxed atmosphere. Restaurant des Thermes (00 33 5 62 68 13 07) in Castéra-Verduzan has regional cuisine, friendly service, and is good value. Nearby farms selling foie gras and local delicacies include Ferme de la Gouardère (00 33 5 62 65 56 51; www.ferme-lagouardere.com) and Terre Blanche (00 33 5 62 28 92 54; www.terreblanche.fr) in St-Puy.

GETTING THERE On A62 take exit 7 or 8. Then, N21 Agen to Auch. In Fleurance, take D103 towards Vic-Fezensac. In Préchac, take a right to Cézan, and follow the road for 2½ miles (4 km). Follow purple signs.

OPEN May–September.

THE DAMAGE 2 people, 1 car (high season) €18. Additional adult €6, child €4.

camping aux mêmes

Camping aux Mêmes, 32140 Bellegarde   00 33 5 62 66 91 45   www.camping-aux-memes.fr

Time seems to expand at Camping aux Mêmes. In days gone by the site was a traditional Gascony farm, set in the heart of the Gers countryside, with rolling hills and magnificent views of the Pyrénées. It was bought by Janet and Peter back in 2003, and they made a home from the farmhouse and opened the land to campers. The rolling hills and views are still there, of course, embellished by a lovely blue pool, a kids' playground, and a bar area, where you can enjoy the site's tranquillity.

Far enough away from the mountains to enjoy the warmer, more settled climate of the south of France, but close enough for days out in the peaks, it's a simple, uncluttered site that's perfect for anyone searching for peace and quiet. The lack of trees means there's not much shade, but there are a couple of pleasant pitches on a lower terrace that are shielded by plum trees. From both areas you get views of the local church and sunflower fields; classic features of the area. Traditional France, in other words, where you can leave behind the stresses and strains of everyday life, and have plenty of time to do all those other nice things.

COOL FACTOR Friendly, family-run campsite in the peaceful Gascony countryside.

WHO'S IN? Tents, campervans, caravans, dogs (on leads) – yes. Groups – low season only.

ON SITE Twenty pitches (8 with electricity), only some shaded. Hot showers, disabled facilities; children's play area, table tennis, swimming pool, shop, wi-fi, bicycle hire, terrace café/bar open all day. Campfires not allowed, but BBQs OK.

OFF SITE Sailing Lac de Thoux St-Cricq (00 33 5 62 65 75 45; www.club.de.voile.thoux.st.cricq.over-blog.fr). Nine-hole golf course (00 33 5 62 66 03 10; www.golfdegascogne.eu).

FOOD AND DRINK L'Auberge d'Astarac (00 33 5 62 65 48 81) at Moncorneil-Grazan does great local food. O Mon Plaisir (00 33 5 62 66 02 14) at Masseube has good local set menus. There are interesting nearby farms to visit.

GETTING THERE D288 from Masseube and follow signs 'Aux Mêmes'. Site 1¾ miles (3 km) from Masseube (signposted).

PUBLIC TRANSPORT Daily bus from Masseube to Auch and trains from Auch to Toulouse.

OPEN April–September.

THE DAMAGE Pitch plus 2 people and car €18; electricity €3; extra adult €6; extra child (up to 11 years) €3.

la vie en vert

La Vie en Vert, 09800 Augirein   00 33 5 61 96 82 66/00 33 6 22 95 95 88   www.lavieenvert.com

If ever there was a campsite destined to be on a postcard, it's this one. The abundance of flowers, the babbling brook running along the back of a lovely old stone house, and 15 immaculately crafted pitches, some right next to the river, make the site a bit of a choccie-box delight. Admittedly it lacks slightly in facilities – there's no pool and no communal room or café – but it does have a small kids' playground, home-made apple juice on tap, and you can have breakfast in the house, if you like. There's also a small library, fresh fruit and veg from local farmers on sale, and a BBQ shack available that you can set up right next to the river.

Then there are Claudine and Charles themselves; an ultra-hospitable pair who know the area well and can give you the low-down on the many local highs: biking and hiking trails, water sports on the Bouigane River, chapels, caves, and a string of picturesque rustic villages in both directions. Castillon-en-Couserans is a 20-minute drive and has regular cultural events in summer. That's if you can wrench yourself away from all the calmness and cuteness, of course.

COOL FACTOR This cute, calm site keeps it (arbo) real.

WHO'S IN? Tents, campervans, caravans, dogs – yes. Groups – no.

ON SITE Fifteen decent-sized pitches, all shaded; 1 tipi; washing machine; old-fashioned toilets (immaculately clean). BBQ area; kids' playground. No campfires.

OFF SITE Hiking and horse-riding arranged from site. Galey has great views and an interesting chapel. Vallée de Bethmal is nice to visit and has a serene lake; good for picnics.

FOOD AND DRINK Claudine is happy to cook emergency evening meals for the odd passing cyclist in distress, but you're expected to be self-sufficient. A bio-breakfast can be prepared for €7 per person. The restaurant in Galey (00 33 5 61 96 71 52) emphasises local produce and has a simple, rustic setting. There are also local cheese and meat farms in the area – ask at reception for info.

GETTING THERE Get to Castillon-en-Couserans and take the road through to Augirein, following the signs for La Vie en Vert. The site is just past the nursery – cross over the bridge and make a left (there are signs).

OPEN July–August.

THE DAMAGE Tent plus 2 people €15 per night. Tipi €32 per night (2 people).

pyrénées

les tilleuls

Les Tilleuls, Impasse Dom-Filastre, 76790 Le Tilleul   00 33 2 35 27 11 61   millet.rosalie@wanadoo.fr

If it's good old-fashioned French family hospitality you're after, then look no further. Run by generations of the Millet family, Les Tilleuls has the kind of open, comfortable atmosphere that makes you feel immediately at home. It's a singularly attractive site too: enjoying sweeping views over a breathtaking mountainscape, taking in Campbieilh, Coumély, Le Cirque de Gavarnie, and a timeless assortment of old stone houses. The main camping area occupies the garden area in front of the Millet's family home. It has been thoughtfully separated into four tiers, all of which have great views, so there's no need to fret over bagging the best spot (although campers thinking of pitching up here in high season might want to grab a spot under one of the few trees, as there's nowhere else to hide from the sun on this campsite). Even the bathrooms have great views here.

Chickens, geese, kids, and the family dog roam around the garden; the stone outhouse has been transformed into a wood-carving museum – another talent and passion that's been passed down the generations; and there's a roulotte (gypsy caravan) available on the other side of the house if you're seeking some creature comforts. Since they have a great deal of experience running their garden campsite, the Millets are also superb sources of information on the surrounding area, offering top tips for restaurants, day trips, and more. With so many glorious places and scenery to explore in the area, there's every chance you'll want to extend your stay. Just don't forget your camera!

COOL FACTOR Cracking valley views.

WHO'S IN? Tents, campervans, caravans, pets – yes. Groups – by arrangement.

ON SITE Fifty-six touring pitches, 30 permanent pitches; a small playground, table tennis, washing machines, dryers. Next to the vegetable garden you'll find a new, modern block containing 4 showers, a sink, a clothes-washing basin and 5 toilets. Campfires not allowed.

OFF SITE It's a 5-minute drive to Gèdre, where you'll find an outdoor pool, an ice-skating rink and a bob luge (00 33 5 62 92 48 54). Small animal theme park in Argelès-Gazost (00 33 5 62 97 91 07, www.parc-animalier-pyrenees.com) and also horse-riding shows in Tarbes. For larger thrills, try a helicopter ride with Pyrénées Copt'Air (00 33 5 59 68 65 19). A 15–20-minute aerial view costs from €120 for 2.

FOOD AND DRINK The artisan shop on the road into Gèdre sells Fleur d'Amour, a sherry-type aperitif *pour rester amoureux*, a bargain at €12. In Gèdre, Le Campbieilh (00 33 5 62 92 23 67; www.lecampbieilh.fr) serves lunches and evening meals. For upmarket cuisine try Les Cascades Gavarnie (00 33 5 62 92 40 17).

GETTING THERE Follow D821 to Argelès-Gazost then D921 through Gèdre. At the end of the village, turn right, then first left towards Saussa. Look out for the almost-hidden left turn to Camping Les Tilleuls.

PUBLIC TRANSPORT The railway station at Lourdes is 26 miles (43 km) away, then a bus to Luz-St-Sauveur. Tarbes-Lourdes-Pyrénées airport is 37 miles (60 km) away or Toulouse airport is 135 miles (217 km), a 3-hour drive, away.

OPEN Mid May–mid September.

THE DAMAGE Tent with 2 people €9.90, child (under 8) €1.80, electric pitch €2, car €2.70.

tipis indiens

Tipis Indiens, 8 rue des Carolins, 65120 Luz-St-Sauveur   00 33 6 15 41 33 29   www.tipis-indiens.com

If you've ever had a Red Indian fantasy as a kid, Tipis Indiens could be the place to live it out. Built by Francis Caussieu, the site is an earnest labour of love: an idea turned reality only after a long search for master craftsmen who could build the kinds of tipis Caussieu wanted. And what magnificent tipis they are! Each one is endowed with not one, but two, double beds plus a small sofa bed (all with thick duvets), wooden chests, dining table and Indian artifacts. It's a small site – only four tipis – but what it lacks in size it makes up for with fine views. When the mist clears to reveal the Cirque de Troumouse, it's hard to believe you're not on some kind of film set.

There's plenty more gorgeous scenery around too, from the ski town of Luz-St-Sauveur to the highest waterfall in France at Gavarnie. The only other thing on site, apart from child-friendly goats in an adjacent field, is a refurbished stone barn, where guests can shower, cook, watch TV, or relax with a good book by the small fire. Not quite so authentically Indian of course, but even hard-core fantasists are allowed to take a bit of a break.

COOL FACTOR In the mountains with goats and tipis.
WHO'S IN? Groups by arrangement, dogs (on leads) – yes. Tents, campervans, caravans – no.
ON SITE One *gîte* is available to all tipi guests, with TV, sofas, kitchen, washing machine, iron, and 2 showers. Guests must bring sheets and pillowcases, or hire linen €5 per bed. Cleaning is an optional €10 per tipi.
OFF SITE Gèdre has an outdoor pool, indoor skating rink, and bob luge. Try a sunrise walk to Gavarnie amphitheatre.
FOOD AND DRINK La Brêche de Roland in Gavarnie (00 33 5 62 92 48 54; www.pyrenees-hotel-breche.com) is good.
GETTING THERE D821 to Argelès-Gazost leads to D921 through Gèdre. At the village end, turn right, then the first left towards Saussa. Continue to 'Tipis' sign on your left.
PUBLIC TRANSPORT The train station at Lourdes is 26 miles (43 km) away with a bus to Luz-St-Sauveur. From there Taxi Caussieu (00 33 5 62 92 97 56). Tarbes-Lourdes-Pyrénées airport is 37 miles (60 km) and Toulouse airport 135 miles (217 km) away, a 3-hour drive.
OPEN May–September.
THE DAMAGE Tipis July/August €85 per night, €195 for 3 nights, €490 per week. May/June/September, €330 weekly (apart from last week in June, which is €390).

lae de haut

Lae de Haut, 64570 Aramits   00 33 5 59 34 63 42   www.selfcatering-pyrenees.com

Margaret and John are new to camping, but they're no strangers to hospitality. In a bid to enjoy a more serene lifestyle, they found this small collection of farmhouses, which they converted into a lovely B&B, activities area, and a couple of budget rooms. They wondered what they could do with the two huge fields before hitting on it: camping! One field is too steep to pitch on, but the other rises to a fantastic plateau that gives panoramic views over the Pyrénées, the village of Aramits, and beyond.

It's a short walk to toilets and showers, but you can play all you like in a wonderful games room (with darts board, pool table, computer, wi-fi, TV, and more besides), an equipped kitchen area, and a large covered activities room with a volleyball court, climbing wall, gym, and table tennis. Oh, and did we mention the large outdoor pool?

Spain is just 15 minutes away and there's plenty to do in the area, from visiting the second-largest cave complex in the world to hiking along the St Jacques de Compostelle path (Santiago de Compostela). Green to camping they may be, but Margaret and John have already got it all sewn up.

COOL FACTOR 'Wild' camping with B&B benefits.

WHO'S IN? Tents, groups – yes. Campervans, caravans, mobile homes – no.

ON SITE Space for a dozen campers on the brow of the hill; 2 shaded pitches on the periphery under a tree. Hot showers and toilets. Outdoor pool, small kitchen, games room, play area, activities room. Bikes to rent. No campfires.

OFF SITE Thirty-two trails in the valley. Kids enjoy Adventure Park (00 33 5 59 34 64 79; www.aventure-parc.fr), as well as the Stade d'Eaux Vives water sports centre (00 33 5 59 40 85 44; www.paupyrenees-stadeeauxvives.com). La Verna, the second-largest cave system in the world is mere minutes away (00 33 6 37 88 29 05; www.laverna.fr).

FOOD AND DRINK Meals on request. Breakfasts from €6. Hôtel le Bristol in Oloran-sur-Ste-Marie (00 33 5 59 39 43 78; www.le-bristol.oloron.ste-marie.com) serves regional food. For Basque treats try Xokottua (00 33 5 59 28 25 75).

GETTING THERE From Aramits, follow the signs to Aventure Parc. A mile (2 km) from the main road, the sign for Lae de Haut is on the left. Site is third house on the lane.

OPEN May–October.

THE DAMAGE 1 person €7 per night; 2 people €10 per night; 3 or 4 people (plus car) from €15 per night.

With 'luxury' and 'comfort' being two heavily bandied buzzwords of recent times, it might seem inconceivable that anywhere could rival the architecture of the hippest boutique hotels. But whereas such grandeur may boast unbeatable neon skylines or the latest in spa fashion, the Pyrénées safeguard something no money can buy – the Great Outdoors.

Mesmerising and spiritual, the mountainous terrain, with all its seasonal temperaments and wildlife, offers an experience that humbles humans to their very core. If, however, you like de luxe comforts to complement your concord with nature, then Camping Pyrénées Natura is just up your street. Even the facilities are a breath of fresh air. The owners have never once rested on their laurels, and they've been going for 10 years. But then you don't become a French 4-star establishment without some effort, and Pascal and Viviane Ruysschaert have devoted their time to creating the kind of campsite they spent their lives looking for, but never found.

In 1995, they bought and restored a 19th-century barn to house a games room, library, and bar, where Pascal mixes up a mean Pyrénées Natura house cocktail – a potent wine and Armagnac concoction. Next, they built a sauna-solarium, a soundproof music room with a top-

pyrénées natura

Camping Pyrénées Natura, route du Lac, 65400 Estaing   00 33 5 62 97 45 44   www.camping-pyrenees-natura.com

notch sound system, and a little shop to sell local produce. The Ruysschaerts decided against a swimming pool, seeing it as superfluous and just plain noisy. Anyway, there are plenty of watery encounters possible in the many lakes in the area, and Arrens-Marsous, 3 miles (5 km) away, has a heated outdoor pool.

In the other direction is the closest town – Argelès-Gazost: a friendly place to stock up on necessities, where cries of *Bonne journée!* seem to resound out of the shops with regular frequency. Estaing was built in 1800 and was used in the Second World War as a stop-gap for evacuees crossing the border into Spain. It's a bewitching

drive up the mountain to get here, passing streams, valleys, cows, and donkeys. It's a shame you can't bottle this air; you could make a killing with it back in Blighty. On arrival, campers and mobile homes are directed to the right of the campsite, on a field set back from the barn. If there are spots available, you could do worse than pitch on the only upper terrace, just in front of where the rows of chalets begin, simply because the views from here are among the best (though none is exactly bad). Since you're up in the mountains, it does get nippy at night, so bring warm gear. On the plus side, the hiking and cycling in the area during the day are phenomenal. Oh, and one other thing

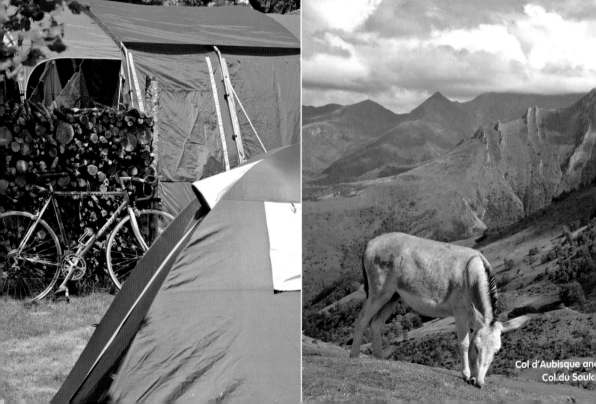

Col d'Aubisque and
Col du Soulo

Pascal and Viviane do upon your arrival is offset the carbon footprint of your journey to the site (no extra charge) by planting trees in Africa. In 2010 they planted 100,000 mangroves, underlining their impeccable eco-credentials even further. It's a campsite that lives up to its name: nature's booty – and beauty – laid out lovingly before you.

COOL FACTOR Eco-camping in the middle of a glorious national park.

WHO'S IN? Tents, campervans, caravans, dogs, groups – everyone welcome.

ON SITE There's room for 45 tents, 15 mobile chalets, and 5 motor homes. Ten showers (clean and made much more charming by a local artist), Internet, a shop, an evening snack bar selling pizzas or main dishes (such as coq au vin or rabbit in mustard, from €4.50), plus a library, table tennis, pool table, telescopes, and an auditorium.

OFF SITE The site organises lots of regular activities, from night picnics at the lake, regular introductions, and hikes through the Parc National des Pyrénées (www.parc-pyrenees. com) with local rangers to horse-riding. The fighting fit might like to cycle around the various *cols* (mountain passes). You can walk to Lac d'Estaing – it's just at the end of the road and makes a highly scenic spot for a picnic. A drive to the 3 *cirques* – Troumouse, Gavarnie, and Vignemale – will leave you feeling no bigger than a pinprick in comparison to these mountain basins, and about as significant. Rafting in various spots around here is fun and furious; it costs between €22 and €65 per person for distances of 6–19 miles (10–30 km) with Ecolorado (00 33 5 62 97 54 54). Take a spin on Le Petit Train d'Artouste (www.train-artouste.com), the highest in Europe, with subsequent jaw-dropping scenery views of some of the highest Pyrénéean peaks at a height of 6,500 feet (2,000 m). It's a popular ride, so it can get busy, but it makes a great adventure for the kids.

FOOD AND DRINK People don't come here to go out to eat, says Viviane, but she and Pascal do recommend locally produced cheese. Pascal will escort you to watch the shepherds at work and to sample their award-winning goats' cheese. The shop, a former watermill, also sells eggs and cheese from the farmers as well as wine, and more, and the bar area will sell you pizzas. Restaurant du Lac d'Estaing (00 33 5 62 97 06 25), right on the lake, offers very good food and views, even if the white plastic chairs and orange awning are basic. Ferme Auberge du Pic de Pan (00 33 5 62 97 45 35) sells local produce. For something more gastronomic try the Basque/Pyrénées cuisine at the stunning Le Viscos in St-Savin (00 33 5 62 97 02 28; www.hotel-leviscos. com) a 10-minute drive away. The associated hotel is fairly nondescript but the restaurant's menu features some of the finest foie gras, cep mushrooms, black pork of Bigorre, and seafood in the region. It has a great terrace, too, featuring views of the Argelès Valley.

GETTING THERE Hire a car and drive via Lourdes to Argelès-Gazost. From there take D918 up the mountain, passing Camping Le Caoussariou, turning left for D13 and right on to D103 towards Lac d'Estaing. You'll see the signpost for the site on your right.

OPEN Mid May–mid September.

THE DAMAGE 2 people with a tent (or caravan), car and electricity €16.50–€25 per night, depending on the season. Under 8 years €3.50 and an additional person €5.25.

useful info

Got the tent, sleeping bag, stove, and corkscrew packed? Don't forget our top tips to keep your cool on those balmy French nights.

THE RIGHT SITE

Know the difference between an *aire naturelle* (campsite with a few pitches on a farm) and a *camping naturiste* (nudist campsite). For campers keen to dip into local life, nothing beats *camping à la ferme*. Limited to six *emplacements* (pitches) for 20 campers, you can hang out with the farmer, taste produce, admire animals, and congratulate *Cool Camping* on yet another fabulous find.

THE RIGHT TIME

Skip French school holidays: spring holidays in April and October/November are reasonably quiet, but sites burst in July and August. Go for early July and bag your slot in advance. Sites generally open March to September or October. France is always one hour ahead of the UK.

RAIN, HAIL, OR SHINE

Watch the weather, particularly in mountainous areas and the south. To check, call 3250; surf www.meteo.fr/meteonet_en; or type your site's postcode into a text message and send it to 73250.

ON THE ROAD

Motorists drive on the right, and vehicles coming from the right have priority. Speed limits are 50 km/h (30 mph) in built-up areas, 90 km/h (55 mph) on the open road, 110 km/h (70 mph) on dual carriageways and 130 km/h (80 mph) on motorways – which cost. To calculate *péages* (tolls) pump your itinerary into www.autoroutes.fr. Children under 10 must not sit in front and must be in an appropriate seat in the back. Chatting on your mobile while driving lands a fine and the drink-drive limit is equivalent to two glasses of wine. Avoid buying pricey autoroute petrol; try a supermarket on a town's outskirts. Leaving the autoroute for lunch likewise leaves a sweeter taste. Motoring on traffic-jammed 'black' days in July and August is grim. Check traffic in advance with Bison Futé (00 33 8 92 68 78 88, France 08 26 02 20 22, www.bison-fute.equipement.gouv.fr) and avoid peak times, particularly Saturday. Tune into Radio 107.7 FM for the latest traffic news.

MAKING THAT CALL

If you're calling from the UK or from your mobile in France, dial the number *Cool Camping* lists, including the international access code '00' and France country code '33'. Calling from a payphone in France, drop the '00 33' and add a '0' before the remaining nine-digit number. French telephone numbers have 10 digits and no area code.

CULINARY NUGGETS

Every village has a market heaped with fresh fruit, veg, herbs, fish, and meat gagging to be cooked on a campfire. Check what the local farmer sells. Few shops open on Sunday and most break for a long lunch on other days. Bread accompanies every meal, though a baguette bought at sunrise is rock-hard by sunset. Every *boulangerie* bakes several times a day. Some campsites serve dinner.

DOWN THE HATCH

Tap water and water in fountains is drinkable unless marked '*non potable*'. In restaurants, ordering a jug of tap water is fine. The French seldom drink beer or tea (bring your own tea bags). The day is kick-started with *un café* (a short, sharp espresso) or tamer *café au lait* (milky coffee), and wine accompanies everything else. Look for *dégustation* (tasting) signs in wine-making areas.

DOWN THE PAN

Women's is *Dames*, men's is *Hommes*. French toilets are not always what they seem so, gals, you might find yourself parading past a man at a urinal. Once in, devices range from bog-standard toilets to a pair of elephant feet. Stand well clear before flushing.

WHAT TO DO IN AN EMERGENCY

(besides yelling 'AU SECOURS! (HELP)'

Fire call 18 from a landline or 112 from a mobile

Police (Gendarmerie) – call 17

Ambulance (SAMU) – call 15

Mountain rescue call 112; better still note the number of the local mountain-rescue squad before setting out

Lost/stolen passport report at the local police station and contact the British Embassy (01 44 51 31 00) in Paris to find the nearest British consulate to get a replacement

Lost/stolen credit card call 08 92 70 57 05, or MasterCard 08 00 90 13 87, or Visa 08 00 90 11 79

---

useful phrases

Campsite un camping
Pitch une emplacement
Large/small tent une grande/petite tente
Campervan un mobil-home/un camping-car
Caravan une caravane
Facility block le bloc sanitaire
Toilets/urinals les WCs/urinoirs
Showers les douches
Washing-up/laundry sink un bac lave vaiselle/lave linge
Drinking water l'eau potable
Recycling bins les bacs de recyclage
Sleeping bag un sac de couchage
Air mattress un matelas d'air
Campfire un feu de camp
Pink/white marshmallows les guimauves roses/blanches
Camping Gaz canister une bouteille de Camping Gaz

Corkscrew un tire bouchon
Tin opener une ouvre-boîte
Mallet un maillet

Where is the nearest campsite? Où est le camping le plus proche?
How much does it cost to pitch a tent here? Combien coûte une nuit en camping avec tente?
It costs a fixed €15 a day for two adults, tent and car. Nous avons un forfait journalier de €15 pour deux adultes avec tente et voiture.
Where are the recycling bins? Où sont les bacs de recyclage?
Do you have a spare tent peg/tin opener/lighter or matches? Avez-vous un piquet de tente/une ouvre-boîte/un briquet de poche ou des allumettes?
Could someone please clean the

toilets? Pourriez vous faire nettoyer les toilettes, s'il vous plaît?
There's no hot water. Il n'y a pas d'eau chaude.
Help! Someone has stolen my wallet! Au secours! Quelqu'un a volé mon porte-monnaie!
Where should I park? Où est-ce que je peux me garer?
Is it OK to build a campfire here? Est-ce qu'on peut faire un feu de camp ici?
What a beautiful view! Quelle vue magnifique!
Where's a good place to eat around here? Où est-ce qu'il y a un bon endroit pour manger près d'ici?
Do you speak English? Est-ce que vous parlez anglais?
Sorry, I don't speak French. Désolé, je ne parle pas français.

index